VOICES OF THE *SCANDINAVIAN WAFFEN-SS*

THE FINAL TESTAMENT OF HITLER'S VIKINGS

OTHER BOOKS BY THE AUTHOR:

Hitler's Legions series

Hitler's Gauls – The History of the French Waffen-SS

Hitler's Flemish Lions – The History of the Flemish Waffen-SS

Hitler's Jihadis – The History of the Muslim Waffen-SS

Hitler's Vikings – The History of the Scandinavian Waffen-SS

Hastings 1066

Death on the Don – The Destruction of Germany's Allies on the Eastern Front 1941–44

The Defeat of the Luftwaffe – The Eastern Front 1941–45; Strategy for Disaster

Voices of the Flemish Waffen-SS: The Last Testament of the Oostfronters

VOICES OF THE *SCANDINAVIAN WAFFEN-SS*

THE FINAL TESTAMENT OF HITLER'S VIKINGS

JONATHAN TRIGG

AMBERLEY

First published 2018

Amberley Publishing
The Hill, Stroud
Gloucestershire, GL5 4EP

www.amberley-books.com

ISBN 978 1 4456 7468 1 (hardback)
ISBN 978 1 4456 7469 8 (ebook)

British Library Cataloguing in Publication Data.
A catalogue record for this book is available from the British Library.

Typesetting and Origination by Amberley Publishing
Printed in the UK.

CONTENTS

PREFACE

This book has its genesis in two parents if you will, the first being *Hitler's Vikings*, a history of the Second World War's Scandinavian Waffen-SS units published in the UK back in 2010, and the second being *Voices of the Flemish Waffen-SS*, my last book, based on a series of in-depth interviews with some of the very few surviving Flemish veterans. The latter, published in 2017, was an attempt to capture and explore the personal memories of men (and women) whose voices will soon be lost forever, and to record them talking about the war in which they served, fought, and survived, in their own words. I found the experience of writing it utterly fascinating, and even before the finished manuscript was with the publishers I had determined to give the Scandinavian Waffen-SS veterans the same treatment.

Having made my decision, the issue was time. Even the famed longevity of Scandinavians – Sweden 82.55 years, Denmark 81.10 years, and Norway 82.10 years (official 2015 figures) – would be tested by men and women who would all now be in their 90s at least. So, if I was going to write this book I needed to get my skates on and go and interview as many surviving veterans as quickly as I could.

My first trawl for potential interviewees did not bode well. A Swedish contact who had conducted an exhaustive study of his own country's Waffen-SS volunteers had concluded that of the approximately 180–200 who enlisted, only one was left alive in 2017, and he had consistently refused every attempt to be interviewed on the subject for several years – perhaps understandable given he hadn't served at the front anyway, having dropped out of training part way through at the vociferous urging of his mother. I also decided to rule out Finland, partly due to my earlier lack of success in sourcing information from Finnish veterans for *Hitler's Vikings*, and also because in my view the Finnish ordeal of the Winter War, the Continuation War, and finally the fighting with their erstwhile German ally in 1944/45, deserved a book all of its own.

That left me with Denmark and Norway, which was no bad thing as between them they provided the armed SS with well over 10,000 men – by far the bulk of what was the Scandinavian Waffen-SS. However, once again I came up empty-handed when I discovered that not one but three of my earlier interviewees had passed away in the interim since writing *Hitler's Vikings*: Christen Dall and Poul Hveger – both Danes and both late of the SS-Panzergrenadier-Regiment Nordland – and Bjørn Østring, one of the most well-known and vocal Norwegian veterans, who had been a personal friend of the executed Norwegian collaborationist leader, Vidkun Quisling. At this point the book's premise seemed to be fast receding, until an armada of extremely knowledgeable and very kind friends and contacts hove into view and began to help me source veterans (please see Acknowledgements for my thanks). Thus began weeks of emails and phone calls with possible interviewees, including exhaustive explanations as to the reasons for the book, its subject matter, scope and timing, etc., and it was during this marathon that I discovered two issues that threatened, once again, to render the book stillborn. The first of these issues was by far the more important of the two, and it was the fear – felt by almost all of the veterans – that the content of the interviews would be used by journalists and various other third-party individuals to launch war crimes probes against them. At first baffled by this belief, I found it was based on events from back in 2015 when the Simon Wiesenthal Centre – renowned for its dogged tracking down of Nazi war criminals – had asked the authorities in Copenhagen to investigate two former Danish Waffen-SS men for their alleged involvement in crimes during 1942–43 at the Bobruisk Camp in present-day Belarus (see the Appendix for an article on the camp by the academic Dr Lea Prais). The men – Helmuth Leif Rasmussen (now called Helmuth Rasbol) and Aksel Andersen, the latter a naturalised Swedish citizen – strongly denied the accusations. The Danish police carried out an investigation that only finally concluded in late 2016, and resulted in the Chief Danish Prosecutor – Steen Bechmann Jacobsen – deciding that no prosecutions would be launched against either man due to a lack of evidence.[1] I make no comment on the case – that is for the relevant authorities – except to say that from the perspective of trying to write this book it made veterans extremely wary of being interviewed, as they understandably did not want the time they have left to be potentially filled with judicial probes into their past. In Rasmussen/Rasbol's case it was especially galling for what I intended, as he had been happy to be interviewed about his Waffen-SS service several times previously, but now point-blank refused to be involved in my project in any way whatsoever.

So, the challenge I had to overcome was to persuade veterans that the intent of the interviews was not to get them into trouble with the law and provide would-be investigators with evidence of their alleged involvement with war crimes, but at the same time explain to them that I would not shy away from asking difficult questions about the Holocaust and Nazi atrocities – to do so would be to desecrate the memory of the millions who were murdered by one of the most blood-stained regimes in history, and abrogate my responsibilities as a historian.

The second issue – and somewhat related to the first – was that the Norwegian-language edition of *Hitler's Vikings* had included a Foreword that several of the veterans believed tarred them and all their fellow volunteers as war criminals. The offending Foreword is, of course, in Norwegian, and I had not read it prior to it being brought to my attention as I scoured the country for veterans willing to talk to me. To say I was flabbergasted would be an understatement. It had not been written by me and it had been inserted without my knowledge or consent.

Both of these factors worked against my efforts, but with the unstinting support of some special people, I was finally able to convince a raft of veterans to agree to be interviewed. They included men who had volunteered in the first waves of enlistees all the way back in 1941 and had fought for most of the war, to some who almost inexplicably joined up as the war turned against the Third Reich, and even some who – mainly due to their extreme youth – had only spent a few months in uniform as Nazi Germany collapsed into total defeat. I also interviewed the 'forgotten half' of the population involved in the war – women; be they nurses in the German Red Cross (the *Deutsches Rote Kreuz* – DRK), female members of Quisling's Norwegian National Unification party (*Nasjonal Samling* – NS) and its related youth organisations, or the widows of veterans. Their experiences and memories were never less than informative and often illuminating and I am extremely grateful for their time.

The insights all of them gave into the war and its aftermath are fascinating and, perhaps surprisingly, they are quite different in many ways from the Flemings I interviewed for *Voices of the Flemish Waffen-SS*. There is common ground between the Scandinavian and Flemish veterans too, of course, most notably that anti-communism was a major motivator to volunteer for all of them, but whereas it mostly came second to the desire for an independent Flanders in the genteel suburbs of Ghent and Bruges, it was *the* key driver in the towns and villages of Jutland, Funen and Hedmark.

However, where the difference between the two cohorts of volunteers was most striking was in how their fellow countrymen and women now – in the 21st century – feel about what they as volunteers did well over half a century ago. In neither Flanders, Norway nor Denmark is there a general feeling among the population at large of *acceptance* at the idea of having been a foreign volunteer in the Waffen-SS, but in the former the existence, size and longevity of the vibrant independence movement has meant there is no widespread revulsion at the *Oostfronters* (as they are known in Flanders) – indeed a sense of curiosity and a certain amount of careful respect tend to be the popular views – however, the same cannot be said of Denmark or Norway, especially the latter. The vast majority of Danes do not look on their Waffen-SS veterans in a favourable manner at all, but over the water in Norway there is a veritable chasm between the bulk of the populace and the minority of Norwegians whose families were involved in the NS and/or the armed SS. That is not to say that all Norwegian Waffen-SS volunteers were NS members – some were not – or that all NS members supported Waffen-SS recruitment – some did not – but it is fair to say that a high percentage of volunteers *were* NS members, and after the war the Norwegian volunteers and NS members were all lumped together by the authorities and identified as 'the enemy within'. This has led to a strong feeling among many of them that they were victimised – unfairly as they see it – to such a degree after the war that even now, some seventy years later, they feel almost alien in their own country. This needs to be put into context, of course, and that context is that for the overwhelming mass of Danes and Norwegians what happened back in the Second World War is not a major topic of conversation now. If the subject comes up at all it is mainly to do with the German occupation, and not to do with their own countrymen or women's involvement – on either side. By contrast, in Flanders the independence movement keeps the Flemish experience during the War alive in some ways, and that cannot be said for the Scandinavians. But it is a reality that some Norwegians – perhaps still some thousands on both sides of the divide – feel an enmity towards each other that is hard to reconcile with the country's image of popular cohesion and social harmony. How else can one view the 'search and destroy' mission carried out in the last couple of years by persons unknown that demolished the cross and simple plaque erected by former front fighters (in Norwegian *frontkjemper* – the term by which all volunteers are now known) on a remote forested hillside on the farm of a former volunteer to remember their comrades who died? There would seem to be little reconciliation in the act. Conversely, the sense of injustice and resentment at both the State and their fellow citizens, felt by many on the 'other side', as it were, is palpable.

The other major difference between the men and women I interviewed in Flanders and Germany, and their 'co-volunteers' in the north, was their own views on being interviewed. What struck me forcefully with the Flemings was that most of them felt very strongly that they ***wanted*** to speak, to be heard, to have their stories told – the same was not true for most of the subjects of this book. Most of the interviewees were pretty circumspect – a bit reserved, to say the least. It was not that any of them harboured any regrets about what they'd done – they had that very much in common with the Flemish – but rather they had no great urge to relate their memories to the world, but would talk about it if asked, and so, ask I did.

One final point that struck me as I criss-crossed the Danish and Norwegian countryside in search of my subjects was that of family. Back in Flanders one of the abiding memories of my research was when an interviewee confided in me that no one in his family – not his children, his grandchildren or even his great-grandchildren – knew that he had served in the Waffen-SS, and he knew that would now all change with the publication of the book. That was not the case this time round, in fact during two interviews it was the subject's own grandchildren who actually acted as translators, and they were not at odds about it at all. As one of them said to me as we sat in his grandfather's apartment, drinking some very good coffee and listening to the quiet hum of the afternoon traffic on the road outside: 'It was a long time ago, you know, and he's my grandfather; what can I say, we're family.'

Notes to the Preface

1. Article in *The Times of Israel*, 4 November 2016, by Jan M. Olsen: *COPENHAGEN, Denmark (AP) — An elderly Dane accused of being involved in the mass murder of Jews in Belarus during World*

War II will not be prosecuted, Danish authorities said Friday, saying they have 'not found evidence he committed or took part in the killings.' The probe had been 'very thorough' but evidence against 91-year-old Helmuth Leif Rasmussen was 'limited,' chief prosecutor Steen Bechmann Jacobsen said. 'To be prosecuted for participation in mass killings requires a closer connection to the crime itself. You do not prosecute a known burglar for lots of burglaries in a neighbourhood simply because he was in the area at the time of break-ins. You need evidence,' he told The Associated Press. 'This is a very sad day,' said Ephraim Zuroff, head of the Jerusalem-based Simon Wiesenthal Center. He said Rasmussen 'must be happy, the relatives of the victims are not.' In July 2015, Zuroff asked police to investigate the case after Denmark's Justice Ministry had turned down a similar request saying it was not their matter. He believed there was a strong case against Rasmussen because of documents found by Danish historians that said he was in the inner circle of the camp run by the Waffen SS where 1,400 Jews died. 'To us (Rasmussen) was part of the operation. That should have been enough to convict him for accessory to murder,' Zuroff told the AP. Bechmann Jacobsen said the 15-month investigation included "pretty good" documents at the Danish National Archives that stores historic sources, but not enough evidence. We have the same requirements for evidence, whether the matter is one hour old or 73 years old,' he said, adding Rasmussen was in the camp from late 1942 to early 1943. 'We have thoroughly investigated the case but there is still no evidence that (Rasmussen) committed a specific crime for which he hasn't already been convicted,' said Bechmann Jacobsen, adding Rasmussen had, among others, been investigated for war crimes under Danish law. After the war, Rasmussen was sentenced to six years' imprisonment for having served as a soldier for Nazi Germany. Now known by the name Rasbol, Rasmussen has acknowledged being among the

6,000 Danish volunteers who joined the Waffen-SS after Germany invaded the Scandinavian country in 1940. Rasmussen, who was not available for comment Friday, has vehemently denied involvement in the killings. One of the authors of the book En skole i vold (A Book of Violence), *Dennis Larsen, says Rasmussen admitted seeing Jews being killed and thrown into mass graves. 'But he always said he was a bystander,' Larsen earlier told the AP. Bechmann Jacobsen added that another Dane who now holds a Swedish passport and who was at the camp at the same time as Rasmussen won't be prosecuted either for the same reasons. Rasmussen, the Swedish national and the Jerusalem-based Simon Wiesenthal Center were informed of the decision Wednesday and Thursday. Zuroff said he was 'strongly considering an appeal' of the decision to Denmark's top prosecutor.*

The 2016 Wiesenthal Center Annual Report had the following on their **List of Nazi War Criminals Slated for Possible Prosecution in 2016:**

- Helmut Rasbol – Denmark (Belarus) – during the years 1942–1943 served as a guard in the Jude lager established by the Nazis in Bobruisk, Belarus, during which almost all the Jewish inmates of the camp were executed or died of the horrible physical conditions.

- Aksel Andersen – Sweden (Belarus) – during the years 1942–1943 served as a guard in the Jude lager established by the Nazis in Bobruisk, Belarus, during which almost all the Jewish inmates of the camp were executed or died of the horrible physical conditions.

ACKNOWLEDGEMENTS

When researching and writing this book I was struck – as ever – by the kindness of strangers, who provided me with tremendous help and support. During my visits to Denmark and Norway in particular I was driven round, fed, watered and generally looked after like a long-lost friend rather than a visiting author, so to all those generous souls I say thank you. I would especially like to thank Hugh Page-Taylor for sharing his unrivalled knowledge of the Germanic SS, Grethe Brörup for allowing me to share interviews with her late husband Erik, to Jökull Gislason in Iceland and Lars T. Larsson and Lennart Westberg in Sweden, Jens Post and Holger Thor Nielsen in Denmark – and Peter Davidsen, Lars Larsen and Jens Pank Bjerregaard who were instrumental in helping me with the Danish volunteers – good luck to the latter two with your upcoming book – and thanks to Århus University and Århus Museum for their kind permission to reproduce details of the occupation and resistance in the Odder district. To Knut Flovik Thoresen and Bergljot Østring in Norway, Sigurd Sørlie at the Norwegian Institute for Defence Studies, Lars Erik Lørdahl at the University of Oslo library, the staff at the Riksarkivet/National

Archives of Norway and lastly Dr Inger Cecilie Stridsklev, who was incredibly generous with her time, her car, her home and her knowledge of her home country and all things NS-related – sorry your dog and I didn't get along, Inger Cecilie!

As ever, my heartfelt thanks to my editor Shaun Barrington who says yes to *almost* every crazy book idea I go to him with, and to Jimmy Macleod who seemingly has contacts, photos and research on just about every topic I write on. I am hugely grateful as well – and as usual – to my friend Tim Shaw for his reprographic expertise, and who shares my love of oysters, chips and beer – the lunch of champions!

Most of all I would like to thank the interviewees themselves; Magnus, Andreas, Elisabeth, Karin, Asbjørn, Stål, Bjørn, Jostein and Bergljot – thank you for sharing your memories with an English scribbler, and most of all to Ivar Corneliussen who unfortunately passed away even as I was transcribing the tapes from our interviews.

As is now customary in my work I want to thank my beautiful wife Rachel and our children, Maddy and Jack. Maddy is now studying at university and has discovered that pub quizzes can be more fun than writing essays – I hope she comes back to the light soon – and to Jack who almost went into shock when his History teacher at school told him he'd actually read one of my books, a feat that neither of my children can lay claim to as yet...

AUTHOR'S NOTE

A few comments if I may on the text and how I have structured it. The Second World War was a gigantic cataclysm – the clue is in the title – and the events involved were not only truly global but also constantly happening – the war didn't stop for a break, not ever. So, I thought it vital to try to place the events my interviewees talk about in a timeline of the war itself; what was going on in the conflict and where, and how this might have shaped the veterans at that time, to give readers a sense of the wider war and hence the veterans' place in it. I have also tried to describe to a certain degree what life was like back in Denmark and Norway under German occupation – this is part of the veterans' story too. After all, they went home on leave, went out for a drink, travelled on public transport, spoke to friends and family – how did all of that tie in with them wearing the uniform of the Third Reich?

The interviews themselves were carried out over a period of several months, and all of them were recorded on Dictaphone – with the interviewees' permission of course. Given the distances I had to cover to see them, I was usually unable to return and ask additional questions, or check any points from the original interviews that I was then unclear on when I was making the transcriptions. I don't think this has detracted from the text, but the reader should at least be aware of it. I have made a great effort to ensure the translation from either Danish or Norwegian (the majority of the interviews were conducted in the interviewees' native languages with a smattering of German and some limited English) is both accurate and achieves fluency. At all times I tried to keep the veterans on a chronological timeline so we would go from their early life, to the German invasion, to their enlistment, to their training and first battlefield experience, and so on, but the interviewees sometimes strayed from this, as memories are not often linear – especially with people in their 90s or with authors! That issue of age is important to remember too – the veterans were describing, and trying to recollect – memories from more than 70 years ago, and inevitably some facts, figures, dates and so on might be a little jumbled or inaccurate – that's just life, and if any readers pick up errors on such things I would apologise but also ask for some clemency, given the very nature of the book – these are the recollections of the people who were there, and not a historian's almanac. Although, having said that, I was repeatedly struck by just how good the veterans' mental faculties really were.

Regarding terminology around the fighting in the east, the Soviet Union was – of course – a country composed of literally hundreds of different peoples and ethnic groups, but the front fighters use the term 'Russian' to cover them all, and so I have left it at that.

As the majority of the book is made up of interviews, I have used a key to identify the veterans, unless it's obvious from the text, so Jostein Berge is 'JB', Magnus Møller is 'MM', etc.

The key is as follows:

Interviewees, place and dates of birth and last achieved rank in the Waffen-SS or German Red Cross:

Jostein Berge (JB): Born in Stange, a few miles from the town of Hamar in Norway, 15 May 1926. Rank: SS-Schütze.

Ivar Corneliussen (IC): Born in Davinde (a small village on Funen Island), Denmark, 8 October 1922. Rank – SS-Rottenführer. He was 19 when he volunteered, and 94 when I interviewed him.

Andreas Lorenz Fleischer (AF): Born in Haderslev, Denmark, 22 August 1926. Rank: SS-Unterscharführer. He was 17 when he volunteered, and 90 when I interviewed him.

Elisabeth Kvaal (EK): Ms Kvaal is the 96-year-old Norwegian widow of Ørnulf Kvaal, a member of Vidkun Quisling's Nasjonal Samling. Ørnulf Kvaal was not a member of the Waffen-SS, rather he volunteered for, and served in, the German Army as a medical doctor, even though his own training was as a dentist. Ms Kvaal was also a member of the NS and now lives on the outskirts of Oslo.

Bjørn Lindstad (BL): Born in Storhamar in Vang municipality (now just called Hamar) in Norway, on 2 February 1925. Rank: SS-Sturmmann.

Karin Matre (KM): Born on 8 May 1924 in Norway. Rank – Schwester-helferin German Red Cross. Ms Matre was 92 years old when I interviewed her.

Magnus Johannes Møller (MM): Born in south Jutland, Denmark, 14 September 1920. Rank: SS-Sturmmann. He was 96 when I interviewed him.

Stål Munkeberg (SM): Born in Honningsvåg, Finnmark, on 23 April 1926. Rank: SS-Sturmmann. (Honningsvåg is Norway's northernmost city. In the 2013 census the population was just 2,415, and legislation effective in 1997 states that to be a city in Norway a place must have at least 5,000 inhabitants, but Honningsvåg was declared a city in 1996, and is therefore exempt from this legislation.)

Asbjørn Narmo (AN): Born in Hamar, Norway, 9 May 1921. Rank: SS-Schütze.

Bergljot Østring (BØ): Ms Østring is the widow of the well-known Norwegian Waffen-SS veteran, Bjørn Østring, who passed away in 2012. The couple met in the 1960s and married in 1966.

I

WHY VOLUNTEER FOR THE WAFFEN-SS?

Asbjørn Narmo (AN): I joined the Waffen-SS because of what happened to the Finns. I tried to go there, to Finland, for the Winter War, but they wouldn't let me as I was too young. I knew what the Russians were like, you see, how terrible communism was, because when I was 10 years old I was with my sister and the rest of my family in the Norwegian Embassy in Moscow and we'd all seen what it was like there – horrible, just horrible. We had to fight it, no matter the cost.

Magnus Johannes Møller (MM): I didn't want to join in the war, but I did want to fight the Russians to help Finland. It was very important for me to help Finland and to defeat communism.

Jostein Berge (JB): I joined mainly because I was being harassed about my NS background, and I wasn't the only one. My father had been an NS member since 1933 and was very badly treated by some neighbours because of it. The ones who got Norway into the war only cared about themselves, and were only trying to get themselves out of trouble. It wasn't just that though, the fact that we were being treated badly and I wanted to get away from them, I also enlisted in the Ski Battalion to go to Finland, I wanted to help the Finns.

Elisabeth Kvaal (EK): My husband Ørnulf felt obliged to go. He felt he had to do his 'bit' – that's what you say in English isn't it? He was so worried about communism. His idealism was so great that he only volunteered when it was clear that Germany was going to lose the war. He knew they were just retreating all the time, but he went anyway.

Stål Munkeberg (SM): My parents were pro-German, so I was too, but by 1944 it was clear that the Germans were losing the war, so I decided to volunteer to help them out, and so off I went.

Andreas Fleischer (AF): A lot of my friends went into the German Army, and I thought I should join too, so I volunteered in 1943. I was in Germany at the time, so I just went to a recruiting office there and joined. I was 17 years old. I volunteered for the Waffen-SS – they were the best, the élite – and that's what I wanted, to be the best.

Ivar Corneliussen (IC): One day I was walking through Odense with a friend of mine and we saw a recruiting office for the Frikorps Danmark, and we thought 'why not, let's join.'

Bjørn Lindstad (BL): My family weren't connected to the NS, and deciding to join the Waffen-SS was the most difficult thing I have ever done. It was all to do with my family and the situation at home. When I joined, they didn't know – they just got my clothes in the mail – that's the way it happened. I don't really want to talk about it, please, if you don't mind.

Herein lies the answer to the question the chapter title poses, or rather the answers – lots of them. Ask any group of soldiers anywhere in the world serving in any army and you'd probably get the same wide range of responses; there is no one overriding reason why young men (and increasingly young women) make the life-altering decision to swap their civilian clothes for a uniform. Soldiers enlist for an endless variety of causes ranging from patriotism and youthful idealism, all the way through to the bafflingly simplistic, such as that it seemed a good idea on a wet Thursday afternoon.

The undeniable difference though, is that the Waffen-SS wasn't just any army; it was the armed wing of Hitler's Nazi Party, and it had been created and built to help deliver the National Socialist goal of a German world empire dominated by the Aryan *Herrenvolk* (master race). This made it different, made those who joined it different, even if they didn't have a real sense of what they were joining at the time, or indeed were given a choice as to where they ended up.

Back in the 1930s, Scandinavia was, like pretty much everywhere else in Europe, experiencing political unrest. There was no civil war, as was tearing Spain apart, and neither was there the street violence and rioting that were convulsing France and Weimar Germany, but there was discontent and political extremism. Denmark had a smorgasbord of far-right parties, among them the Danish Unity and Corporatist Party (in Danish *Dansk Samlings og Korporationsparti*), the Danish National-Socialist Party (*Dansk National-Socialistisk Parti*), the National-Socialist Workers' Party (*National-Socialistisk Arbedjer Parti*),[1] and the largest of them all, Frits Clausen's[2] Denmark's National-Socialist Workers' Party (DNSAP – *Danmarks National-Socialistiske Arbedjer Parti*) – all at odds with their opponents on the far-left and the political centre. As for Sweden, it mirrored its southern neighbour with a plethora of parties that formed, split and reformed with bewildering speed, organisations such as the Neo-Swedish National Socialist League,[3] the Swedish Opposition (*Svensk Opposition*) the Sun Wheel (*Solkorset*), and Sven Olov Lindholm's[4] Swedish Socialist Union (SSS – *Svensk Socialistisk Samling*). Norway was different in that one far-right party dominated – Vidkun Abraham Lauritz Jonssøn Quisling's NS. Apart from that, there was a short-lived home-grown Nazi party – the *Norges Nasjonal-Socialistiske Arbeiderparti* – that appeared in January 1934 and just as quickly disappeared that October.[5]

Mussolini and his Italian fascists were Europe's leading far-right movement at that time – Hitler and his Nazis were still the new kids on the block – and in an attempt to herd cats, the Italians tried to corral the Clausens and the Quislings with the likes of France's Marcel Bucard, Britain's Oswald Mosley, Belgium's Léon Degrelle and Ireland's Eoin O'Duffy, and bring them all together into an Italian-sponsored International Fascist Congress – but as is the nature of extremist parties of both left and right they all enjoyed fighting each other far more than finding a common cause to rally around.[6]

Context is all here, though, as yes, there were a lot of far-right parties in Scandinavia at the time, and yes, most of them had youth and paramilitary wings that wore military-style uniforms and held rallies with marches, bands and flags and so on, but there was never the sort of vicious mass gang warfare between them and their opponents as was common in Germany and France, for instance. It is also true to say that there was no overwhelming popular support for any extremist party across Scandinavia – be it of the far left or the far right. So, in the Norwegian general election of 1933 the Communists polled 22,773 votes, while Quisling's brand-new NS got 27,850 – a far cry from the Labour Party's winning tally of just over half a million. To the east in Sweden, three years later, the Social Democrats romped home with around 1.3 million votes, against the Communists on less than 100,000 and a combined total for a number of fascist parties at less than half that. Again, three years later in the Danish general election, Clausen mustered 31,032 votes, to the Communists 40,893, with the winning Social Democrats polling 729,619. All over Scandinavia the extreme right and left were there, but they were only really nibbling at the edges of the political landscape.

However, being in the minority bound many of these voters together, as sometimes happens, and these ties were reinforced by the treatment they often seemed to receive from the mainstream – treatment that still rankles with many of the Norwegian ex-NS members in particular.

EK: Being an NS member in school wasn't much fun I can tell you. The other children would always pick on me, and I remember one day when the BBC – you British – broadcast a radio report about me, **me** *of all people – it was supposedly about a young Norwegian girl giving the Hitler salute, you know, the right arm raised, but that wasn't what I was doing at all. We were proud of our Norse heritage and in those days – you know, back in Viking Norse times – people would greet each other with a raised, open right hand to show they had no weapons and came in peace – that was what I was doing, not a Nazi thing at all – it was a complete accident. No one wanted to listen to my explanation though, and the next thing I knew the school was closed for the* *day – the day the broadcast went out – and suddenly there was a big gang of kids chasing me down the street. They had batons, sticks and some even had knives – knives, can you believe it, for a young girl? I ran for my life, I can tell you, and I somehow managed to reach a fruit shop run by some other NS members. They locked the door behind me and called the police to come and protect us all. I was lucky and didn't get hurt. The other families must have listened to the report on banned radios, because only NS members were allowed to have them. We had one, of course, and sometimes we listened to the BBC too, but not my father, when the BBC came on he would always leave the room. Anyway, after I took my exams in 1941 I decided no more school for me and I left.*

Karin Matre (KM): I joined the NSUF[7] in September 1940, my membership number was 654. It was like being in the Scouts. Some of my friends didn't like me being in the NSUF at all, they were very anti-NS, and some friendships ended, but I made a lot of new friends in the NSUF so it was OK. We lived in different groups here in Norway, you were either NS or not NS; we didn't mix much, which was a real shame.

JB: I was in the NSUF from 1940–41, my future wife, Ingeborg, was in the NSUF too. Lots of people didn't like that. I remember one time, me and my brother – years ago – before the war, we were in a football team and we had a team photo taken, anyway after seeing the photo in the local paper or something I was invited to go and meet another team. I arrived to meet them and as I was waiting I helped lay out the place settings for lunch; coffee cups, plates, etc. One of the other boys helping asked if there was enough settings and I said yes there was, as I was one of those invited for the lunch – he then recognised me and left as he knew then that I was NS.

This enmity between those with a background in the NS, and those who didn't, was a theme I came upon again and again in my interviews in Norway. Strangely enough, it was not the same in Denmark with ex-members of the DNSAP, in fact the legacy of mistrust and resentment I felt very keenly in Norway was almost entirely absent in its southern neighbour.

I was introduced – if that's the right word – to this issue almost as soon as I landed in Norway. My host and companion was Dr Inger Cecilie Stridsklev whose own family was heavily involved in the NS; her mother, Lucie, was an NS member and a local leader in her area of the party's female section, the *Kvinnehird*, her maternal grandfather Anders was a member, and another relative – Arne Stridsklev – fought in the SS Wiking Division and was later sentenced to three years' hard labour for his wartime service. Now, Dr Stridsklev runs an association-cum-support group for the families of former NS – it even has its own website: http://www.nsbarn.no/.

The doctor took me to my first appointment, which was with Bergljot Østring, the widow of Bjørn Østring, a veteran who after fighting on the Leningrad front with the Norwegian Waffen-SS formation – the *Den Norske Legion* (DNL, or in German the *Legion Norwegen,* and in English the *Norwegian Legion*), went home and served in Quisling's bodyguard. I had written to Mrs Østring many times during the writing of *Hitler's Vikings*, and on several occasions since, and I was very much looking forward to meeting her having found her both helpful and polite during all our correspondence. Her flat, in a modern four-storey block overlooking a local school on one side and beautiful stretch of woodland on the other, sits in a small town called Høvik, just outside Oslo. The flat is uncluttered, but 'busy' if I can put it like that; there is shelf after shelf of books, lots of photo albums and books on photography – of which she is a keen student – and quite a few romances. Bergljot herself was well-dressed in dark blue trousers with a dark blue short-sleeved blouse; she had short-cropped grey hair and wore glasses. It was lunchtime when we arrived at her home and our hostess had very kindly prepared lunch for us; open sandwiches, tea, salad and pickles – all very Norwegian – which perhaps is only remarkable in the sense that she herself is not a 100 percent native Scandinavian, having been born in Germany to a Norwegian mother and a German father (Gerhard) – and not just any German, but a Baltic German, that tribe of Teutons that had settled across Estonia, Lithuania and especially Latvia in the days of the crusading Livonian and Teutonic Knights, and then again in the expansion of the mercantile Hanseatic League. Gerhard had joined the *Sturmabteilung* (the SA – Hitler's Brown Shirts) before the war, but not the Nazi Party, and had subsequently worked for Alfred Rosenberg's *Ostministerium*[8] on account of his expertise on the Soviet Union. Seemingly not a convinced Nazi, he had been invited to join the anti-Hitler conspirators, of whom Claus von Stauffenberg was one, but he had declined. Over lunch and some aromatic coffee, Bergljot talked about her family, and about her late husband, whose loss she still clearly felt keenly. It was during this conversation that several themes cropped up that would echo in so many of the interviews I would do in Norway – firstly, the feeling that the NS and its members were made scapegoats after the war; that the machinery of government, the press and the media have unjustly pilloried them; and secondly that post-war justice had been far from blind but instead had been used to serve the wishes of the victors. Whether these charges are true or not is a judgement this book is not intended to adjudicate on, but if I have learnt anything from the history I have studied, it is that injustice – be it real or perceived – is like a cancer in public life and sows the seeds of mistrust within a society. And with that observation, I will leave that particular kettle of fish there.

Less controversial was what turned fringe Scandinavian far-right parties and their supporters (some but not all) into future recruiting grounds for the Waffen-SS. It was, in essence, three words, of which the first was '*Finland*'. Moscow had determined to invade its tiny Nordic neighbour, and concentrated a huge force of more than 450,000 men and masses of tanks, guns and aircraft to do it. Then, on the order from the Kremlin, the Red Army surged over the border on 30 November 1939. Expecting an easy victory, the Soviets were dumbfounded to find themselves facing a Finnish military that although mainly equipped with the 1930s version of bows and arrows, managed to exploit its intimate knowledge of the endless lakes and forests of its snow-bound land to give them a bloody nose.

As one of the invading Soviet infantryman, Georgy Uritski, recalled in an interview with the historian Lloyd Clark in August 2009:[9]

> *It was a winter that I have tried to erase from my mind ... My company was wiped out. Attacking a Finnish position without artillery support we were cut to tiny pieces. Again, and again we attacked until we ran out of men ... My life was spared, but I lost my right hand.*

Uritski was indeed lucky, in total the Soviets suffered an astonishing half a million casualties, to the Finns 90,000, and despite their eventual victory the following spring, their military confidence took a severe knock. Much of the blame for the Red Army's shortcomings could be laid at Stalin's door, with the purge he began of the military back in 1937 gutting the Soviet armed forces almost to the point of no return.[10]

As it was, Soviet aggression was a profound shock to the peoples of Denmark, Norway and Sweden, and resulted in the 'radicalisation' of thousands of young men who stepped forward and enlisted in units that were specifically created to go to fight the Red Army. The Swedish Volunteer Corps for Finland (SFK for short) was one such force, and it alone received almost 13,000 applications[11] from would-be volunteers. The Swedes would be joined by more than 2,000 Danes and Norwegians who stepped forward. Not all were accepted as fit for military service, and the war was over before many others reached it but nevertheless, it created an environment in which Soviet communism was seen as a real enemy, and where it was socially acceptable in some quarters for young men to volunteer to combat it. Indeed, in Dr Inger Stridsklev's own excellent questionnaires to former Norwegian Waffen-SS veterans, more than 80 per cent of respondents cited the assault on Finland and anti-communism as their prime motivators for volunteering.

The second word was '*invasion*' – not of Finland this time, but of Denmark and Norway themselves as Berlin launched *Unternehmen Weserübung* (Operation Weser Exercise) on the morning of 9 April 1940, and defeated the outmatched Danes in approximately six hours. Their veteran Prime Minister, Thorvald Stauning, went on air with the king, Christian X, to announce the country's surrender, and to call on their fellow Danes to cease all resistance. After that, the Germans were content to leave the Danes – whom they viewed as 'fellow Aryans' – much to themselves, and so the existing government stayed in office, parliament continued its work, and the control of both domestic politics and the central authorities, including the courts, remained largely in Danish hands. The police were, however, obliged to co-operate with the occupiers in maintaining order and investigating any anti-German activity.

Under the new arrangements public opinion was in a sort of stasis; on the one hand there was definitely no groundswell of support for the Germans among the population generally, but neither was there widespread opposition – in some ways it was as if the invasion hadn't happened. The Social Democratic politician Frode Jakobsen, who would go on to establish the *Ring* resistance network, wrote down his own experiences of the invasion and its immediate aftermath some 30 years later:

> *We were still lying in bed that morning when we heard the airplanes. I remember making a thoughtless remark to my wife: 'Are they German or British planes?' I didn't mean it because I was sure they were Danish. Ruth had to go to the Radium Centre in Østerbro, where she worked, but around midday I had difficulty reaching her. Outside on the street there were crowds and people talking loudly. The noise of airplanes was gone, but I was aware that it was not an ordinary morning. We had no radio, so it would be a few days before I could listen to London. Outside I was told what had happened: the Germans had landed. I had to see it. I immediately took my bike and cycled off. I went to the harbour and saw the* Langelinie *[Author: the ship had brought invading German troops ashore], it was a depressing sight. There was no hostility, no anger over what had happened. German guards stood everywhere. Everything was calm. But what angered me most was the clusters of people stood around the German soldiers. They talked, they smiled, they gave the Germans*

cigarettes. They were eager to show their neighbours that they could speak German. I went from group to group, listening, registering the reaction. I had had enough. I went up to one group and said loudly and indignantly to the German: 'Sie verstehen wohl, dass dies nicht das danische Volk ist, sondern den danische Pöbel!' *(In English: 'You understand don't you, that this isn't the Danish people, but the Danish rabble?') He looked at me amazed. Would I be arrested? Or was it as if he understood me? I was not a young man. He did nothing. The Danes were partly angry, partly ashamed. I went on my way. Much later I realised that maybe I had done some of the people a favour. The majority of the population didn't understand Nazism, or what had happened to the country, and it wouldn't surprise me if a few years later some of them ended up in the ranks of the freedom movement. What would now happen in Denmark? The statements from politicians angered me. But they could then be nothing but honestly meant. The idea behind the parties' policy would then be to quietly work on another line, a kind of underground resistance. The fact that the parties that professed democracy – I even stood in the Social Democratic Party – found that they had to put a good face on it – for a time, so we could prepare our underground struggle. It was a strange day. The winter had been so terribly harsh. There was still ice in Kastelsgraven. Today was the first day of spring. We had woken up to such a beautiful spring morning, but even though the sun continued to shine, the world was different. I waited for the lunch break at the Radium Centre. I had to see my wife, I had to talk to her. I was there at twelve. It was a moving reunion – after five hours. So much was different. Also, something special for the two of us had changed, we stopped speaking German to each other, it had previously been our common language; Ruth had not been able to speak a word of Danish when we first met. But we stopped on April 9 – for the neighbours, for the sake of the Germans, for the sake of ourselves.*

Jakobsen wasn't alone in feeling a sense of shame and embarrassment at the ease in which Germany occupied the country – nor the lack of active resistance to it from the population. Down in Hjortkaer, not that far from the German border, the 21-year-old farmhand Vagn Husted felt the same.

On April 9, 1940 I was at home with my parents in West Jutland. It was a Tuesday. We had had a long and very severe winter and I was out spreading fertiliser ready for sowing grain.

Early in the morning aeroplanes appeared flying low over my head and going north. I couldn't make out what they were as there was a lot of fog at that time… I've quite forgotten now what I thought about the planes at that point, I hope you will forgive me and understand that I was concentrating on my work that morning.

A little bit later my mother came into the field to see me. She had been listening to the radio and told me that the Germans had come over Denmark's southern border. On the way to see me she had talked to our neighbour's son, Carlo Bertelsen, who said that we were in real trouble now the Germans were coming.

I thought we could still resist and said to my mother: 'We must listen to the radio tonight, maybe I will get called up!' I had done my national service and was a reservist, which meant I was due in Haderslev in November for more training.

I continued my work and when the morning fog lifted I could see the swastikas on the big aeroplanes which continued to fly north, which we later realised were on their way to Norway.

Everything then went very differently than I perhaps naively expected. In the evening we heard King Christian X on the radio and also Prime Minister Stauning. The king said we should stay calm and carry own and I was very angry. My parents took it better, as did Mr Nielsen the teacher, who came around later in the evening and said we had to black out all the windows.

In the evening I went to my work at Lisbeth and Svend Lyndgaard's ... Svend Lyndgaard was very shaken by what had happened, more than my parents had been, and he said we had to go to bed with our clothes on as no one knew what could happen. He and I went on patrol around the farm, each of us armed with a heavy cudgel, and we went to bed with clothes on.

The lawlessness we feared didn't happen, but neither the help we hoped for from England. I don't know how long Svend kept his truncheon by his bed, I threw mine out after about a week. Svend slept with his clothes on the first eight nights. I didn't persevere for so long and after three nights I took my clothes off when I went to bed.

In Denmark we didn't experience the terrible brutality against the population that the Germans practised in other occupied countries, like Poland for example. That was because the German soldiers had very strict orders that they should behave politely and correctly here, which was due – we soon discovered – to their plan to use Denmark as a pantry to help supply their large population and their mighty armies ... In addition, I believe that Heinrich Himmler, who harboured a kind of fanatical admiration for all things Nordic, naively expected some fair-haired and blue-eyed young men to enlist in his SS corps.

But even if everything went relatively quiet here in the days after April 9, 1940, that did absolutely not mean that I took the situation calmly. I wondered all the time on what I could and should do. After about a week or so, I had a plan ready. There was nothing else to do but to try to get to Sweden and from there to go to England and volunteer.

I had been hired by Sven on a year's contract and I wouldn't run from that, so I decided to tell him and my parents about my plan … I thought we could speak about it calmly and although I knew that neither Svend Lyndgaard nor my parents had quite the same attitude to the war as I did, I thought they were definitely on the same page as me.

First, I spoke to Svend Lyndgaard about my plan and I told him I had to make a contribution to beating the Germans together with Europe's other peoples. It was now that I realised that my approach was a big mistake. Svend Lyndgaard didn't understand my views at all. He said that on top of everything else was he now to lose his worker – that would not help. He also said I would be immediately reported to the police if I went and he got very angry. I had never seen Svend Lyndgaard, who was otherwise a friendly and quiet man, so upset. I didn't expect his violent reaction and it unnerved me as we had always had an extremely good relationship with each other.

Now, all these years later, I can see that Svend was completely thrown off balance by the shock of April 9, and I was just increasing that shock. There was nothing more to talk about, I understood, and I was immediately aware that I should have left without saying anything, as we obviously couldn't even talk about it. But at the same time, I was very disappointed that Svend didn't give me credit for wanting to talk to him about it openly. I was prepared that my parents would be very concerned about it, but I knew that I could talk to them about, but now Svend had completely broken my courage.

> *I went and thought about it for a few days, but it didn't take long before the Germans had complete control over everything in Denmark, and I had lost my chance.*

Norway was invaded the very same day as Denmark, with the *Kriegsmarine* (the German Navy) sailing up Oslo fjord in an attempt to land troops on the quayside and take the capital by storm. As an operation it was a disaster. The German flagship, the heavy cruiser *Blücher*, was fired on by the obsolete defences of the Oscarsborg Fortress and sank with heavy loss of life. Norway would go on to resist for two more months until forced to capitulate when an Anglo-French expeditionary force sent to help them had to abandon the country.

A native of Oslo, Karin Matre was a 15-year-old schoolgirl at the time, and would go on to become one of the approximately 500 young Norwegian women to join the German Red Cross as a nurse – of whom some 20 would lose their lives in the fighting.

> *KM: We experienced bombing, at first by the Germans, and people were shocked, but nothing much seemed to happen. The king and the government escaped to London, and they took all the country's gold from the Bank of Norway. On 10 April 1940 there were rumours that the British were going to bomb the city, and lots of people left just in case, but everything was still pretty calm. We left as well and came across columns of marching German soldiers coming from the airport. They were very smart and well-turned out, plus they were well-disciplined and behaved very well – they even gave sweets to the children who ran beside them in droves. The Germans then took over all the schools for their soldiers so the children had to be taught in church buildings and in private houses.*

For Denmark, in particular, there were far-flung consequences from its defeat, as its ancient north Atlantic empire disintegrated. First to go were the Faroe Islands, that sheep-strewn archipelago sitting in the cold, cold ocean almost 1,000 kilometres from mainland Denmark. The British Navy appeared in the island's capital Torshavn on 12 April and that was that, except for the tiny handful of young Faroese men who volunteered for the Waffen-SS, one of whom was the late Sverri Djurhuus.

> *I was a volunteer in the Waffen-SS. I was in Denmark when the war started and stayed there during the war, and then in March 1941 I enlisted. After my training I was sent to the Frikorps Danmark in August that year. Later on, I was transferred to the Regiment Danmark, and I was with them right up until the end of the war. On 5 May 1945 I was in Denmark when the war ended, and was arrested and spent two years in prison. Apart from me there were three other Faroe Islanders in the Waffen-SS that I know of – two were killed in Russia and the other died a few years ago.*

Next to go was the vast semi-continent that is Greenland. Erik the Red's poster-boy discovery was handed to the Americans as a virtual protectorate on 9 April 1941 by the Danish envoy to the United States, Henrik Kauffmann, who signed a treaty authorising the USA to defend Greenland and construct military stations there.

Last, and never least, was the jewel in Copenhagen's crown – Iceland. The home of the oldest national parliament in the world, the *Althing*, Iceland was Danish and self-governing from 1918, and was then occupied by Great Britain in May 1940, who promptly handed it over to the USA to be used as a north Atlantic staging post and weather station. Iceland formally separated from Denmark on 17 June 1944 when its most celebrated politician,

Sveinn Björnsson, announced the island's independence in front of a crowd of 30,000 Icelanders, and immediately became the first President of the new republic – embarrassingly for Sveinn though, his eldest son was in Copenhagen at the time, and rather than banging the drum for Icelandic independence and Allied co-operation, he was actually wearing a Waffen-SS uniform and broadcasting Nazi propaganda back home – more on him later.

The third and last word that transformed the politics of the region and paved the way for the Scandinavian Waffen-SS was '*Barbarossa*'. The largest invasion in history, Barbarossa thrust anti-communism to centre stage – although the much-vaunted 'European Crusade against Bolshevism' was not a big part of the original German campaign, and only really began to be used by the Nazis as a rallying cry when they failed to win the quick victory they anticipated – then it was all the rage as a recruiting tool.

In terms of a European, non-German, SS perspective, what Barbarossa did at first was encourage the *Schützstaffel* (SS) to build on the foundations laid in the occupied countries by the Germanic SS with the creation of armed national legions in the Waffen-SS. Already in the autumn of 1940, the *Allgemeene-SS Vlaanderen* and the *Nederlandsche-SS* had been set up in Flanders and Holland respectively to act as the future Germanic élite of their lands. They were joined in May 1941 by the *Norges-SS* in Norway, but not until the spring of 1943 did the Danes get on board with their *Schalburg Corps* (originally called the *Germansk Korpset*). Initially locally controlled, the former three were taken under Himmler's direct leadership in late 1942 and renamed: *Germaansche-SS in Vlaanderen*, *Germaansche-SS en Nederland* and *Germanske-SS Norge.*[12] Given tasks at home such as supporting the police to maintain order and root out resistance, service was voluntary, unpaid, and was performed after work or at weekends, with uniforms being supplied by the Germans. These Germanic SS organisations effectively became recruiting pools for their national Waffen-SS units, which for Denmark and Norway respectively meant the *Frikorps Danmark* and *Den Norske Legion.*

Notes to Chapter One

1. Littlejohn, David. *Foreign Legions of the Third Reich Vol. 1: Norway, Denmark, France,* p89, R. James Bender.
2. Frits Clausen (12 November 1893 – 5 December 1947), born in Åbenraa, at that time when it was part of Germany, Clausen served in the German Army during World War I. After the war he studied medicine in Heidelberg and became a doctor in 1924, after which he returned to Åbenraa, which had become part of Denmark in 1920, and set up a practice. Clausen entered politics advocating causes that favoured the German minority in southern Jutland. He became a member of the conservative party, but resigned and joined the DNSAP in 1931. Two years later, Clausen ousted the leadership committee of the party and became its sole leader. Under Clausen's direction, the party essentially called for a stronger relationship between Denmark and Nazi Germany, and much of Clausen's support was from the German minority in Denmark. At its height the DNSAP had about 20,000 members and 20,000 sympathisers. However, the party fared relatively poorly in the 1939 elections, winning only three seats in the Danish parliament, the *Folketing.* A year later, when Germany invaded Denmark, Clausen became a strong supporter of the German occupation. The Germans attempted to reward Clausen for his services by trying to persuade Christian X to let him and his followers have roles in the nation's government but the king opposed any such moves. Much to Clausen's chagrin, the Germans were unwilling to forcibly put him in charge of Denmark. The Germans did hope, however, that Clausen would

legally take power in the 1943 elections, but the DNSAP performed poorly, again winning only three seats in the Folketing. After the elections, Clausen joined the German Army (again) and saw active service on the Eastern Front as a surgeon. He returned to Denmark in the spring of 1944, at which point his political career ended when SS-Obergruppenführer Dr Werner Best, the Plenipotentiary of the German Reich for Denmark, convinced him to step down as leader of the party and replaced him with a three-man committee. When Denmark was liberated in May 1945, Clausen was captured and sent to Frøslev Prison Camp. He was later tried, but was in poor health due in large degree to his alcoholism, and he died of a heart attack in the Vestre Fængsel, a prison in Copenhagen, before the trial concluded. Ravn, Ole, *Fører uden folk: Frits Clausen og Danmarks National Socialistiske Arbedjer-Parti*, University of Southern Denmark, 2007.

3. Larsson, Lars, T. *Hitler's Swedes: A History of the Swedish Volunteers in the Waffen-SS*, p17–19, Helion.
4. Sven Olov Knutsson Lindholm (8 February 1903 – 26 April 1998), born in Jönköping municipality, Lindholm was a sergeant in the Swedish army before joining Konrad Hallgren in setting up the *Sveriges Fascistiska Folkparti* (Swedish Fascist People's Party) – which became known as *Sveriges Fascistiska Kamporganisation* (Swedish Fascist Cause Organisation). He visited Nuremberg in 1929 and as a consequence abandoned Italian fascism in favour of German National Socialism and would then play a leading role in both the National Socialist People's Party of Sweden and its successor the Swedish National Socialist Party. The six percent Lindholm captured in Gothenburg in the 1932 election represented a high point for the Swedish National Socialists. However, Lindholm had grown tired of the leadership of Birger Furugård. In 1933 he formed the *Nationalsocialistiska Arbetarpartiet*. This new group, which adopted

the swastika, took an anti-capitalist line and organised its own youth group, the *Nordisk Ungdom* (Nordic Youth). By 1938, Lindholm had become more critical of Berlin and attempted to reorganise the group as more Swedish, reinventing them as the *Svensk Socialistisk Samling* (Swedish Socialist Union). He returned to the army in 1941, opposed the Nazi invasion of Denmark and Norway yet also helped to recruit volunteers for the Waffen-SS. The SSS continued to be active until 1950, after which Lindholm went into semi-retirement, with only minor involvement in far-right youth groups. He died in 1998. Rees, Philip, *Who's Who in the Extreme Right Since 1890: An International Biographical Dictionary,* p233–234.

5. Littlejohn, David. *Foreign Legions of the Third Reich Vol. 1: Norway, Denmark, France,* p8, R. James Bender.
6. Dorril, Stephen, *Blackshirt*, p237, Penguin Viking.
7. The NSUF – the NS's youth wing – NS *Ungdomsfylking.*
8. The Reich Ministry for the Occupied Eastern Territories (German: *Reichsministerium für die besetzten Ostgebiete* or RMfdbO, or Ostministerium for short) was created by Adolf Hitler in July 1941 and headed by the Nazi's supposed ideological expert, Alfred Rosenberg – a Baltic German. The ministry was created to control the vast areas captured by the Germans in Eastern Europe and the Soviet Union. It also played a part in supporting anti-Soviet groups in Central Asia. In reality it lacked power and strong leadership, and its occasional support for peoples such as the Ukrainians – whom it hoped to win over to side with the Third Reich – was fatally undermined by Nazi brutality across the conquered lands.
9. Clark, Lloyd, *Kursk: The Greatest Battle – Eastern Front 1943*, p64, Headline.
10. Stalin's Great Purge of the Soviet armed forces began with the arrest of the 44-year-old Marshal Mikhail Tukhachevsky on 22 May 1937. He was tried with seven other high-ranking colleagues on

11 June and all were then executed just after midnight that same day. Stalin asked Nikolai Yezhov (head of the NKVD): 'What were Tukhachevsky's final words?' 'The snake said he was dedicated to the Motherland and Comrade Stalin, then he asked for clemency.' Stalin was silent for a moment and then belched. Tukhachevsky's wife, Nina, and his brothers Alexandr and Nikolai (both instructors at a Soviet military academy) were all shot. Three of Tukhachevsky's sisters were sent to the *gulag* and his underage daughter was arrested when she reached adulthood and remained in the *gulag* until the 1950s. Following Tukhachevsky's execution, the rest of the Soviet officer corps was crushed: three of the five marshals created in 1935 were shot, along with 15 of the 16 Army commanders, 50 out of 57 Corps commanders, 154 out of 186 divisional commanders and 401 out of 456 colonels – senior Party members were not exempt either; of the 1,966 delegates to the XVIIth Party Congress in 1934, some 1,108 were executed in the purges. Bellamy, Chris, *Absolute War – Soviet Russia*, p32–3, MacMillan.

11. Westberg, Lennart, & Gyllenhaal, Lars, *Swedes at War*, p217, Aberjona.
12. McNab, Chris, *Hitler's Elite: The SS 1939–45*, p105–107, Osprey.

2

FIRST INTERVIEW – MEETING MAGNUS

Flying into Copenhagen, I picked up my hire car – a one-step-off-the-bottom diesel Ford Fiesta – plugged in the TomTom satnav I had brought with me (already pre-loaded with a map of the country), and headed west to the small apartment in the town of Vejle that I had rented for a few days. This was my first visit to Denmark and much as I tried to keep my eyes on the road, I seemed to spend most of my time looking at the country through which I was driving and constantly saying to myself: 'It looks just like England.' Denmark's countryside is rich, the contours of the land are undulating, so much of it looks like an unmade green duvet dotted with neat farms and prosperous villages. It wasn't what I expected in a strange sort of way. I didn't expect grinding poverty of course – this is Scandinavia after all – but I was surprised by just how much it resembled my own country – not all of it, I live in the midst of the Peak District and the Yorkshire Moors after all, but it felt like being in the Cotswolds, or the wealds of Sussex. Maybe because I'm a history geek, but the first thing that sprang to my mind at that point was a question: Why did the Danish Vikings leave this place to come and raid and invade England?

I had always been taught that those same Vikings had struggled to scratch a living in their own desperately poor homelands, and that was the wind that filled the sails of their dragon ships as they crossed the North Sea. But looking around me that couldn't be the case, it seemed far more likely that on reaching England's shores the first Vikings would have seen the land and said how much it looked like home. The only time this image was swept from my mind completely was when I crossed the Great Belt. This combined road and rail bridge is an absolute marvel of engineering, seeming to go on and on ad infinitum, and so high that a big car ferry passed underneath as I drove over it. Having said that, the toll I was charged was also so high I felt as if I was personally paying for its upkeep – but enough of my parsimony. I arrived in Vejle, made myself comfortable in the flat, walked around town to orientate myself and then drove north to Århus – Denmark's second-largest city – to meet two local contacts who had arranged for me to interview my first veteran – Magnus Møller.

Magnus had volunteered for the Danish *Frikorps Danmark* (in German *Freikorps Danmark*, and *Free Corps Denmark* in English) pretty much as soon as the unit was established in 1941,[1] and had then gone out with it to the Russian front and fought in the long-running Demyansk encirclement. When the *Frikorps* was disbanded in 1943, he had left the Waffen-SS and gone home. During my preparations for the trip I had come across him in a YouTube video in which he was talking about the war, and I had also seen photos of him on a battlefield tour he had gone on back to Russia, and the basic impression I had formed of him was of an elderly but still physically imposing man with an excellent memory of events. As I went up the stairs to his flat I had high hopes for the interview. So when I walked into his apartment I was shocked by what – or rather who – I found. This couldn't be the man I had seen in the posted video, he had been upright and vigorous, while this figure was ailing, his torso almost fallen in on itself – a balloon deflated – his stare vacant and dull, the flesh wasted off his bones, his dark grey trousers and blue roll-neck hanging off him, his lower jaw jutting, wisps of white hair on a paper-thin scalp, and over-sized feet tucked into well-worn black slippers. Yet it was, this was indeed Magnus Johannes Møller, 96-year-old veteran of the Danish Waffen-SS, and survivor of the terrible fighting at Demyansk and Velikiye Luki. Trying to compose myself, I looked around the flat – I must admit that this was partly to buy time before we began – it was open-plan with a big lounge-cum-dining area, and an en-suite bathroom with a disabled toilet you could look right in on. Large windows made the place light, but also showed how sparse it was; a few cabinets filled with books, some knick-knacks, a handful of photos. I checked out the books; I always do, it can be quite instructive, and never less than interesting, to see what people read. For Magnus, most of the books were about the Danish Waffen-SS, including one on the Danish Knight's Cross winner, Søren Kam,[2] and a well-thumbed copy of Dan Brown's *Da Vinci Code*. I was brought back to the interview when Magnus began to scrape his long fingernails on the edge of his lunch tray – something he would do repeatedly throughout the interview – making a noise akin to scratching a blackboard, and he then started to talk:

MM: I am from the southern part of Denmark, near the German border, the Germans call it Schleswig. You must remember Herr Trigg that we Danes share a border with the Germans, and we're very close to each other in lots of ways. My father had served in the German Army in the First World War, and I had enormous respect for the German Army – to me they were the best – but despite that

> *I didn't want to join the Germans, I wanted to be part of a Danish unit, so when they announced the establishment of the Frikorps I signed up straightaway, on the very first day in fact – I am proud to say I was one of the very first to join the Frikorps – it was Danish you see, a Danish unit approved by the government*[3] *and made up of volunteers, like me. It was part of the Danish Army – yes, we were Waffen-SS, but not 100 percent Waffen-SS, we were just volunteers who had to wear Waffen-SS uniforms. It was for Denmark, and for Finland, and we all wanted to help Finland – it wasn't so much to help the Germans. As for politics I was already a member of Frits Clausen's DNSAP, as was my father, and lots of local people – it wasn't a strange thing to be a member, not in our part of Denmark anyway.*
>
> *Yes, I was a Nazi back then, but that was a very long time ago and so much has changed and I'm not so much a Nazi now, not 100 percent. There were quite a few other Nazis in the Frikorps – not everyone of course – but a few, and some of them believed in Nazism very much.*

There it was, right in front of me, a former Waffen-SS volunteer admitting he was a Nazi when he joined up. This shouldn't have been news, this shouldn't have been shocking, and yet it was. This was the first time in any interview I had ever conducted with a volunteer where this admission had been made. Normally, former volunteers would say they were *anti-communists*, they were *patriots, nationalists*, anything but Nazis – my Swedish contact had always told me that the volunteers he interviewed told him that they were *against* communism and not *for* Nazism. That isn't to say all these reasons and justifications weren't true – I'd interviewed a number of Flemish ex-Waffen-SS men for the book prior to this one [see *Voices of the Flemish Waffen-SS*], and I had no doubt that their almost unanimously stated view that they had enlisted to further their cause for an independent Flanders was indeed the truth, but this wasn't what had motivated Magnus Møller. Yes, he had joined primarily to help the Finns fight the Soviet Union, but he had also joined because he fundamentally believed in the founding ideology of Hitler's Third Reich. This was a revelation.

However, some of Magnus's comrades in the *Frikorps* were less than enamoured by their erstwhile Nazi countrymen. One of them, the former Danish Army *Gardehusar* Regiment officer Erik Brörup, who had also volunteered for the Waffen-SS, and who I interviewed for *Hitler's Vikings*, said about it all:

> *When Operation Barbarossa started, the invasion of the Soviet Union of course – all the Danish Nazis wanted to join the glory trail, and they started up the Frikorps Danmark. I had already received my marching orders for Bad Tölz,*[4] *but at the last minute they were changed and I found myself in the Frikorps. I didn't mind so much, but these Danish Nazis really pissed me off. I've never been interested in politics and I think that politicians are the lowest form of life along with pimps and preachers.*

MM: My joining was complicated you see, as I said I was a Nazi back then, but that wasn't the only reason I joined the Frikorps. I wanted to help Finland, again as I've said, and we were poor too. We lived in the countryside and I was born on my parents' farm. We had no money before the war, we weren't alone in that, there were a lot of people without any money at that time, there was a terrible crisis in Europe you know, a depression, and so many people didn't have a job – there was very little work – so we were lucky in a way, as we were poor but had the farm, and we worked hard I can tell you, I was the oldest of six children and we all worked on the farm, very long days, hard physical labour. I didn't mind it so much though, and the best thing about it was working with the animals – I loved that – especially the horses. I love horses, they are such wonderful animals; beautiful, strong, loyal, I've always thought horses and me are bound together in some way – anyway, I was told that if I joined the Frikorps I could carry on working with horses as they had quite a few of them, for the officers mainly, so at Langenhorn and Treskau[5] *I looked after the officers' horses.*

Leaving home wasn't easy. My father had no problem with me joining the Frikorps so when I went to leave he was fine, but my mother wasn't happy at all. She was very sick you see, her legs were paralysed, and she wanted me to change my mind and stay at home on the farm. But I'd volunteered and that was that, so off I went. First of all, they sent us to Langenhorn, near Hamburg, and not very far from Denmark; while we were there we got our uniforms, we had a bed, a roof over our heads, the food was good and there was lots of it, and we got paid too – not much, and all in German Reichsmark of course, but you couldn't complain. There weren't many German officers there at that point, and we thought we would be commanded by Danes, but we were all very surprised when they began to train us and the orders were all given in German. As our farm was near the German border I could speak German, but a lot of the lads couldn't and they had real problems. The Germans didn't care though, we soon realised that the Germans really thought they were the best, better than anyone else – the master race – and that we Danes weren't as good as they were. They didn't really want the Frikorps – we found that out from our German instructors – they didn't respect us as soldiers and they thought they would win the war without us – we were a distraction, nothing else. They didn't really like us either, and to be honest we didn't really like them too, it was a clash of cultures you understand, we Danes wanted to have a drink sometimes and have some fun, whereas the Germans were all about the rules, always rules, rules, rules, and lots of them! We especially didn't like the way we were treated by the German officers in Langenhorn, they just wanted to control everything. But the officers liked me because I could speak their language and help them with the other volunteers, and because I was good with their horses. As for the training itself, it was very tough, very hard. We tried to do as little as possible, you know, to do just enough to get through it.

Other Scandinavian volunteers such as the Danes Ivar Corneliussen and Andreas Fleischer, and the Norwegian Bjørn Lindstad, had the same view on the training as Magnus:

IC: Training was hard. One of my friends didn't look after his rifle properly so the instructor told him to hold it above his head and run around this field we were in again and again and he had to shout all the time at the top of his voice – 'I must look after my rifle, I must look after my rifle,' again and again.

AF: The training was hard, very hard, I can tell you. After the war I became a sergeant in the Danish Army and most of the men used to complain about the training, saying it was hard and so on, and I used to say to them 'you know nothing, this training is nothing compared to what I did during the war.' We were trained to follow orders, no matter what they were, we had to follow them, it was about discipline – that made training hard, so if we were told to jump down into the mud or into ditches full of water, then we did it. We were also trained never to leave a wounded comrade behind, we had to get them and carry them back to be treated, no matter what. And, we were told 'never steal, not ever'. I remember once an Army soldier came up to me and said 'Hey, I thought you Waffen-SS boys never stole anything, but you have, you've stolen from us.' I just looked at him – looked him in the eye and said, 'you better get away from me, man, or there'll be trouble, we SS don't steal, so go away.' That was that, he went away – that was at the front.

BL: I had trouble with the language as all the training was in German. I was used to physical labour so that wasn't a big problem, I'd been working with my hands for quite a while before I volunteered, but the language made it hard.

Not all the volunteers found the training extremely hard though. Asbjørn Narmo was one of about 700 young Norwegians who joined the Waffen-SS as a ski trooper, and one of the 500 or so who survived the war:

AN: I found the training pretty easy – I'd been cutting trees down for a long time beforehand as a job, and so I was already fit and fairly strong – and we had to do a lot of skiing in the training too, and I was used to that as well. Almost everyone I trained with was Norwegian like me, so that helped too, with the language and everything.

The volunteers trained all over Europe – Germany, Austria, Poland and so on – however, the majority, particularly those who enlisted from 1942 onwards, spent at least some time at the former French Saint Andre mental institution and now-Germanic Waffen-SS training area at Sennheim (modern-day Cernay) in Alsace-Lorraine, at that time an annexed region of

Nazi Germany, having been ceded to France at the end of the First World War.[6] Sennheim was specifically designated as the initial training base for all non-German European Waffen-SS volunteers, with a battalion structure that was composed of *Kompagnie Nord* for Danes, Norwegians and Swedes, and *Kompagnie West* for Dutch and Flemish recruits. A volunteer would usually spend four to six weeks at Sennheim learning marching and drill, doing fitness and sport and having some political classes on Nazi ideology. They would then be sent to other barracks, such as Klagenfurt in Austria, for further combat training and weapons familiarisation.

IC: We didn't have much money when I was young, and I was a bit of a tearaway as a child, I didn't behave well and was always getting into trouble. I wanted to be a sailor in the Danish Navy, I wanted to serve in a submarine, so me and a friend hitchhiked our way to the Danish naval base in Copenhagen and spent a couple of weeks there going through all the tests, but an x-ray showed a spot on one of my lungs from when I was a child and had had a lung disease, so I was discharged and sent away as 'unfit for service'... When my friend and I went into the recruiting office of the Frikorps they asked us what they could do for us and we said we wanted to join, and we did the paperwork there and then, and that was it, we were in the Waffen-SS. We were asked to sign up for two years, for four years or for the duration of the war, and I signed for the duration of the war – 'auf Kriegsdauer' contracts they were called. I found out later that most of the Norwegian volunteers were serving on one-year contracts, whereas the majority of us Danes had signed up for the whole war. I can't remember my friend's name now – I can see his face, not a problem, but I can't remember his name, it will come to me and I'll tell you. Anyway, within a week a Danish SS-Schütze [Author: private soldier] showed up at my house and collected both my friend and I and took us to Sennheim for recruit training – there were about eight or 10 of us on the transport to Sennheim. I did my recruit training there and was then sent to Klagenfurt in Austria for further training.

AF: So, I was sent to Sennheim barracks in the Alsace for my basic training – most people there spoke French and I don't know the language – and then, after that, I was sent to Poland for more training – on all sorts of weapons including anti-tank guns, heavy machine-guns and infantry cannons as well.

BL: I was trained at Sennheim in Alsace. There were 40 other Norwegians there at the time, and so I made a lot of friends. We all thought we were going to the Legion[7] *– and we were meant to be in Sennheim for six weeks, but instead we ended up staying for 12. Normally recruits weren't given weapons in Sennheim, but because we were there for so long we were trained with weapons. We were then sent to Mitau [modern-day Jelgava in Latvia] – it's called something else now, it was 30 kilometres south of Riga. But we had only just arrived when we were sent back to Germany – typical military! So, all together we were travelling for two weeks.*

For all the volunteers, training ended with them taking an oath of loyalty to Adolf Hitler.

JB: We didn't swear an oath to Adolf Hitler personally, but to him as the supreme commander of the armed forces, it was different.

The actual oath taken by all members of the Waffen-SS was intended to be as follows:

> *I swear to you, Adolf Hitler, as Führer and Chancellor of the German Nation, loyalty and bravery. I vow to you and to my superiors designated by you, obedience to the death. So help me God.*

However, there were some exceptions, such as for the original *Frikorps Danmark* oath which was altered by Christian Peder Kryssing (the *Frikorps*'s first commander), with Hitler's name replaced with the term 'German Commander in Chief'. Not that all the veterans went straight into the Waffen-SS; two of my interviewees first joined the *Germanische Landdienst* (the Germanic Land Service)[8] and were sent to occupied Poland to both carry out war work on the land, and to help prepare the conquered East for its planned future as Nazi *lebensraum* (living space).

The first of those Land Service volunteers I interviewed was the former DRK nurse and NS member – Karin Matre, now 92 years old. We arrived outside her four-storey apartment block of sand-coloured brick and bright flower boxes, and then had to wait for the best part of half-an-hour for her as she was out on a walk with her local rambling group – it was our fault, we were early.

Her flat was almost a carbon-copy of everyone else's I had seen: clean, light, adorned with family photos and mementoes – in her case lots of porcelain figurines, a tribal face mask and Egyptian statuette picked up on a foreign holiday back in the day. There was no television, just a huge wall calendar, and there on the lone chest-high bookcase were the collected works of Jonas Lie – including his detective novels.[9] Karin herself was a bit stooped – arthritis or osteoporosis I thought, probably the latter. Nevertheless, she was very lively, with very blue eyes; her pink shirt, flower-patterned trousers and sleeveless denim jacket were capped by her smile. It was a warm day, the balcony doors were open and the noise from the communal gardens being mowed wafted in on the breeze.

KM: After the Germans arrived lots of things changed, of course. People started buying too much – panic buying – so they brought in rationing to try and control it, but everyone had enough to eat. If you had children you got extra food, and we all grew food too, wherever we could – we had two allotments, after all we had four children to feed. We read about the war in the papers, but we only trusted some of what we read. As NS we were allowed to have radios, but we didn't listen to London, though other people did.

I joined the Germanic Land Service early on, not that long after the Germans came here. As an NS member, I was encouraged to join. It was natural, we talked about it at home, and there were lots of nice people in it, so it was a normal thing to do. My whole family was NS; my mother and father, my two brothers and my sister she was younger than me – and like me she joined the NS's youth wing, the Ungdomsfylking. My elder brother ended up serving in Quisling's bodyguard – the Førergarden[10] *– with Bjørn Østring – and my younger brother, who was two years younger than me, he did Land Service too and then went to a school for very bright children in Gjøvik. Later on in the war a recruiter went to the school to try and get the boys to volunteer for the SS Ski-battalion.*

Anyway, I was sent to Posen [Author: modern-day Polish Poznan] in the Warthegau,[11] *it was a nice place, where we were sent. I led a group of 25 other young people: Norwegians, Danes, Dutch and some Flemish. The Poles who lived there had signs on their clothes to identify them as Polish – it was the letter 'P' on a yellow badge. We worked with the local Volksdeutsche*

[Author: ethnic Germans] who'd lived there for generations. We worked on the farms, harvesting grain, hay and rape seed for the oil. It was hard work but fun.

So far so good – it all sounded like good, healthy fun – a very Nazi image of lots of clean-limbed blond youths marching to the fields singing, all smiles as they bring the harvest in and eat picnics next to hay wains – except there was another side to this particular coin, and as so often with the Third Reich it was a dark one.

The Nazis had a plan for the Warthegau – and the local majority Poles had no place in that plan. Under the slogan 'By the sword comes the plough', the whole region was to become 'Aryanised' – and Norwegians were integral to that process. The Holocaust Centre researcher, Terje Emberland, pointed out:. 'Heinrich Himmler and the SS idealised Norwegians, whom they believed were actually ancient Vikings and conquerors. Therefore, they wanted Norwegian blood to help colonise the east.'

The programme called for Jewish Poles to be rounded up and deported to the Łódź ghetto, where they were to be used as slave labour and systematically starved. Those who survived that process were to be murdered at a later point when the extermination camps were up and running. The rest of the Poles were to be sorted into two groups: 'racially useful' and not. The Nazi's regional governor – the megalomaniac sadist Artur Greiser – was then to 'Germanise' the former, allowing them to stay with the 16.7 percent of the population classified in the 1921 census as ethnic Germans. They were to be joined by trainloads of other ethnic Germans shipped in from the Baltic countries, Romanian Bessarabia and Bukovina and other far-flung provinces, to become the 'new' German population, taking over the farms, homes and businesses of the previous occupants.

Those 'previous occupants' were to enter the past tense by being forcibly expelled to the dumping ground in the east that the Nazis christened the General Government – *Generalgouvernement*. There they would be exploited as a labour pool until they dropped dead. To aid in that process the Nazis set ration levels in the area at 2,310 calories per day for a German, and 654 for a Pole – a Jew got just 184 calories.[12]

KM: We didn't know then that the idea was to take over all the land for people of Germanic descent. I went there for a year, and then signed up for another year, but things were changing in the war and the Swedes wouldn't let us travel through Sweden anymore so I had to come back early – I was there for 18 months in the end. I then went back to Norway and was asked to try and persuade others to volunteer for the Land Service. They sent me to Bergen first, and I managed to convince some others there to join, but I can't remember how many. I was then meant to go back to the Service myself but it was cancelled.

Another Land Service volunteer was the tall and strapping 17-year-old Jostein Berge – a native of Stange, near Hamar in southern Norway. He found himself in occupied Poland in 1943, called out to take part in an operation where German troops were evicting local Polish farmers.

JB: We never saw anything wrong in joining the Land Service, on the contrary, I think it was a bit of a sacrifice for us, as it was not a particularly popular thing to do. On this day we were armed with small calibre rifles, but we had no ammunition. But we carried the weapons anyway, and we were also in uniform. We just stood guard, but I saw at least one case where a man was thrown out of his house. I know they protested, I could hear them shouting and crying, but there was nothing we could do.

The Norwegian magazine that printed the interview with Jostein that included his response above, had managed to track down one of the Poles who had been evicted – not in that same operation, as he was forced out in 1940 – but from the same region, and his name was Herbert Kurczewski.

I was just six years old at the time and we lived in constant fear that the Germans would suddenly come – probably at night – and send our parents to concentration camps. Then, one day, German soldiers appeared and were running to all the major farms. One came to our farm and ordered us to pack all our belongings within two hours, and leave the farm. They brought Germans from Latvia and Estonia with them who were to take over our farm. We left a big house, all our animals and 50 hectares of land behind us. The Germans sent us to Rabka – hundreds of us, all from our region.

Berge was very clear that – as with Karin – he did not know about the 'master plan' of deportation and extermination – and given the Nazis obsessive secrecy about their final goals there is no reason to doubt their sincerity. Even so, it was hard for Berge to come to terms with what he took part in.

JB: It is not easy to understand what went on at that time, it's easy for people to criticise it now of course. But I was very young – we were all very young – and while that does not excuse the problems those poor people had, it does at least explain it a little on our part. But also, I cannot stand here and simply say 'I regret what I did, and if only I had known, and so on…' That would be too easy. One must stand up for what one has done and know that you did it because at the time you thought it was right and the best thing to do.

As it turned out, the settlers, already transported from one homeland, were to reap a whirlwind of vengeance in their new one. By 1945 nearly half a million *Volksdeutsche* had set up home in the Warthegau, but with the advance of the Red Army they hurriedly threw their most valued possessions onto wagons, carts and their own backs and took to the roads west. Thousands died from the cold, or were killed in Soviet air raids, artillery strikes, or general massacres. Those who clung on until peace finally came, found themselves utterly despised by the returning Poles and were expelled in turn as part of the mass ethnic cleansing of German-speaking peoples that scarred central and eastern Europe after the war.

Notes to Chapter Two

1. The DNSAP's newspaper – the *Fædrelandet* (in English *Fatherland*) – announced the formation of the *Frikorps Danmark* on 29 June 1941, seven days after the Nazi invasion of the Soviet Union.
2. Søren Kam (2 November 1921 – 23 March 2015) was a very well-known Danish Waffen-SS volunteer, having become only the third Dane to be awarded the Knight's Cross in 1945 while a company commander in the SS-Panzergrenadier Regiment Germania for 'especially decisive action in the battle against the enemy', and being wanted in Denmark for the murder of the newspaper editor Carl Henrik Clemmensen. Kam originally joined the Waffen-SS in June 1940 and served with the SS-Wiking Division in Russia, winning the Iron Cross 1st and 2nd Class, along with the Infantry Assault Badge, the Close Combat Clasp and the Wound Badge in Silver.

After the war he settled in West Germany under the pseudonym Peter Müller. Still wanted, Denmark applied for his extradition in 1999 and again in 2007, but it was refused by the German authorities. Kam gave his only recorded interview to the BBC World Service in February 2008 for a programme entitled *The Danish Nazi* in which he declared: 'I am a good man, I never did anything wrong.' Kam wrote his memoirs and had a middle man hand them over to the Royal Library's head of research, John T. Lauridsen, and the respected historian Mikkel Kirkebæk, so they could publish them after his death. Kam died in Kempten, Germany, at the age of 93.

3. Lidegaard, Bo, *Dansk udenrigspolitiks historie. Overleveren – 1914–1945*. Danmarks Nationalleksikon.
4. The *Frikorps Danmark* was sanctioned by the democratically elected Danish government and members of the Royal Danish Army were authorised to join it (many did, including 77 officers). The *Frikorps*'s first commander, the Danish artillery officer Lieutenant-Colonel Christian Peder Kryssing, made a public appeal for volunteers to come forward on 5 July 1941: 'Men of Denmark, with the approval of the government, I have been placed in command ... I call upon you to join the ranks of the *Frikorps Danmark*...' In total, 12,000 Danes would volunteer, with only half being accepted. Of these 6,000 some 1,500 were from Denmark's ethnic German minority.
5. SS-*Junkerschule* Bad Tölz was the premier officers' training school for the Waffen-SS. Established in 1937 the school was located about 30 miles south of Munich in Bavaria. The school operated until the end of the war.
6. Langenhorn (Hamburg) and Treskau (modern-day Owińska in Poland) were military barracks where the *Frikorps Danmark*'s recruits underwent their initial training.
7. The border region of Alsace-Lorraine was ceded to the new German Empire following its victory over France in the Franco-Prussian War

of 1870–71. It then became French again under the provisions of the Versailles Treaty in 1919, and was then yet again taken over by Germany after the defeat of France in 1940. It would revert to being French in 1945.

8. *Den Norske Legion* – DNL (in English the Norwegian Legion, German: *Freiwilligen-Legion Norwegen*) was formed by the Waffen-SS on 29 June 1941 in German-occupied Norway – the same day as the *Frikorps Danmark* was announced. Volunteers were assured that it would be a Norwegian unit with Norwegian officers, uniforms and language and that its area of operations would be Finland. Instead, the Norwegians were deployed to Russia, initially taking part in the fighting on the Leningrad front.
9. With the urging of the Norwegian Minister, Axel Stang, about 500 Norwegian teenagers between the ages of 16 and 18 joined the international *Germanische Landdienst*, and were sent to occupied Poland in 1942/43 to be trained as potential future 'Aryan colonisers'. They joined several thousand other young people recruited into the service from Germany, Denmark, Holland and Flemish Belgium. The service emblem was an Odelsrune pierced by an upward pointing sword. Littlejohn, David, *Foreign Legions of the Third Reich Vol. 1*, p65, Bender.
10. Jonas Lie (31 December 1899 – 11 May 1945) was the Minister of Police between 1941 and 1945 in the *Nasjonal Samling* government of Vidkun Quisling. He was an early Waffen-SS volunteer and served with the SS Leibstandarte in the Balkan campaign. The grandson of the novelist Jonas Lie and the son of the writer Erik Lie, he himself wrote a number of popular detective novels under the *nom de plume* Max Mauser in the 1930s. In 1942, he also published *Over Balkans syv blåner*, an account of his Waffen-SS service in the Balkans.
11. The *Førergarden* was one of the two regular units of the NS *Rikshird* (main national paramilitary part of the NS, like the Nazi SA),

and consisted of 150 hand-picked hirdmen who volunteered to perform six months full-time duty as guards at Quisling's two official residences. Karin's younger brother served in the SS-Schijäger-Bataillon and survived the fighting at Kaprolat and Hasselmann Hills in 1944.

12. The Warthegau – also called the *Reichsgau Wartheland* – was a Nazi administrative zone carved out from the western parts of Polish territory annexed after the invasion of 1939 and named after the main river running through it: the Wartha.
13. Official figures for food distribution in the General Government as of December 1941.

3

FIRST BLOOD – DEMYANSK

Barbarossa – the Third Reich's grand plan to destroy the Soviet Union and occupy the country to a line extending from Archangel in the north to Astrakhan in the south – had died in the winter snows of 1941/42. A far from beaten Red Army had defied Hitler's predictions of its imminent collapse and had launched attacks all along the front that had cost the Wehrmacht tens of thousands of its best men and much of its equipment. One of these Soviet offensives in the north had failed in its stated objective of encircling Ernst Busch's entire Sixteenth Army, but had succeeded in trapping much of Walter Graf von Brockdorff-Ahlefeldt's II Army Corps and some of the X Army Corps. In total about 90,000 soldiers and 10,000 auxiliaries (mainly personnel from the Organisation Todt and the Reich Labour Service) were surrounded in what became known as the Demyansk Pocket – an area of swamp, and forests of pine and birch roughly the size of the Danish island of Funen. Alongside the five Army infantry divisions in the Pocket (the 12th, 30th, 32nd, 123rd and 290th), was Theodor Eicke's SS Division *Totenkopf*, and as heavy defensive fighting in February, March and April 1942 ground down the Totenkopf in particular, the decision was made to reinforce the pocket with the by-now-trained *Frikorps Danmark* and its Danish volunteers – Magnus Møller amongst them.

What Magnus and his comrades didn't know at that time was that they were about to be thrown into a battle of unusual ferocity – unusual even in the context of the utter brutality of the Eastern Front. At Demyansk, Soviet and German infantrymen fought each other hand-to-hand amidst the stink and slime of seemingly endless marshes, and a roof was a luxury as the Soviet Airforce bombed every building in sight to deny it to the enemy. For the men inside the Pocket, reinforcements and supplies of food, ammunition and spare clothing were at a premium and what little did get in, usually arrived via the 800-metre-long airstrip hacked out of the undergrowth, or on the *Rollbahn* (German military parlance for main supply route) built in the spring, which was mainly made of birch logs laid side by side in the mud. Opening that roadway had cost the Germans close on 20,000 casualties – the Red Army suffered approximately three times that number trying to stop them – and the Danes were focused on helping to keep it open and functioning.

The near-1,000-strong *Frikorps* suffered its first loss early on – 10 May to be exact – when an ex-French Foreign Legionnaire in its ranks, 'Morocco' Jensen, was killed by a mine splinter in his neck – 136 more Danes would die before they were withdrawn, and another 400 would be wounded. Most of the rest would contract some sort of illness, such as swamp fever or typhus. Hardly anyone got out unscathed.

Some of the fiercest fighting occurred in the middle of July as SS-Sturmmann S. Larsen of the *Frikorps*'s 2nd Company recalled:

I was in a platoon that fought near the Rollbahn – it was some very heavy fighting, suddenly we could hear engine noise and the rattling of chains, and out of a cloud of diesel smoke a T34 came into sight about 50 metres ahead of us. The turret turned slowly back and forth, and I saw that the crew had caught sight of two Danes hiding behind some tree trunks. The T34 fired a shell that hit just in front of the stack of logs with a gigantic bang. Both the logs and the two Danes disappeared in a thunderous explosion. Through an opened hatch the tank commander's head and upper body appeared, by reflex I fired at him and hit him, and he sank back down into the tank. Shortly after that the hatch closed and with a roar the T34 turned back into the woods again.

We ran over to the two Danes and found that both were still alive; I knew one of them, he was Hans Peter Fischer [Author: SS-Schütze Fischer volunteered for the Frikorps on 20 July 1941 in the first wave of recruits] and the other was a new man I didn't know. The new man had been wounded by shrapnel in the abdomen, while both of Fischer's legs were badly injured. We put both of them on makeshift tent stretchers and evacuated them to the battalion command post, where they were examined by SS-Obersturmführer Dr Konrad Lotze, who could not do more for them than first aid and then send them on to the main Totenkopf Division hospital at Lotnitzi. Martinsen gave me orders to go with the two wounded to the hospital, and then 'get your ass back here as fast as possible'.

For transport we went in the back of a Tatra truck, and along with the two wounded were the driver and me. Fischer lay semi-conscious on a tarpaulin, and the new man sat curled between my legs, so I could keep him wrapped up, Lotze had said that the wound in the abdomen was so large that he had to sit bent over to stop his guts falling out, so it was very important that he didn't straighten himself out. Lotnitzi was about 10kms away, and the trip was pure torture for the two wounded because the fighting meant we had to leave the road and drive most of the way down the Robja river bank. The new guy quickly lost consciousness, but I could see that Fischer was still alive but bleeding a lot, and the pool of blood around him grew larger and larger. At one point he fumbled around with his hands at his throat, almost as if he could not breathe, I yelled 'what the hell are you doing? Lie still for God's sake'. He carried on fumbling around at his neck and it was only when we reached the hospital did I find out he was a Catholic and had been trying to reach the crucifix he wore around his neck. But by the time we reached the hospital it was too late – he was dead – having bled to death on the truck bed. The new man was still alive when he was brought to the doctors, but only for a short time I think, I am almost certain that he died later. The hospital was too scary to be in, so after a quick smoke break we drove back to the front.

Larsen's 1st Company comrade – SS- Schütze Anton Hansen – thought much the same of the hospital:

It was like walking into a slaughterhouse, outside lay the dead side by side in long rows, many of the most seriously injured were also placed there, waiting to join the lines of the dead.

For the ex-Danish Army dragoon – Werner Bircow Lassen – this was his first real experience of the front:

So far, I had seen very little fighting, I had mainly been in reserve, and most of my impression of war had been through my ears –

hearing the explosions and gunfire, but now I saw it; trees had been torn up by shellfire and everywhere there were heaps of corpses, Germans and Russians, dead horses, smashed vehicles and tanks, discarded weapons and scraps of uniform.

SS-Sturmmann E. H. Nielsen had an even more visceral experience of the realities of combat in the Demyansk Pocket:

The wounded lay screaming with blasted legs or with shrapnel in the stomach or in the lungs. When I was going past, I had to just shut out compassion or human sensitivity, but it just wasn't possible. I still remember – perhaps because after all I was shaken to the bone marrow – that I saw a young handsome guy of the type that the girls would never leave in peace – and he had his hands clutched where his genitals used to be, and he just kept screaming 'I will never be a man again, I will never be a man again' – he quickly bled to death.[1]

Magnus's introduction to the Pocket was less dramatic.

MM: Ninety percent of the Frikorps flew into Demyansk, on Auntie Jus[2] *but I was in a motorcycle unit and so we went by train from Staraya Russa into Demyansk. We put our bags and our kit onto the train and off we went, we even slept on the train. We went to the front in May 1942, I'd been in the 1st Company in Langenhorn for about one month, and then I was transferred over to Heavy Weapons, to the 4th Company of the Frikorps, and my boss there was Kobe Martinsen.*[3] *It was good to have a Danish officer, and Martinsen, he was a good officer, without a doubt, but not everyone liked him as he had to be tough sometimes and some of the troops didn't like that.*

In the *Frikorps* itself, Kryssing had been replaced as the Germans felt he was not pro-Nazi enough. His replacement, Christian Frederick von Schalburg, was an experienced ex-SS Wiking officer and, by all accounts, a charismatic leader of men who proved to be a very popular choice amongst his Danish and German subordinates.

IC: I don't know why my friend and I weren't sent to the Frikorps Danmark, no one ever told us why; we were just sent to the SS-Westland Regiment. One of the reasons we wanted to join the Frikorps Danmark was because of Von Schalburg, you have heard of him? We had heard of him – lots of good things – and we wanted to serve under him very much, but it never happened.

MM: Von Schalburg was Danish,[4] *but he was born in Russia you know, and then came back to Denmark and went to help Finland against Russia, just like most of us Danes wanted to – help Finland and fight the Red army. Von Schalburg though was very popular, he was very idealistic, and everyone liked him.*

Popular he may have been, but his tenure in command was over before it had really begun. He was killed in action less than a month after leading his men into the Pocket.

MM: I wasn't with Von Schalburg when he was killed, I was in the Heavy Weapons Company, not a rifle company, so when Von Schalburg was killed in the attack on the bridgehead I was behind the attack supporting it with fire. As it was, his death was the result of a big mistake. The attack itself was a success, but Von Schalburg saw some of our soldiers going back to the rear, and he thought they were running away because the attack had failed, so he shouted at them to turn around and go forward again, but they weren't running away, they were carrying wounded comrades back to the dressing station. Then it got worse because some of the Frikorps soldiers were running into a minefield, and before they knew it Von Schalburg had stood up and ran towards them shouting to get back into the attack – 'Attack! Attack!' He was shouting again and again at them, and the next thing he stood on a mine and bang, off it went and blew him up. His right leg was completely gone, and he was lying there, and then the Russians attacked again, lots of artillery fire came crashing down and a shell landed right where he was and that was it – he was gone, just gone, in an instant.[5] *He was a good officer but he shouldn't have been acting like he did, as an officer he should have been further back, looking at the whole picture of the battle, and not been right up at the front in so much danger – he was too careless with his life, he wasn't even wearing a helmet, just a cap! We buried him near there, near where he fell, right there.*

We went back there three years ago you know, back to where we buried him. It was a great trip,[6] *we met a Russian whose grandfather had been killed by the Germans in an air raid on Leningrad during the war, and he wasn't angry at us at all, not a bit, he just said that it was war and there was nothing you could do about it. I also met a Russian woman and she made me the best pancakes I have ever tasted, wonderful. There really was no anger towards me there for what I'd done. I was a bit surprised, but pleased to be honest.*

At that point Magnus's voice – never above a faint, rasping whisper during the whole interview – lapsed into silence. After a few minutes he shook his head slightly and began again.

MM: Anyway, when Von Schalburg was killed there was a lot of chaos amongst the other officers because no one knew who was in charge now. In the end Martinsen took over and it all settled down. The fighting in Demyansk was very hard, very hard. I remember one day I was out on patrol with a friend of mine from Copenhagen, and for some reason we swapped places, and then the very next thing a shell landed and he was killed. It could have been me! It was so random, all just chance. We buried him there. Another time we tried to attack a Russian light machine-gun position. I was a messenger at the time, running between the different companies, it was a dangerous job, with the Russian snipers out there to get you, and all the shellfire...

His voice dropped off again, this time due to the entry of a nurse who had come in to check up on him. She was young and friendly, helping move Magnus's cushions and bringing him a glass of water, which he didn't touch. Reassured all was fine, she left and a minute or so later we carried on.

MM: I left Demyansk with the rest of the Frikorps in August I think,[7] *or it could have been September, I'm not sure, it was a very long time ago. We then had leave in Denmark, September/October time, but first we had a parade right through the centre of Copenhagen, the whole Frikorps, with our flags flying and a band playing.*[8] *But we were a bit worried that local communists might try to attack us as we marched, so we were told to keep six bullets in our rifles; five in the magazine and one in the breach, so if anyone did try to attack us we could at least shoot back. But it was only really in the big cities there was any trouble, any resistance, down in the south where my parents lived there wasn't any trouble at all, and we were left alone.*

In fact, so hard had the Demyansk fighting been, that the majority of Germans and Danes who survived it were reduced to physical wrecks, as attested by the Totenkopf's SS-*Hauptsturmführer* Dr Eckert – medical officer for Max Simon's 2nd Battalion, 1st Regiment – who wrote a memo to his commanding officer outlining the results of the medical examinations he carried out on 281 Totenkopf survivors from the Pocket. He detailed that no fewer than 88 were unfit for further military service, the average weight loss was 20 pounds per man, and that they were all weak and listless due to inadequate shelter, food and the incessant cold. In a telling observation he even said the men resembled the concentration camp inmates he had seen during his previous tour of the camps.[9]

The *Frikorps* Copenhagen parade coincided with the so-called Telegram Crisis between Nazi Germany and Denmark that saw the relationship between the two countries worsen dramatically, and led to the Germans taking a far tighter grip on their northern neighbours. The crisis was a diplomatic spat triggered by a telegram sent from Christian X of Denmark to Adolf Hitler, acknowledging Hitler's congratulations on the occasion of the king's 72nd birthday on 26 September 1942. Hitler wrote a lengthy personal letter to the monarch, but was enraged when the only reply he received was the proverbial one-liner saying '*Spreche meinen besten Dank aus. Chr. Rex* (English: 'Giving my best thanks, King Christian'). Hitler recalled Berlin's ambassador from Copenhagen and expelled the Danish ambassador from Germany. Attempts to placate Hitler, including a proposal to send Crown Prince Frederick to Berlin to apologise to Hitler personally, were refused by the Nazi dictator. In early November 1942 Cecil von Renthe-Fink, who had been Berlin's senior official in Denmark as the Reich Plenipotentiary (in German *Reichsbevollmächtigter*) was replaced by Dr Werner Best, and the commander of the German forces in Denmark, Erich Lüdke, was replaced with the more heavy-handed General Hermann von Hanneken. All remaining Danish troops were ordered out of Jutland, and under German pressure Vilhelm Buhl's government was dismissed and a new cabinet put in place led by non-party member and veteran diplomat Erik Scavenius, whose pro-German outlook was far more to Berlin's liking.

Best's appointment in particular was a big shift in Nazi policy towards Denmark. An ex-judge with a PhD in law, his background was in the Gestapo, and according to the historian Frank McDonough he was, 'a key figure in transforming the Gestapo into a modern and efficient instrument of terror'.[10] Several Gestapo officers – among them Karl-Heinz Hoffmann and Otto Bovensiepen – testified after the war that whilst, 'brutal treatment and torture were strictly prohibited' during most investigations, under Best's direction in Denmark they had carried out a large number of 'enhanced interrogations', and that 'the application of torture in certain cases in order to get a confession out of a prisoner' became far more common, especially against people involved in the resistance.[11] Best remained in Denmark until the end of the war.[12]

However, away from the salons of power, most Danes were just focused on day-to-day life. Getting around, to work, to see friends etc., was a chore. Fuel was in very short supply and the use of private cars had been banned anyway, so everyone tried to get where they needed to go by train, bus, tram or by bike. This made bicycle tyres a very important commodity, but rubber was scarce, so people began to improvise, using twisted straw, compressed paper and even plain wood, as one Dane put it, 'It was tiresome trying to find something to run on.'

The travails of transport aside, like everywhere else in Europe at the time, by far the biggest issue for the Danes was food, or rather the lack of it. People tried everything to fill their empty stomachs; waste ground was turned over to public allotments for food production, and payment plans were put in place by local councils to enable the poorest people to buy a half or quarter of a pig in instalments. As sugar disappeared off the menu, bee-keeping took off for the honey, roasted grain and chicory were ground up and used as coffee substitutes, and people drank tea made from blackcurrant leaves (this would probably be classed as a luxurious organic fruit tea these days and cost a small fortune!). In an age when smoking was very widespread, a lack of tobacco was akin to a national emergency, so the population began to grow its own – so much so that town councils had to organise people to go around and harvest it all. Scarcity and hunger weren't helped by rising unemployment. Factories that used to export to now-Allied nations had to cut back on labour, as did those enterprises now lacking in necessary raw materials such as slaughterhouses and all manner of retail production and distribution. Again, local councils did their best to try to alleviate the worst of the labour problems by putting men to work in municipal schemes such as firewood-cutting – trees in public parks and lining roads were the first to go – one such woodcutter said of it: 'They provide heat twice, first while taking them up and collecting all their branches, and second when they go into the stove.'

The Germans were quick to capitalise on this surplus of labour too, offering work in German factories to unemployed Danes, and about 20,000 packed their bags and headed south.

Nevertheless, crime increased, particularly theft, most often of ration cards, bicycles, bicycle tires, fuel and food – so-called 'pantry thefts'. But Denmark still got off pretty lightly, and life went on.

The strains of the occupation also began to impact the Danish media, as popular entertainment began to change to match the public mood. Danish cinema – placed under German supervision after the invasion – became much darker, while also putting more focus on Denmark as a nation. Documentary filmmaking expanded, and it became the norm to show documentaries as short films in theatres. Many more German films were shown, but incredibly not all movies from Allied countries were banned until the end of 1942. The Danish films produced during this period couldn't, of course, criticise Nazi Germany, so the filmmakers responded by avoiding the situation of the occupation as a topic and moving to making crime and suspense films such as Bodil Ipsen and Lau Lauritzen Jr's dark psychological *Afsporet* (1942), and the thriller *The Melody of Murder* (1944). Often sitting in the darkness watching these films were local Danish girls and their new-found German Army boyfriends – they say love conquers all, and for several thousand '*tyskerpigerne*' ['German girls' as their fellow Danes disparagingly christened them] walking out with a German was the way to go. The local Danish police and the German authorities found common cause in trying to stop this fraternisation as they feared both the spread of sexually transmitted diseases and the inevitable friction with the populace, but they might as well have been Cnut trying to order back the tide.

Over the water, life in occupied Norway was a deal harsher than in Denmark. The Norwegians had resisted their invasion for longer than France, and so were not allowed to simply carry on as before by their German conquerors, although the country was still considered 'Germanic' enough to be run by a civilian German commissioner – Josef Terboven – rather than by a military governor. Hermann Goering, head of the Luftwaffe and supremo of the Reich's Four Year Economic Plan, announced in August 1940 that what was needed was 'a mutual integration and linkage of interests between the German economy and those of Holland, Belgium, Norway and Denmark'. But considering that by his own admission Goering's usual policy towards other national economies was plunder, loot and plunder some more, it's difficult to see what he meant by this grandiose statement.

The reality on the street in Oslo or Trondheim was shortages – shortages of clothes, goods, equipment, and most especially food, with hunger becoming such an issue in Norway that the Danes sponsored the setting up of soup-kitchens across the country called *Danskehjelpen*, specifically to feed thousands of undernourished Norwegian children.

The average Norwegian spent an awful lot of time trying to sort out basic necessities so that they had clothes on their backs, a roof over their heads, food in their stomachs and they could get to and from work. In the cities the threat of air raids was ever present, so shelters were built and black-out curtains put up. The occupying German soldiers had very clear orders to behave properly towards the locals, but they could still arrest anyone they thought was acting suspiciously, and requisition whatever they wanted – including apartments, houses, public buildings, etc. New rules and regulations were constantly being introduced, with harsh punishments for non-compliance; reading banned newspapers was illegal, listening to the BBC was illegal, and in any case only NS members and their families could own radios – break the rules and you could be imprisoned or even executed. Informers were encouraged by the authorities, engendering a climate of fear and suspicion: 'You're a traitor!', 'You're a collaborator!' – The accusations and counter-accusations were hurled about by friends and neighbours alike.

The economic consequences of the German occupation were severe too. Norway lost most of its normal, pre-war trading partners the moment it was occupied, with Nazi Germany suddenly becoming the main destination for all goods, but even the Reich couldn't make up for all the lost import and export business. While production capacity remained largely intact, the German authorities confiscated the majority of the output anyway, leaving Norway with only 43 percent of its production being freely available to the populace. Combined with a general drop in productivity, Norwegians were quickly confronted with a scarcity of basic commodities, including food of course, and there was a real risk of famine. Fishing and hunting became more widespread as people looked to find their own food from the wild; the black market also provided a flow of goods at extortionate prices for those who could afford it, while everyone else learned to use *ersatz* products for a wide variety of purposes, ranging from fuel to coffee, tea, and tobacco – just as in Denmark.

One resident of Oslo wrote:

I remember there was nothing to buy in the shops. The growing of potatoes, Swedish turnips and carrots became a normal activity for anyone who had a small garden. The municipalities distributed allotments in parks and outlying fields, and beautiful rose beds were replaced with useful potato fields. Natural resources were exploited to the fullest; berries were picked to provide vitamin supplements during the winter months, even though the jam from them was very sour due to the lack of sugar. The magazine of the NS women's organisations – 'Heim og ætt' – [Home & Family] used to include lots of recipes, tips and advice for housewives regarding cooking, sewing and using what was

> *available such as the use of wild plants like goutweed [ground elder], thistle and wild caraway in dishes and horse chestnut as soap. The use of newspapers for sewing is another example. Having rabbits, hens and pigs became usual in the cities, even though space was limited and access to fodder was poor. It was so widespread that there were even regulations regarding having these so-called 'villa pigs'.*

To try to make sure that the few goods available were distributed fairly, the Department of Supplies oversaw the introduction of rationing. Each household was given one ration book per family member, allowing people to buy a certain amount of particular food items in the book. Rations varied with age, gender and special needs such as for infants, pregnant women and people with hard physical jobs. You had to take your ration book with you wherever you went just in case you saw a shop selling something you needed, or wanted to go into a café or restaurant – no book, no food or drink, was the rule.

This would have been irksome at the very least, if there had been enough to fill everyone's rations, but there wasn't; what was the point of a meat ration when there wasn't any meat to buy? When news came of a shop having received a shipment of some sought-after items, people raced to get there and stand in a queue for hours in the hope of being able to buy something – almost anything – if it was scarves and you didn't need a scarf then fine, you'd buy one and trade it for something you did need, after all if someone had had their scarf stolen, to qualify for another one the victim had to produce witnesses who would testify to both the theft and their need for a new scarf!

Sugar, coffee and flour were rationed first, and then all imported foodstuffs, as well as bread, fat, meat, vegetables, eggs and then milk, and it was this last item that sparked trouble in the autumn of 1941. When milk rationing was announced on 8 September that year there was widespread outrage, and workers at the Akers shipyard walked out on strike in protest. By the next day they had been joined by thousands of other workers from approximately 50 sites. The Germans reacted immediately, declaring martial law in Oslo and Aker and arresting two of the ringleaders – Viggo Hansteen and Rolf Wickstrøm – both were union men. With the barest of legal formalities, the two were tried, convicted and shot by an SS firing squad for their role in what became known as the Milk Strike (Norwegian: *melkestreiken*). In Nazi parlance, Norway was to be taught that leniency did not mean weakness, and the Germans were not afraid of exacting reprisals for resistance if they deemed them necessary.

This was never more evident than in the small fishing village of Telavåg on the coast of western Norway. With a population in the low hundreds, it was used as a link in the clandestine boat traffic between Norway and Great Britain, often acting as a shelter for agents or couriers.

In late April 1942 the Gestapo found out that two Norwegian agents of the British SOE-sponsored Linge Company – Arne Meldal Værum and Emil Gustav Hvaal, codenamed Penguin and Anchor respectively – were being hidden in the village. The Germans searched the place and a gun battle broke out that left Værum and two Gestapo agents – Gerhard Berns and Henry Bertram – dead. Hvaal was wounded and later executed.

As punishment, every building in the village was torched, every boat was sunk or confiscated, and even the wells were levelled. Having been made to watch their homes being burnt down, all 72 local men were sent to the Sachsenhausen concentration camp, where 31 of them died. The women and children were imprisoned for two years. For good measure, 18 other Norwegian prisoners held at the Trandum internment camp were also shot.

Away from the realities of occupation, and back in the Soviet Union, Magnus and his *Frikorps* comrades had been sent to take part in the bloody fighting at Velikiye Luki, near Pskov in northern Russia. Just as at Demyansk, a Red Army offensive had encircled German troops in the city, albeit on a much smaller scale. Magnus and the *Frikorps* were part of the forces sent to relieve the garrison in an operation codenamed *Totila*.

> *MM: I remember being in Velikiye Luki from October '42 to March '43, the fighting was very hard, but the Russian civilians there were very kind to us. I was still in the 4th Company then, and still a Sturmmann, I never got promoted higher than that, you know! Our commander was a German at that time. Anyway, the local Russians cooked food for us, and when we had any spare food ourselves we shared it with the local people. In fact, the civilians there were afraid of the Red Army soldiers and not us. They told us that the Red Army men treated them badly, beat them and raped the young women too, while the Germans and us were very correct with the locals. We were also told by our officers that we weren't allowed to have any dealings with the local girls, but of course we did anyway!*

Magnus laughed at that point, a dry sound, his head bobbing slightly on his all-too-thin shoulders. It was clear that he was very tired now, and the hip he had broken a week before when he'd slipped in the bathroom seemed to be giving him some pain. I thought it was time to leave and stood up, but he motioned me to sit back down – he wanted to end his story.

MM: In 1943, after Demyansk and Velikiye Luki, it all changed, you know. The Germans decided to disband the Frikorps, they wanted us to become full members of the Waffen-SS, and I didn't want that. When I'd first volunteered my contract was for the duration of the war, but in a Danish unit, not a German one, so as far as I was concerned the contract was no longer valid. I spoke to some other Danes and they all agreed and said it was OK for me to leave, but the Germans weren't happy, not happy at all. They said I had signed up for the whole war and that was that, I couldn't leave. They didn't threaten my family or anything like that, but there were several other volunteers who were very loud in saying they wanted to leave and that the Germans had broken their word when they disbanded the Frikorps,[13] *and they ended up being sent to prison. As for me I ended up writing a letter to my officer – it was Martinsen – telling him I wanted to get out, but before I heard anything I was sent to work on a farm near Grafenwöhr as a kind of punishment to try and get me to change my mind.*

When I came back from the farm the Germans tried again and told me that I would have to join the 8th Company of the Regiment Danmark, but I said no, I wanted to go home. Then in August 1943 the whole Nordland Division, along with the Regiment Danmark of course, was sent to Croatia, and at that point I went to another officer in the 8th Company, a Danish one – Ole Peter Kuna – and told him again that I wanted to leave and he said to me that he didn't want anyone with him who didn't want to be there and who didn't want to carry on fighting. So, the next day I was sent to Graz in Austria on the first leg of my journey back home to Denmark, I ended up never serving in the 8th Company. I did nothing at all in Graz, they took good care of us even though we'd left the Waffen-SS – I wasn't the only one, there were several of us Danes. I went to Graz at the beginning of August '43, and was finally sent home on October 6, 1943. I had to hand my uniform in, and then I went back to my parents' farm. Some people knew what I'd done, some neighbours and friends of my family, but no one made me feel bad about it; it was just accepted. I was in a kind of 'union' at the time, and they helped me fit back into civilian life, to find work on a farm again, and just get on with normal life.

It was definitely time to go now, Magnus's lower jaw was hanging slackly, his food tray untouched as the daylight in the room faded. My companion and translator-when-needed – Jens – left the room, clearly desperate to get outside and light up a cigarette. I packed up my gear, thanked Magnus, and was about to switch off my dictaphone when he suddenly grabbed my arm, his blue eyes flashing with new energy:

MM: Hitler was the biggest idiot there ever was! If he had been a bit cleverer he could've won the war, could've won it easily, but he kept on making mistakes, again and again, the same ones – the fool. The Germans murdered the Jews in Russia, but we Danes just wanted to fight the Red Army. You must understand that the Jews were allied to the communists – not all the Jews, just some of them. But even so, what Hitler did to them was wrong, all that killing, it was so wrong, and it wasn't just Hitler that treated the Jews badly you know. I knew two Jews, they were from eastern Poland and they tried to emigrate to the United States, but weren't accepted, so one ended up in Australia....

Then his thin voice, so weak, trailed off again. Somewhat taken aback by Magnus's outburst I once again turned to leave, only for Magnus to spring one last surprise – he flung up his right arm in a Nazi salute, and smiled; 'You English would never have given the Hitler salute would you? Not then and not now.' I thanked him for his time and walked out of his room and into the gathering gloom, my footsteps echoing quietly on the polished floor tiles.

Notes to Chapter Three

1. The above quotes from the four *Frikorps Danmark* veterans are reproduced here from the www.Freikorpsdanmark.dk website by kind permission of its author – Lars Larsen.
2. Affectionate Wehrmacht slang for Junkers Ju-52s, the three-engine workhorse of the Luftwaffe's transport fleet.
3. Knud Børge Martinsen – the Danish veterans shortened and joined his first two names and pronounced them as 'Ko-bay'. Martinsen (30 November 1905 – 25 June 1949) was a Danish Army officer and one of the four commanders of *Frikorps Danmark*. Born in Sandved in 1905, he joined the Army in 1928, rising to the rank of captain and attending the general staff course at the Frederiksberg Palace just before the German invasion. Two weeks after the invasion he joined the DNSAP and took part in several demonstrations in his uniform, which annoyed his superiors and blocked any future promotion. He resigned and joined the Waffen-SS and initially commanded *Frikorps Danmark*'s 2nd Company. He then moved to command the 4th Company. Martinsen was temporarily commander of *Frikorps Danmark* between Christian Peder Kryssing's resignation and Christian Frederik von Schalburg's appointment, and then again between Von Schalburg's death and Hans Albert von Lettow-Vorbeck's appointment. When Von Lettow-Vorbeck was killed only two days after his appointment, Martinsen took over as commander and remained as such until the disbandment of *Frikorps Danmark* on 20 May 1943. Together with most of *Frikorps Danmark* he was transferred to SS-Panzergrenadier Regiment 24 Danmark in the 11th

SS Volunteer Panzergrenadier Division Nordland, but left in July and returned to Denmark to establish and command the Schalburg Corps as a recruitment unit for the Waffen-SS. In October 1944 he was relieved from his position, arrested and imprisoned in Berlin by the Gestapo. He escaped and returned to Denmark. On 5 May 1945 he was arrested in his home for his involvement in the Schalburg Corps and for two murders. One of the murders was the shooting in March 1944, in the headquarters of the Schalburg Corps, of a fellow member, Fritz Henning Tonnies von Eggers, whom Martinsen believed had had an affair with his wife. He was sentenced to death and on 25 June 1949 at 01:00 he was executed by firing squad in Copenhagen.

4. Christian Frederik von Schalburg (15 April 1906 – 2 June 1942) was a Danish Army officer and brother of Vera von Schalburg, who served as an agent during the war for the security services of the Soviet Union, Nazi German and finally Great Britain. Born in Zmeinogorsk in Imperial Russia, Von Schalburg's father was Danish, his mother Russian. He served in the Tsar's cadet corps and lived in Russia until the October Revolution of 1917, when he fled with his family to Denmark. Originally deemed unfit for military service, he became an officer in the Royal Danish Life Guards. From 1939 he headed the youth branch (NSU) of the DNSAP, and he and a group of NSU members called '*bloddrengene*' (the 'blood boys') were among the Danish volunteers for the Finnish Winter War against the USSR in 1939–1940. In September 1940, with the consent of the Danish Army and the king, he joined the Waffen-SS, served with the 5th SS Division Wiking as an SS-Hauptsturmführer, and was awarded the Iron Cross 1st and 2nd Class during Barbarossa. On 27 February 1942, Von Schalburg reported to the *Frikorps Danmark* in Treskau and on 1 March he took command. He introduced language lessons in German and Russian, and instituted physical training every morning for the volunteers.

5. Von Schalburg was killed on the 2 June 1942. He suffered extensive injuries, including one leg torn off at the hip and the foot missing from the other. Christensen, Claus Bundgård, Poulsen, Niels Bo, Smith, Peter Scharff, *Under hagekors og Dannebrog: danskere i Waffen SS 1940–45*, p152, Aschehoug. He was replaced by the German SS-Obersturmbannführer Hans von Lettow-Vorbeck who was himself killed in action after only two days in command. Vorbeck was ordering a withdrawal when he was hit by a Soviet machine-gun; the first burst hit him in the upper body and left upper arm – a shoulder blade was shattered and shards of bone penetrated his lung. A Danish NCO put him on his shoulder to try to get him to the nearest dressing station, but another burst of fire hit the NCO (who survived) and killed Vorbeck outright.
6. Magnus returned to Demyansk in the autumn of 2014 accompanied by Lars Larsen and Jens Pank Bjerregaard.
7. The bulk of the *Frikorps* left Demyansk on 4 August 1942.
8. The parade was held on 13 October 1942, but casualties had been so severe in the Demyansk fighting that only 10 officers, 28 NCOs and 171 men were able to take part out of the roughly 1,000 men who fought at Demyansk – the first contingent into the Pocket in May was 702 strong.
9. Sydnor, Charles, W. Jr., *Soldiers of Destruction: The SS Death's Head Division, 1933–1945*, p230, Princeton.
10. McDonough, Frank, *The Gestapo*, p39, Coronet.
11. Ibid, p249–251.
12. Arrested at the end of the war, Best was convicted by the Danes in 1948 of the murder of the newspaper editor Christian Damm on 30 December 1943, and the subsequent murders of the poet and Lutheran pastor Kaj Munk on 4 January 1944, and the engineer Snog Christensen in August 1944. Munk was murdered for defying a Nazi ban on preaching the first Advent sermon at the national

cathedral in Copenhagen. His body was found in a roadside ditch in rural Hørbylunde near Silkeborg with a note pinned to it that read, 'Swine, you worked for Germany just the same.' Sentenced to death, Best was released in 1951 as part of a general amnesty for war criminals. He then went to West Germany where he got a job with a leading insurance company, eventually becoming its Managing Director. As part of the de-Nazification process he was fined 70,000 Deutschmark in 1958, but went on to become a senior economic legal adviser to the Hugo Stinnes Trust and an expert in the West German Foreign Office. Rearrested by the West Germans in 1969 for war crimes, his subsequent trial was adjourned in 1972, and additional delays meant no further action was carried out against him before his death in 1989. *The Brown Book – War and Nazi Criminals in West Germany*, p78, Verlag Zeit im Bild.

13. The *Frikorps Danmark* was officially disbanded on 20 May 1943 after having lost a total of nine officers, 17 NCOs and 133 men killed in action over its lifetime. The Germans expected the surviving legionnaires to transfer en masse over to the newly-established SS-Panzergrenadier Regiment 24 Danmark, but were disappointed when Magnus and 310 other Danes asked to be released and sent home. For more information see Trigg, Jonathan, *Hitler's Vikings*, p151–152, The History Press.

4

MORE FIRST BLOODS – CROATIA AND SOUTHERN RUSSIA

As Magnus was fighting in Velikiye Luki – not knowing it would be his last hurrah before leaving the Waffen-SS – a new generation of Scandinavian volunteers was enlisting, and two of them were Magnus's fellow Danes, Ivar Corneliussen and Andreas Fleischer. Connected by their part-German ancestry – Corneliussen was half-Austrian on his father's side, whilst Fleischer was a classic Danish ethnic German from the southern border region – the two men joined the Waffen-SS for very different reasons and ended up serving in very different units; Corneliussen in the semi-multinational Wiking Divisions' Westland Regiment – traditionally the home of Dutch and Flemish volunteers – and Fleischer in the Totenkopf Division, one of the first, and perhaps also one of the most controversial, of all the Waffen-SS formations. Interviewing the two men was wildly different too; Corneliussen was quiet, a bit forgetful and clearly a man in his 90s, while Fleischer was forceful and possessed of an energy and intensity that belied his age – talking to Ivar was like having a conversation with an amiable great-uncle, while with Andreas on occasions I wasn't sure who was interviewing who. Meeting veterans for the first time it is always difficult not to make comparisons with other, past interviewees, and in Andreas's case it was well-nigh impossible as he reminded me so forcefully of a Waffen-SS volunteer I had met for my previous book on the Flemish veterans – his name was Dries Coolens. Both men were not the tallest, but had the same stocky, powerful build and also the same practical air of men who got things done and weren't afraid of breaking a few eggs to do it – perhaps it was no surprise that both had been senior NCOs – most such men have a similar stamp. As with Coolens, the overriding impression I had of Fleischer when I interviewed him was of a man who felt no regret for what he'd done, who wouldn't compromise, and who was going to tell me what he wanted to tell me no matter what – and it was my job to listen. Several times during the interview he would fix with me an unsmiling, stony stare and reply to one of my questions with 'Is that really necessary?' None of the questions he replied to in that manner were controversial, it was more he clearly thought they were unrelated to his story and so not worth him answering. To be fair to him, he was also a very hospitable host, generous with his time, and always ready with a smile or a joke – yes, very much a senior NCO.

AF: Before we begin Herr Trigg I must tell you that I read quite a few books about the fighting in World War Two; this last year I've read books on the fighting in northern France from 1944 onwards, three of them actually, one by an American, one by a German and one by an Englishman. One of them had a story in it about a British tank commander – I can't remember where the battle was, somewhere in France – anyway, he was in his tank and he said he knew something was wrong, that just over the hill were two German panzer divisions, and if they attacked he and his men were finished. But they didn't attack, and you know why?

Fleischer put his right forefinger to the middle of his upper lip almost conspiratorially and said, 'The man with the little moustache, that's why!' Then he laughed.

> *That man was always doing things wrong!*
>
> *I've been to Scotland you know, several times, it's beautiful there, and I've been to England too, and Ireland. I read books while I'm travelling, I read so many books, and some of them are on war and fighting you know? Well, some of these books don't speak the truth, they don't know what they're talking about. I've been in a war, a big war, with the Russians, and I know what it's like, and some of these books don't know anything about what it's really like I can tell you.*
>
> *Mind you, we stayed at this one place in Scotland, and the lady there fed us so much food, and I said to her, 'Please, not so much food, we can't eat it,' and she looked at me and said 'Eat what I give you!' And that was that.*

He laughed again.

> *AF: My father was born in eastern Germany, in East Prussia. He was a soldier in the First World War, in the German Army, and afterwards we moved here to Denmark, and I was born here. Do you need to know more about my parents? Is that necessary?*

A flick of his hand in a dismissive gesture and we moved on.

> *AF: We lived near the border, near Christiansfeld, and we from the German minority were asked to join a youth organisation, like the Hitler Youth, almost the same. We were told they met every Saturday, but my brother and I thought they just made loud*

speeches all the time. Then when I was 15 in 1941, I got a job in Germany, in Flensburg, as an apprentice blacksmith. I was working in the dockyard there, where they built U-boats for the Kriegsmarine. Narrow things they were those U-boats, no room inside, I didn't like the idea of being in one of those things, not one bit. A lot of the friends I'd made over there then went into the German Army, and I thought I should join too, so I volunteered in 1943. I was in Germany already, so I just went to a recruiting office there and joined. I was 17 years old.

Ivar's story was strikingly similar in many ways:

IC: For me it all started at the beginning of September 1942, that's when I volunteered. We lived in eastern Denmark, right by the sea, but my father was from Austria, so I was half-Austrian I suppose, but I have always thought of myself as Danish. But when the Germans came to Denmark in 1940 they told me I wasn't just a Dane anymore, I was a volksdeutsche,[1] *because of my father, I guess. I have a half-sister in Innsbruck too. By the way, I must tell you that my mind is a little slow at times, I'm sorry about that, I'm old!*

Anyway, my father came to Denmark for work, and he met my mother here and wanted to take her back to Germany, but my grandmother said 'no, she mustn't go, she must stay!', so my father stayed too.

These two young men – teenagers actually – had thus entered the vast octopus that was the Third Reich's military, but they had both volunteered for a specific part of it; not the Army, the Luftwaffe or the Kriegsmarine, no, they had both put their crosses next to something quite different – the armed SS. Beginning as a small adjunct to the Nazi Party itself, this avowedly political force had grown out of all recognition by the time Ivar and Andreas walked into their respective recruitment offices in Odense and Flensburg. By this mid-stage of the war the Waffen-SS was an established part of the German military with divisions of men – almost all of them fighting on the Eastern Front, where they would build a reputation both for military excellence and brutality in almost equal measure.

That same fighting in Russia was consuming men at a Somme-like rate; almost 48,000 Germans killed or missing in the same month Ivar enlisted, and the Waffen-SS was as desperate for manpower as all other elements of the Third Reich's war machine. Frustrated at the machinations of the generals to stifle its growth, Himmler and his subordinates had cast their hooks into those pools of potential recruits that were open to them; *Volksdeutsche* living outside Germany's borders, and those Europeans viewed as 'fellow Aryans' – Andreas and Ivar were both in this sweet spot. Given their Danish nationality they both should have been funnelled towards the SS-Wiking Division's *Nordland* Regiment – home to most of the Scandinavian volunteers as the *Frikorps Danmark* and DNL were closed down, but that presupposed a standard of efficiency that was wholly lacking in National Socialist bureaucracy – the fact is that the myth of Nazi efficiency is largely exactly that – a myth – Nazi *inefficiency*, would be a better term, and even better if conjoined with the phrase 'bureaucratic labyrinth'. So it proved with Ivar and Andreas, as instead of being sent to serve alongside their fellow Danes in the Nordland, Ivar went to the SS-Westland Regiment – supposed home of the Dutch and Flemish volunteers – while Andreas went completely off-piste and ended up in the 3rd SS-Panzer Division Totenkopf, a unit that was theoretically meant to be composed entirely of German nationals.

AF: They didn't ask me what unit I wanted to join in the Waffen-SS, they just said to me 'You will join the Totenkopf.'[2] *That was that, I was sent to the 3rd Company, 3rd Battalion of Regiment Theodor Eicke.*[3] *Totenkopf was a panzer division at that time, it was special I can tell you. There were more than 20 of us who were like me in the same boat – ethnic Germans from Denmark – and we weren't treated any differently than anyone else. We all spoke German, so we didn't mind, and the Totenkopf was an élite unit, and that was what we all wanted, to serve with the best, to be the best.*

IC: I did my training at Sennheim and Klagenfurt, and was then posted to the Wiking Divisions SS-Westland Regiment, to the Machine-Gun Platoon of the Heavy Weapons Company – 4th Company, 2nd Battalion. There were other Danes in the unit, and Norwegians and Dutch, and Flemish, and there were lots of Germans too – I'd say the majority of men were German.

One thing you might find interesting: I don't have a blood group tattoo – you know the blue SS blood group tattoos we were all meant to have? They said that it would make things easier and quicker if we were wounded and needed a blood transfusion – they wouldn't have to ask us our blood group, or test us or anything like that, they'd just look at our tattoo – unless you'd lost your arm I suppose.

Anyway, on the day when we were all meant to get them me and a friend were sent to a farm to do some work, so we missed it, and while everyone else got their tattoo we didn't.

From Klagenfurt me and the other reinforcements went by train all the way to the Caucasus – it took three weeks – and we finally arrived there on Christmas Eve 1942. As soon as we arrived we 'organised' – and by that I mean we stole – a couple of chickens from the locals, and a comrade that had been a cook back in civilian life managed to cook us a Christmas dinner. We also got presents from the Regiment; one bottle of schnapps and some cigarettes to share between us. That was good, there was a great atmosphere in the Company, we all liked and respected each other as soldiers, and we felt the same about our officers – our view was that we were all a very long way from home and we were all in the same boat, together.

This period of time was the zenith of Hitler's drive east, with soldiers of the Wehrmacht crossing over into Asia for the first and only time. The rest of the Eastern Front was in a bloody stalemate, but elsewhere the death knell for the Axis in North Africa had been tolled by Montgomery's defeat of Rommel at El Alamein, and the Operation Torch Anglo-American landings in Algeria and Morocco. Even more significantly for Ivar and his Westland compatriots, the Red Army had encircled the huge German Sixth Army in Stalingrad in late November, and the Red Army's follow-up Little Saturn offensive was not only annihilating the Italian 8th Army on the Don River, but was threatening to cut off all of Army Group A down south in the Caucasus[4] – including, of course, the Westland.

In an admission of defeat, the German offensive to capture the Soviet Union's Caucasian oilfields was cancelled, and the troops sent marching hell for leather northwest to escape certain destruction.

For Ivar it was a sobering welcome to the war.

IC: I remember the first time I came under artillery fire, they were katyushas[5] – Stalinorgeln we used to call them, [Author: it is the same word in Danish, Norwegian and German] and I was very scared. We had to run through the explosions, but I took cover and stayed on the ground, and when I looked up there was this big, black boot next to my head, it was a Dutch Rottenführer, and he was shouting at me; 'What are you doing? Get up and get running!' So, I got up and ran, but I was scared I can tell you.

It was a terrible time. We were very far from home and our supply lines were very long, so supplies only got to us very slowly; food, ammunition, fuel and so on. We had a field kitchen that did their best to serve us one meal a day but they didn't always manage to do that, so we had to buy, trade or steal food from the local Russian civilians. Going to the toilet wasn't easy either. If we could, we made a ditch, either by digging if possible, or if not, we used explosives to blow a hole. If we couldn't do either, then we just had to go off with a shovel on our own and take a shit wherever we could. We hadn't been issued winter clothing or boots and this proved to be a real problem as many of us got frostbite in our feet or toes because the iron nails in our boots would attract the cold – our boots were 'drawing-in' the cold like magnets so we soon learned either to wrap cloth around our feet to keep them warm, or to find felt boots on dead Russians and take them for ourselves.

At the beginning of January 1943 we were ordered north, to help the besieged Sixth Army trapped in Stalingrad. We went over the Kalmyk steppes. It was a cold journey, there was lots of snow and there were no roads, so our vehicles only made slow progress. The thing I most remember about that journey though wasn't the cold, but that we had a pig – a dead one of course – hanging off the side of the vehicle, and to cut any meat off it, so we could cook it and eat it, we had to use an axe – it was frozen solid, you see.

It soon became clear we couldn't get to Stalingrad in time to help the Sixth Army so we were ordered to go to Rostov instead [Author: Rostov-on-Don]. But there was a problem, the route over land was cut off, so instead we had to walk over the ice of the Azov Sea to the south of the city to what is now the country of Ukraine. We were all worried about the ice breaking, and we were bombarded by Russian artillery and were attacked by Russian aircraft a couple of times, so we went over that ice as fast as we possibly could. Once we got to the city, the thing I most remember about the place was just how icy the streets were – we had to crawl along on all fours on the streets sometimes just to get around. The food wasn't good either, we kept on being fed the same diet of meat and bread with no vegetables, so a lot of us got jaundice as a result and looked like Asians with yellow skin. It was always some kind of stew they fed us, and it was poured into our mess tin, and then we had relish or whatever put in the lid, and a couple of slices of bread of course, and on the odd times we got potatoes we put them in our side-caps.

With so many of us being ill we were all sent to the lazarett [Author: military field hospital] in Rostov to get de-loused and washed as we were filthy after our journey from the Caucasus. We were issued new uniforms and given vitamin tablets and grape sugar to help get rid of the jaundice, and after a couple of days of this treatment we were all declared fit and were sent back to the regiment. After that we were finally shipped to Taganrog where we were re-organised and sent south to Panzer Corps South [Author: Ivar probably means Army Group South].

Ivar was far from being the only Scandinavian who served in the Caucasus. Another was the Icelander Björn Sveinn Björnsson. The son of the most senior politician in his home island, he had been living in Germany for several years when the war broke out, and his reaction was to step forward to volunteer for the Waffen-SS in October 1941. The SS authorities seemed to think that both his talents and his family connections made him more useful in the field of propaganda rather than serving in a frontline unit such as the *Frikorps Danmark* (where as an 'official' Dane at the time he should have been sent), so instead he was posted to the SS war correspondent battalion – the *SS-Kriegsberichter-Abteilung* – itself the forerunner to the SS-*Standarte Kurt Eggers* created in December 1943. Björnsson was then sent to the Russian front and made several broadcasts from there to be transmitted back to Iceland to help drum up support for the Nazi war effort and aid Waffen-SS recruitment amongst his countrymen – although with a total population in 1941 of approximately 122,000[6] it's difficult to imagine any number of Icelandic volunteers tipping the balance in the fight against the Soviet Union! Only one recording he made at that time survives and a very helpful Icelander sent it direct to me. The recording was made in late 1942 in the Caucasus, and in it Björnsson interviews two supposed local Cossack farmers about the evils of the Soviet Union – I recommend a search on YouTube to find it. Björnsson himself later wrote in his memoirs of the Russo-German war:

> *For me this was a campaign against the threat of Bolshevism, and the Germans were fighting a life-and-death struggle. I felt that this was an enemy that I wanted to fight, and should fight.*[7]

He obviously impressed his superiors because before the end of 1942, he was sent to Bad Tölz to train as a Waffen-SS officer, and from there onwards to Copenhagen in 1943, where he eventually became the Director of Radio Denmark after the previous incumbent had been sacked by the Germans for taking part in the famous Danish General Strike of that year.

After completing his training and joining the Totenkopf, Andreas Fleischer also experienced his first taste of life at the front as the *Ostheer* [Author: the German Army and Waffen-SS in the East] retreated out of the Soviet Union and back into Romania.

> *AF: From Poland we went down to Romania, to the Black Sea coast. I was just an infantry soldier, I started off with a rifle, and then as I was promoted I was given a machine-gun, an MP40.*[8] *We used to patrol against each other, us and the Russians, and we always tried to destroy each other's machine-guns. One night one of our patrols went out to destroy a Russian machine-gun position. I told the rest of the men in the line the route the patrol were going to come back on so they didn't shoot them. We didn't have many men then, and were always careful to avoid casualties if we could. Anyway, later on, I don't really know how it happened, but I was checking the line and one of my men who was on guard duty was asleep as I came to him – he had fallen asleep on guard duty! That was a serious offence in itself, but it was also a real problem. It was very dark and we couldn't see anything and I wasn't sure what to do, so I spoke to my friend, he was the next-door platoon leader, and he said 'shoot a flare up, so you can see what's going on'. I did that, and Jesus Christ! There were Russians everywhere! We opened fire and that was that, they were swept away, and they didn't get my machine-gun!*

Another volunteer, like Andreas of the 1943 vintage, was a young fresh-faced Norwegian who had enlisted believing he would be going to serve with his fellow countrymen in Den Norske Legion, but would actually end up in an altogether different formation – the brand-new SS-Panzergrenadier Regiment 23 Norge. This was Bjørn 'Bubi' Lindstad.

Lindstad is pretty unique amongst the veterans I have interviewed for my books – not because he is hospitable, friendly and has no regrets about his service – although all those things are true – but because the reason he volunteered, what motivated him to fight the Soviets, was so ill-defined, so, if you like, private. Yes, he was anti-communist before he enlisted, but not *deeply* so as with so many other veterans, nor was he politically motivated in terms of party membership – he wasn't a member of the NS or any far-right organisation, and neither were any of his immediate family, none of whom volunteered either, and that was when 'family' was often a key driver for many Scandinavian volunteers. For example, a serving Danish soldier, and amateur historian himself, Holger Thor Nielsen, said of his own background:

> *My grandfather, on my father's side, was a district leader of the DNSAP on the island of Funen. In November 1943 he was badly wounded in an assassination attempt, after which he moved to Copenhagen and worked as a civilian clerk for 'Landstormen'.*[9] *He survived the war but died in 1955. My father was a Waffen-SS volunteer from June 1940 to May 1945. Obviously, he survived the war, since I was born in 1961. He died in 1998. My father's younger brother, my uncle, was a Waffen SS volunteer from March 1941 to October 1943, when he transferred to civilian service and worked for the Gestapo in his home town of Odense. He was assassinated in November 1943. My father's youngest brother, another uncle, served with the Hitler Youth in Kiel, Germany, from June 1943 to October 1944, when he was transferred to the Luftwaffe. He survived the war, but died in 1986. My grandfather, on my mother's side, was an NSKK*[10] *Mann with the OT*[11] *from September 1941 to February 1943. He survived the war but died in 1995.*

Granted, this is something of an extreme, but Lindstad wasn't even a watered-down version of this, or anything else for that matter. Normally when I interview veterans they have a stock answer ready for me to what is a stock question – why did you join? But not Lindstad, who seemed to join to get *away* from something, rather than to fight *for* something – and it was only later in his service, much later as it turned out, that he almost 'stumbled' on to a *reason* to fight.

As for his life today, he lives in what can only be described as a Brothers Grimm log house out in the Norwegian back woods. To find it we had to first drive along a main road, then turn onto a side road, then onto a track and finally onto a dirt drive shrouded by pine and fir trees. Lindstad himself was standing on the porch waiting for us; a short man – particularly so for an ex-Waffen-SS soldier, where height was highly prized – he looked remarkably young, despite being in his 90s. He was smiling, and I would soon realise that was his usual expression, he was definitely not a morose individual. The word I would use to describe his build would be 'compact' – he was well turned out; in his case in jeans, trainers and a pressed blue short-sleeved shirt, no glasses or hearing aid, his grey hair well-combed.

We went into his house and the log cabin theme continued – everywhere you looked in the house there was wood; the ceiling was wooden beamed, the walls were wooden panels, all the furniture was made of the stuff, and the surfaces were covered in wooden spindles, wooden picture frames, etc. – you get the idea. I looked out of the window to see a pair of red squirrels and a woodpecker quietly munching the nuts and seeds left out for them by the Lindstads, and before I sat down I almost tripped over a big, shaggy-haired dog, which covered a good chunk of the floor – the Lindstads were dog-sitting for a football-crazy relative who is a Manchester United season ticket holder and had flown over to see his team play – given the date it was probably the August 2017 game against West Ham that United won 4–0. There was another Manchester connection in the family; Lindstad doesn't speak English so I needed a translator, and his granddaughter was fulfilling that role on the day as she had married a Mancunian and speaks English superbly. I asked her when and how she had found out about her grandfather's service, and she told me that when she was 16 she had told her father she wanted to study languages so she could speak German like her grandfather – she then asked him how grandpapa had learnt German and her father replied that she had best ask him that herself – so she did, and he told her. At first, she was shocked and tried to just ignore it, but when she later moved to live and work in Israel she began to email her grandfather about it all, and even read the manuscript of the book he was writing about his service in the Waffen-SS.[12] She told me that she began to understand what he had done and why, and she ended up accompanying him back to the Narva battlefield in Estonia where he had fought.

Narva!

There was that word, that place – the place where so many of the Waffen-SS's non-German European volunteers had fought in 1944. The Dutch fought there, the Flemish, and, of course, the Scandinavians. Casualties had been very high, so finding a surviving veteran is hugely difficult, and it looked as if I had struck lucky with my very first veteran interview in Norway – I was tempted to throw an extra nut to the red squirrel happily dining outside!

The interview proper then started as several others have, with a compliment and a correction:

BL: I liked your book Herr Trigg, [Author: he was referring to Hitler's Vikings*] it is better than most I have read on the*

Scandinavian Waffen-SS, but, if you don't mind, I would like to make some corrections? In the book you say that two of the Norge Regiment's Norwegian panzer grenadiers, Lage Søgaard and Kasper Sivesind from the 12th Company, managed to escape Berlin just before the final surrender – I'm sorry but that is not correct. I knew them both you see and I can tell you that Søgaard was captured in Berlin by the Russians but managed to escape when his guards got drunk, and he made it safely to the British Embassy. As for Sivesind, he hid in a cellar for a week, living off stolen food and licking water that was dripping down into the corner of the cellar. Then, one night, he escaped from the city, got to the north German coast and hitched a lift on a boat to Denmark, where he was arrested.

I thanked him for the corrections; that kind of detail is priceless to an author, and he then went on:

BL: However, the biggest problems I had with the book are its title – I don't like 'Hitler's Vikings' – we weren't Hitler's, I definitely wasn't, and then there was that Foreword. The man who wrote it said that Norwegians were involved in putting down the Warsaw Uprising, and that just isn't true. There were a few Norwegians there at the time, but they were being trained as X-ray technicians, as radiologists, they weren't there to fight the Poles. It was pure coincidence.

I explained the issue with the Foreword – and once again inwardly cursed the writer – and we swiftly moved on.

BL: I joined the Norwegian Legion on the 1st of February 1943, the day before my 18th birthday, but it was disbanded shortly after I enlisted so I never served in it – we were just told one day, 'that's it, it's disbanded' and I ended up in Grafenwöhr [eastern Bavaria], in the Heavy Weapons Company of the 2nd Battalion of the SS Regiment Norge. I was in infantry cannons, that's what they trained me for [Author: the standard establishment at the time was one infantry cannon company of about 180 men per regiment]. The job of the cannons was to sit about 1,200 metres or so behind the frontline, with an observer out front giving them directions where to fire – that was my role, as an observer. The cadre of my battalion was from the 2nd Battalion of the Nordland Regiment from the Wiking Division, so, all the quartermaster staff, the field kitchens, some of the NCOs and officers and all that. They were very experienced, all of them had been to Russia, down in the Caucasus,[13] *and some of them had even been in France, back in 1940, although not in the Wiking at that time. My company commander was Walter Körner, he was Austrian; he was a good officer. We found him very difficult to start with during our training, very hard and tough with us, but then when we got to the front he was a real buddy and we understood why he'd been so hard with us during our training. He won the Knight's Cross, you know; he caught some Luftwaffe men deserting and was shot by one of them and wounded, he died later.*[14]

We all got on, there was no trouble between us and the Germans and Austrians, but we didn't have enough Norwegians for sure, it would've been great to have more of us but there wasn't the volunteers back home, you see. They brought in Volksdeutsche from Romania to fill the gaps – these people had been in Romania for hundreds of years and they didn't speak German too well, but they were treated as Germans and drafted in. I got on with the Volksdeutsche boys from the very beginning, they were just soldiers like everybody else. They often got blamed if something went wrong, even when it wasn't their fault, and that wasn't fair, but I liked them. I had two Volksdeutsche working with me in my role as an observer, and they were the closest comrades I had. We had a field telephone with a line that went back to the guns, and their job was to keep that line working. One of them was called Samuel Sutoris and the other was called Samuel Schuster – we called them both 'Sam' for short, they were cousins from Siebenbürgen in Transylvania – you know, Dracula's home.[15] *The village where they came from is called something else now – I'm sorry if I can't remember everything now; it's my age, you understand – anyway, I went to look for them after the war and I found the sister of one of them in their village, and the other one's cousin – you see all these tools here on the wall, and this spinning wheel, they are all from their village – anyway, I found out that one of them died in Riga during the war, and the other died from arthritis in the 1950s.*

I was mostly trained in Germany, but for the last part of our training we were all sent to Yugoslavia, to Bosnia, to a town called Bos Novi.[16] *I was there from the end of August until the beginning of December 1943. General Steiner*[17] *was in command of us all and he told us that our priority was our training, but if we were attacked by Partisans*[18] *then we had to fight back. We were based in the hills surrounding the town itself, but also came down into the town for some of our training.*

I remember the town came under fire once when I was in it – someone was firing at us, I couldn't see who at first – and there were civilians everywhere, running, running, trying to get away. There was a Wehrmacht train in town with three wagons on the front; the front two were empty and were meant to detonate any mines put on the tracks, and the next one had a 20 millimetre cannon on it to protect the train from aircraft attack or from

Partisans.[19] *I was ordered to walk beside the train to help protect it from the shooting, and then the cannon gunner used tracer rounds to shoot at the ruins of a farm where the firing was coming from – there were two people firing at us from there. I had some binoculars and I could see someone running out from the ruins, but it wasn't clear, I didn't know if it was a child with a doll or a woman with a child. I watched as the cannon gunner got the first shooter, then he hit the woman or whoever it was, and then he got the second shooter. That was the first time I had seen any action. I wasn't scared, I was more curious than scared. The whole time the firing was going over my head.*

A child with a doll? A woman with a child? Was this an atrocity, a war crime? It sounded like it. Both sides were firing, both sides couldn't identify exactly what they were firing at – did the Partisan fire hit any civilians in the town, did the cannon gunner shoot an innocent? There are no answers to these questions, and in this instance it is the unknown cannon gunner – and not Lindstad – who must search his conscience for resolution, and, perhaps, absolution.

What we do know without a shred of doubt was that the war in the East – including in Yugoslavia – was unfathomably brutal. It was conceived by Hitler and the rest of the Nazi leadership as an ideological war, a war of racial extermination. The goal was not to right a historical wrong – real or perceived – it wasn't for spoils, it wasn't to conquer territory – although both of these objectives were wrapped up into it, no, the overriding aim of the Nazi invasion of the Soviet Union was nothing less than the annihilation of vast swathes of humanity that they deemed to be *Untermenschen* – inferior races – including Slavs, Gypsies and the biggest Nazi bogeyman of them all – the Jews. This book is not a history of the Holocaust or the seemingly endless litany of massacre and counter-massacre that characterised the Russo-German war, but in so far as it played a role in the story of the Scandinavian Waffen-SS veterans it has a place all of its own.

There has been, and there continues to be, an ongoing debate about whether the Waffen-SS was part and parcel of the SS murder machine that was epitomised by the notorious killing squads of the SS-Einsatzgruppen,[20] or if they were simply soldiers doing their duty. Again, that debate is not the subject of this work, but again what can be said definitively was that in the minds of the majority of the men and women who fought in the Red Army there was no distinction – they were just SS – and the SS was something to be feared.

As one Soviet soldier wrote in a letter home: 'Whatever happens I don't want to fall into the hands of the SS.'

The dreadful reality was that both sides had good reason to be fearful of the treatment they would receive at the hands of the other. From the launch of Barbarossa to the Nazi capitulation in 1945, in excess of 5.5 million Soviet soldiers went into German captivity, of whom between 3 and 3.5 million died; murdered, starved or dead from disease.[21] Conversely, of the 3 million Germans who went the other way into Soviet imprisonment, one third perished.[22] It made for a war with very little mercy or compassion. The German Army infantry officer, Karl Hertzog, recalled of the fighting in Russia:

We feared the Partisans. They were ruthless... On one occasion I led a patrol into a known Partisan stronghold and just escaped with my life. My platoon was slaughtered. Ten were killed on the spot, 15 were taken prisoner, and the remainder – including myself – managed to escape. Three days later, by the side of the road, we found the dismembered corpses of those men who had been captured.[23]

IC: We got on well with the Russian civilians, and sometimes we were quartered in their homes, they were very friendly and shared whatever they had with us – including their lice! Sometimes we took Prisoners Of War that were sick of the war, just like we were, and our orders were that all POWs were to be sent back to collection camps. I never went to any of those camps or had any contact with them, so I don't know what they were like. But once I was ordered to shoot two Partisans that we had captured and had then been questioned; one was an older guy, say around 30 or maybe even 40, and the other was just a kid, maybe 15 or 16. We were still pretty new at the front, and were told to go to headquarters and pick these guys up. Anyway, me and another Dane were told by some officers to take them into the forest and shoot them. We marched off and when we were a good distance into the woods we looked at each other – me and the other Dane – and then we just said to the two partisans 'Davei davei!' (Run run!), and we fired our rifles into the air as the two ran off – I never saw anyone run so fast I can tell you! After that we went back and said 'order carried out'. There was no way we were going to shoot unarmed men, especially when one of them was just a boy.

We heard rumours of attacks on Jews; mass deportations, mass shootings and concentration camps, that sort of stuff, but these things were not a subject we talked about much at the front. We had enough to think about just trying to stay alive. It wasn't until after the war that I realised the atrocities that had been going on in Russia.

> *We travelled through villages where Russian civilians had been shot or there had been hangings, but we never did these things, and I never witnessed them personally.*

At this point Ivar went silent and sat there on his sofa, absentmindedly clenching and unclenching his fists, and then he started up again:

> *IC: There was one time in Russia where we had counter-attacked and retook a village, and we found, we found...*

He lapsed into silence. Through my interpreter, I pressed him about what he had found, but it was clearly a memory too far:

> *IC: I don't want to talk about it, I won't be able to sleep tonight if I even think about it, no.*

He shook his head so vigorously his glasses almost came off, his hands waving around as if swatting imaginary flies, and then he just looked out of the window through the outside lean-to to the hedge beyond, his mouth twitching, but without any sound coming out.

I am ashamed to say that as I sat there in front of this very old man whose mind was obviously trying as hard as it could to block out so painful a memory, all I could think of was how could I get him to talk about it, how could I get him to open up and get it all on tape. The answer, as it turned out, was simply to wait and keep quiet. Ivar's hands stopped shaking, and he turned his head to look down at the coffee table in front of him.

> *IC: The thing I remember most of all is mutilated genitals – people's genitals – and mostly women's genitals. Look it up, that's all I'll say, it was at Grischino; it's well-documented.*

Ivar lapsed into silence once more, and that was definitely that this time – I moved on with my next question.

The note had been made, though, and I did indeed research Grischino after the interview and wasn't surprised to discover a tale of carnage almost too typical of the Russo-German war, but what made this one stand out, perhaps, was that the Germans had called in neutral international observers to document it so that it could be broadcast to the world to demonstrate the savagery of Soviet communism. In essence, in February 1943 the Germans counter-attacked and recaptured the eastern Ukrainian towns of Krasnoarmeyskoye, Postyschewo and Grischino. In the latter town, Ivar and his comrades found a total of 596 murdered Axis personnel who had been unable to escape the place before it was liberated by the Red Army. The total included 508 soldiers; mostly Germans but also 89 Italians, nine Romanians and four Hungarians, and a large number of paramilitary and civilian workers, among them two Danish Organisation Todt members, and a number of female nurses and signals staff. The women had been raped and mutilated; a German military judge who witnessed the scene stated in an interview during the 1970s that he saw a female corpse with her legs spread-eagled and a broomstick rammed into her vagina. As for the men, noses and ears had been cut off and penises removed and stuffed into their mouths.[24]

Lest we in the West seek to sit atop our moral high-horse and put all of this down to some sort of Russo-German atavism that has nothing to do with us, we should look at our own record too, as witnessed by an American Army corporal fighting in Nijmegen in the Netherlands during Operation Market Garden in 1944: 'Old German men grab our M1 rifles and beg for mercy, but they were shot point blank.' And a comrade of his in the Screaming Eagles

101st Airborne in the Ardennes a few months later: 'We took no prisoners, we mowed them down as if they were weeds.'

While Lieutenant Paul Fussell of the American 103rd Division described how some of his men found 15 German soldiers cowering in a deep crater in the forest on the Franco-German border. 'Their visible wish to surrender – most were in tears of terror and despair – was ignored by our men lining the rim ... Laughing and howling ... our men exultantly shot into the crater until every single man down there was dead ... The result was deep satisfaction.'

It wasn't just Americans either. One Canadian soldier's letter home said: 'When the Jerries come in with their hands up, shouting "Kamerad", we just bowl them over with bursts of Sten fire.'

Patton himself wrote at the time of 'some unfortunate incidents in the shooting of prisoners (I hope we can conceal this)'.[25]

Andreas Fleischer summed it all up rather well:

AF: What can I tell you, war is shit, it's the worst thing man has ever invented.

Notes to Chapter Four

1. *Volksdeutsche* – in Nazi terminology these were 'Germans in terms of people or race', regardless of citizenship and thus included Germans living beyond the borders of the Reich, as long as they were not of Jewish origin. This is in contrast to Imperial Germans (*Reichsdeutsche*), German citizens living within the 1938 borders of Germany itself. The term also contrasts with the usage of the term *Auslandsdeutsche* (Germans abroad/German expatriates), which generally denotes German citizens residing in other countries. According to German estimates in the 1930s, about 30 million Volksdeutsche and Auslandsdeutsche were living outside the Reich.

A significant proportion of them were in Central Europe: Poland, Ukraine, the Baltic States, Romania, Hungary and Yugoslavia, and even Russia. McKale, Donald M., *The Swastika Outside Germany*, Kent State University.

2. Quite a few *Volksdeutsche* were sent to the SS-Totenkopf Division despite the opposition of its then-commander – Theodor Eicke. He felt they were not good enough for his beloved division, and first complained in a letter to higher SS authorities about Volksdeutsche recruits on 15 November 1941 when he claimed that they were weakening the Totenkopf because 'they were lazy, politically ignorant and inferior physically, they slept on guard duty, and acts of cowardice and self-inflicted wounds were common among them.' Sydnor, Charles W. Jnr, *Soldiers of Destruction: The SS Death's Head Division 1933–1945*, p230, Princeton.
3. Totenkopf became the 3rd SS-Panzer Division Totenkopf in October 1943, and SS-Panzer-Grenadier Regiment 6 'Theodor Eicke' – formerly SS-Totenkopf Regiment 3, was re-named by Hitler in Eicke's honour in his eulogy after his death in action on 26 February 1943.
4. Trigg, Jonathan, *Death on the Don: The Destruction of Germany's Allies on the Eastern Front, 1941–44*, The History Press.
5. The Katyusha multiple rocket launcher is a type of rocket artillery first built and fielded by the Soviet Union in World War II. The Katyushas of World War II were usually mounted on ordinary trucks. Because they were marked with the letter *K* (for Voronezh's Komintern Factory), Red Army troops adopted a nickname from Mikhail Isakovsky's popular wartime song, *Katyusha*, meaning 'Little Katie' about a girl longing for her absent beloved, who has gone away on military service. The song was made famous by Soviet forces sweetheart Lidiya Rusanova, who reportedly paid for two batteries herself. German troops coined the nickname 'Stalin's organ'

after Soviet leader Joseph Stalin, comparing the visual resemblance of the launch array to a church organ, and the sound of the weapon's rocket motors, a distinctive howling sound which terrified the German troops, adding a psychological warfare aspect to their use – Clark, Lloyd, *Kursk: The Greatest Battle – Eastern Front 1943*, p140, Headline.

6. Statistics Iceland – main official institute providing statistics on the nation of Iceland.
7. *My Life and the Story that Could Not be Told*. The book came out in 1989 and was recorded by Nanna Rögnvaldurdottir.
8. The MP40 – *Maschinenpistole 40* – was a submachine gun developed in Nazi Germany and used extensively by the Axis powers during World War II. Designed in 1938 by Heinrich Vollmer with inspiration from its predecessor the MP38, it was heavily used on the Eastern and Western Fronts. Its advanced and modern features made it a favourite among soldiers and popular in countries from various parts of the world after the war. It was often erroneously called 'Schmeisser' by the Allies, despite Hugo Schmeisser's non-involvement in the weapon's design and production. From 1940 to 1945, an estimated 1.1 million were produced by the Erma Werke.
9. 'Landstormen' – a group led by Max Arildskov, which had broken away from the DNSAP after Clausen's poor results in the March 1943 election. They joined the Danish People's Defence (in Danish: *Dansk Folke Værn* or *Dansk Folkeværn*), which was the civilian arm of the Schalburg Corps, active from April 1943 to August 1944, in support of the German occupation of Denmark. It was made up of civilians, some of whom were expected to provide financial backing. The founding of *Dansk Folkeværn* commenced in April 1943, with Knud Børge Martinsen among the first *Dansk Folkeværn* leaders. *Dansk Folkeværn* functioned as the political propaganda arm of the Schalburg Corps, and was open to both men and women.

10. The National Socialist Motor Corps (German: *Nationalsozialistisches Kraftfahrkorps*, NSKK) was a paramilitary organisation of the Nazi Party that officially existed from May 1931 to 1945. The NSKK served as a driver training organisation, and its members served in the transport corps of various German military branches.
11. The Organisation Todt (OT) was a civil and military engineering group in the Third Reich from 1933 to 1945, named after its founder, Fritz Todt, an engineer and senior Nazi figure. The organisation was responsible for a huge range of engineering projects both in pre-Second World War Germany, and the occupied territories from France to the Soviet Union during the war. It reached its maximum strength in November 1944 when it consisted of a total of 1.35 million members, including fulltime 48,500 Germans (of whom 4,000 were female) and 12,800 non-Germans, 313,000 German and 680,700 non-German civilian personnel in contracted firms, 165,000 POWs and 140,000 workers including Jews who were classed as 'petty criminals' and were forced labour. McNab, Chris ed., *Hitler's Armies: A History of the German War Machine 1939–45*, p235, Osprey.
12. Lindstad, Bjørn, *Den Frivillige – En Frontkjemper Forteller Sin Historie*, Kagge Vorlag.
13. The Wehrmacht's major 1942 summer offensive – codenamed Operation Blue – had had seizing the oil fields of the Caucasus as its main objective. The Wiking had been heavily involved in the failed offensive.
14. SS-Haupsturmführer Walter Körner was the Regimental Adjutant of the SS-Freiwilligen-Panzergrenadier Regiment 23 Norge. He was killed in action on 6 March 1945 and his Knight's Cross award was dated the 11 May 1945. The nomination by his unit was received by the *Heerespersonalamt* (HPA—Army Staff Office) at the end of March 1945. There is no entry date listed on the file

card nor in the book *Verliehene Ritterkreuze* (*Awarded Knight Crosses*). The HPA created a nomination request with the number 4980, which does not exist anymore, and according to the file card was submitted for further processing on 4 April 1945. No further comments or notes indicate that the nomination was finalised. On 20 July 2004, a spokesperson from the German Federal Archives stated that it cannot be verified that Körner received the Knight's Cross. The German author, and key member of the Association of Knight's Cross Recipients, Walther-Peer Fellgiebel, assigned the presentation date.

15. The Transylvanian Saxons are a people of German ethnicity who settled in Transylvania (in German *Siebenbürgen*) from the mid-12th century onwards. The main task of the German settlers was to defend the south-eastern border of the Kingdom of Hungary. The colonisation continued until the end of the 13th century. Although the colonists came mostly from the western Holy Roman Empire and generally spoke Franconian German dialects, they were collectively known as Saxons because of the Saxon Germans working for the Hungarian chancellery. After 1918, when, following the Treaty of Trianon, Transylvania was separated from Hungary and became part of Romania, the Transylvanian Saxons, together with other German-speaking groups in the newly enlarged Romania; – Banat Swabians, Satu Mare Swabians, Bessarabian and Bukovinan Germans – became part of that country's 750,000-strong German minority.
16. The town's full title at the time was Bosanski Novi, it is now called Novi Grad. It is a town and municipality in the northern portion of the Republika Srpska entity of Bosnia and Herzegovina. The town is situated on the Una River, on the border with Croatia, opposite the town of Dvor. In the 2013 census the municipality had a population of about 30,000 people. Yugoslavia was created at the end of the

First World War and comprised Serbia, Bosnia Herzegovina, Croatia, Slovenia, Montenegro, Macedonia and Kosovo. The country was dismembered after the Nazi invasion in 1941, reunified following the end of the war, and split again from 1991 onwards.

17. Felix Martin Julius Steiner (23 May 1896 – 12 May 1966) was an *Obergruppenführer* in the Waffen-SS during World War II, who commanded several SS divisions and corps. He was awarded the Knight's Cross of the Iron Cross with Oak Leaves and Swords. Together with Paul Hausser, he contributed significantly to the development and transformation of the Waffen-SS into a military force made up of volunteers and conscripts from both occupied and un-occupied lands. Steiner was chosen by Heinrich Himmler to oversee the creation of and then command SS Division Wiking. In 1943, he was promoted to the command of the III (Germanic) SS Panzer Corps.
18. The Yugoslav Partisans, or officially the National Liberation Army and Partisan Detachments of Yugoslavia, was the Communist-led resistance to the Axis powers (chiefly Germany) in occupied Yugoslavia during the Second World War. It is widely considered to have been Europe's most effective anti-Axis resistance movement during Second World War, often compared to the Polish resistance movement, albeit the latter was a mostly non-communist autonomous movement. The Partisans were led by the Communist Party of Yugoslavia and its commander was Marshal Josip Broz Tito.
19. Following the Allied advance up the boot of Italy during 1943, the United States Army Air Force (USAAF) and British Royal Air Force (RAF), including the Balkan Air Force (BAF), began to carry out air attacks in Yugoslavia in support of the Partisans. These attacks became intense in May–June 1944, and dozens of Yugoslav cities and towns were bombed, many repeatedly. There was also a bombing campaign against transport infrastructure in September 1944 as the *Wehrmacht* withdrew from the Balkans.

20. The SS *Einsatzgruppen* were paramilitary death squads responsible for mass killings in the East, primarily by shooting. First operating in occupied Poland, they went on to follow the invading troops into the Soviet Union at the launch of Barbarossa. Their victims were mainly Communists, Jews and Gypsies. Under the direction of *Reichsführer-SS* Heinrich Himmler and the supervision of *SS-Obergruppenführer* Reinhard Heydrich, the *Einsatzgruppen* carried out operations ranging from the murder of a few people to operations that lasted for days, such as the massacre at Babi Yar where 33,771 Jews were killed in two days. Historian Raul Hilberg estimates that between 1941 and 1945 the Einsatzgruppen and related auxiliary troops killed more than 2 million people, including 1.3 million Jews.
21. Calvocoressi, Peter, & Wint, Guy, *Total War.*
22. Overmans, Rüdiger, *Soldaten hinter Stacheldraht. Deutsche Kriegsgefangene des Zweiten Weltkriege*, p246. Ullstein.
23. Clark, Lloyd, *Kursk: The Greatest Battle – Eastern Front 1943*, interview with Dr Karl Hertzog, p100, Headline.
24. The towns were overrun by the Soviet 4th Guards Tank Corps on the night of 10/11 February 1943, and recaptured by the SS-Wiking Division, with the support of the 333rd Infantry and 7th Panzer Divisions on 18 February 1943. While a large part of the investigation file is lost, some of the evidence remained in a German Foreign Office file currently stored in the German Federal State Archive (*Bundesarchiv)*. De Zayas, Alfred, *Wehrmacht Investigative Body*, p318, Universitas Munich.
25. Atkinson, Rick, *The Guns at Last Light: The War in Western Europe, 1944–45*, Abacus.

5

THE TIDE TURNS

From the beginning of 1942, up to the early summer that year, the Red Army lost a staggering 1,400,000 men killed, missing or taken prisoner, with 600,000 gone in May alone. The Ostheer on the other hand ***only*** suffered 190,000 casualties in the same period. The maths told the story – on that basis Moscow would run out of men before Berlin did. However, the second half of 1942, and the first few months of 1943, saw the balance tilt decisively in the Soviets' favour after their victory at Stalingrad. Hitler's forces in the east – which had stood at the beginning of Barbarossa at 3,800,000 men – had been ground down to 2,700,000, while the Soviets could still field 6 million – and those 6 million were increasingly better equipped from the factories now at full production behind the Urals, and an American industrial leviathan that was fast becoming one of the man-made wonders of the world. Now it was Berlin's turn to do the sums, and they all said the same thing – the Soviet Union would outlast them.[1]

Nazi Germany now stood at a crossroads in the war.

The Soviet offensives in the south in late 1942 and early 1943 had destroyed the German Sixth Army, and taken big chunks out of their Second Army and Fourth Panzer Army. Their main allies in the East were more or less wiped out, with the Romanians having lost their 3rd and 4th Armies, the Italians their 8th, and the Hungarians their 2nd [see *Death on the Don* by Jonathan Trigg]. Erich von Manstein – probably the Wehrmacht's finest strategic brain of the war – urged Hitler to go onto the defensive for the remainder of the year, to trade space for time, and adopt a flexible, mobile defence that would allow still-superior German tactical ability to win victories such as his at Kharkov in the previous months.

Manstein was to be disappointed.

The dictator's decision was to more or less gamble the Wehrmacht's entire offensive punch on one grand throw of the dice – Operation Citadel (*Zitadelle* in German). Massing 800,000 men, 10,000 guns and 3,000 panzers, the Ostheer planned to use its tried and tested pincer attack to capture the city of Kursk and kill or capture almost a quarter of the whole Red Army. Hitler was so nervous about it all he even said to one of his generals, 'Whenever I think of this attack my stomach turns over.'[2]

Pardon the pun, but he should have listened to his gut. Citadel was a total and utter disaster. Called off after just one week of bitter fighting, more than 50,000 Germans lay dead in the midst of hundreds of their burnt-out armoured vehicles. The German *panzerwaffe* (panzer force), arguably the only chance they had of achieving victory in the east, would never recover. The flower of seventeen Army and Waffen-SS panzer divisions was ground into the steppe.

The 5th SS-Panzergrenadier Division Wiking (soon to be converted to a full panzer division), took no part in Citadel, being employed further south in vicious defensive fighting of their own. Ivar Corneliussen was with them.

IC: We took part in lots of fights with Red Army soldiers from town to town until the 5th of July 1943, and we always beat them back, but we suffered dead and wounded too. Our fallen comrades were buried on the spot, the wounded were sent back by horse-drawn cart, first to the main dressing station and from there further back, to the hospital if they needed it. We were then put into reserve about 50 kilometres west of Kharkov, and then, on the 18th of July we took part in a major offensive. We were given these little inflatable dinghies and sent across the River Donetz to attack a Russian bridgehead there – this was in the Voronezh/Orel area. I remember that it was a beautiful morning that day, with just a light mist on the river and across the land. Everything was silent when we paddled across the river, the Russians didn't hear us coming. On the far side of the river, the bank was a steep slope with blackberry bushes on top. We climbed the bank and went into position just at the top of the slope. I was a Stuurman at this time and normally I would be the commander of a Gruppe [Author: roughly equivalent to a British Army section] of 10 men, but on this day there were only eight of us.

We were pretty heavily armed, and we all had stick grenades – the German ones – I never liked them though, I much preferred the egg grenade, like the British had, as it had more shrapnel in it and could do more damage.

I was lying in the middle of the group and to my left was my second-in-command, armed with a scoped rifle. To my right was a heavy MG42 – a 'Hitler saw' – it shot as many as 1,200 to 1,800 rounds a minute, but this meant we constantly had to fetch ammunition for it. So, with the MG42 was the gunner number one, and to his left gunner number two, who was supposed to reload the ammo belts and be ready with a spare barrel when the one on the machine-gun got overheated – that happened a lot because of its high rate of fire. The barrel used to get so hot, it would glow red, and then we'd have to change it or we couldn't fire it anymore. Then I had four riflemen; two on each side of the machine-gun, and they were at the same time allocated to bring fresh ammo to the MG. That was always the problem with the 42; we had to constantly change the barrels as they overheated, and it just used up ammunition at a terrible rate. All we seemed to do was feed it ammo, again and again, belt after belt after belt. We also had a Panzerschreck.[3]

Anyway, I looked up and there was an open area with a Russian farmhouse in front of us. When everything seemed quiet I gave the order to move out and go forward. After about 100 metres I saw to my right a small outbuilding and behind it was the back-end of a Russian tank, a T34. It was parked up and couldn't use its machine-guns on us as it was facing the other way, but its turret was turning towards us to fire. I shouted to my men 'Take cover!' and we all threw ourselves down on the ground, but I was stupid. We had all learnt to keep our heads down and cover our faces with our arm in situations like that, but I put my head up to look and right at that moment the tank shell exploded close to me and a shrapnel splinter hit me in my left eye.

The next thing I remember is waking up in the aid station. My comrades had taken me there. I was told later on that one of my men had blown the T34 up with the Panzerschreck. I was lucky though, as I think the shell was an anti-tank one and not high explosive, if it was high explosive then I think I would have been killed.

As it was, I was operated on by an SS-Sturmbannführer and he removed my left eye – that was on the 19th of July – and he also removed some more shrapnel from my head and the rest of my body, but he didn't take it all out as I had lots of little fragments in me. When I was in the hospital they X-rayed me, and told me that these bits would constantly move around – look, here's one you can see and feel in my hand.

At that point Ivar stretched out his left hand towards me, and there on the outside of his wrist was a distinct lump the size of a grain of wheat, and when I touched it you could feel it was hard as stone, even as it moved around a bit under his skin. Ivar began to chuckle:

IC: I was X-rayed in Germany once – a few years ago when I was there to have my eye changed[4] *– and the doctor looked at the X-ray and asked me if I had ever been shot by a shotgun, and I said: 'Why would you think that Herr Doctor?' and he said because your body is full of tiny balls of lead, like buckshot – and I said: 'Oh that! No, it wasn't a shotgun, it was a T34 tank shell!' I couldn't stop laughing, I tell you!*

As an aside, Ivar wasn't the only Scandinavian volunteer who had his doubts about the ammunition-heavy MG42 – his fellow veterans Andreas and Bjørn had made the same point:

AF: We were issued MG42s, you know the heavy machine-guns. We didn't like them. We much preferred the old MG34s. On the 42, as soon as you pressed the trigger, just like that, brrrrrrrrrrrrr, that was it, fifty rounds gone right there, it sounded like starting a car. We were always having to carry ammunition up to it, so much ammunition, we were always running back to the frontline ammo dump, and that was always at least a few hundred metres back, picking up more and running forward with it again. We would have eight men at a time just servicing one MG42 – it was 'munitionsverschwendung' [Author: roughly translated as a 'waste of ammo'].

BL: MG42s – firing at 1,500 rounds a minute, oh the noise of it! They used to stop the Russian infantry for sure, but after 300 rounds they used to get too hot to fire, we then had to change the barrel, that happened a lot with that machine-gun, so we had to fire it in bursts, and it used up ammunition in massive amounts.

Away from the Eastern Front, and the veterans' musings on their favourite machine-gun, 1943 was also a turning point year in occupied Europe. After the fall of Tunis in May, the Anglo-Americans landed in Sicily and then on mainland Italy. Over in the Balkans, the coalition of German/Italian/Croat Ustasha and Serb Chetnik forces had failed to eliminate Tito's Partisan army at the Battle of the Neretva, and over the skies of Germany itself the British RAF was in the process of dropping 34,000 tons of bombs on the Ruhr industrial region.

In Denmark, the so-called 'politics of co-operation' still held sway in the first half of the year. German troops were stationed in the country, but to all intents and purposes it was the Danish authorities who carried on governing, administering and policing the country on a day-to-day basis. Active resistance was very limited, although some sabotage did occur; this was split into two types – military-economic (industrial sabotage) and military-tactical (railway sabotage). The main objective of those who did resist was to demonstrate to the Allies that Denmark was with them, and also to remind the Danes themselves that the world was at war. But to be clear here, this was no national rising as in Yugoslavia, great care was taken by the Resistance to avoid shedding German blood so as not to provoke Nazi reprisals, and the same went for Danish civilians, and Danish property – damage and destruction was at all times to be carefully controlled. The other side in this game was Danish too, with the local police having the lead responsibility for combating sabotage and resistance. It was the police who investigated acts of resistance, made arrests, and then it was Danish courts who tried and convicted perpetrators – although the Germans did occasionally intervene if they felt the case warranted it. The situation was described by Assistant Police Chief E. Lemvigh-Müller – who was deployed to the municipality of Odder[5] in 1943 by the State Department – as a liaison between the German troops in the area and the local magistrate, local police and the parish council.

When I began my work as a liaison officer on the 1st of June 1943, about 400 Germans were billeted in Odder, some two companies of Wehrmacht troops under the command of a Hauptmann Bredenförder. The German HQ was located in the Hotel Phoenix in Rosensgade. The day after my arrival I paid a courtesy visit to Hauptmann Bredenförder, to whom I explained the various complaints arising from German soldiers' actions. It was then only about trifles, however, but was extremely irritating to the local population; such as German soldiers unceremoniously violating road traffic regulations, driving on the pavements or cycling without bike lights after dark, etc., and to a lesser extent damaging private property or confiscating fuel and the like. The Hauptmann apologised, and explained that part of the problem lay with Wehrmacht ignorance of Danish legislation, and he issued an Order of the Day for his soldiers to abide by the instructions they received from the Danish police, as he admitted they had a right to take action against infringements committed by German soldiers. He asked that in future all minor problems like this be reported to him and not to higher authorities so they could be settled in this manner to the satisfaction of all parties. This assumed, of course, that both parties acted in good faith towards each other, even though both parties were somewhat sceptical of each other, as witnessed by the fact that there were always at least two participants from each side present at all negotiations. As a witness to the negotiations, I always took Sergeant Grønnebæk Petersen, while the German commanders always had an aide.

That issues could be settled in this way required knowledge of German mentality. The Germans' respect for titles, uniforms and insignia has always been great. It was therefore necessary to act correctly, address them as soldiers and appeal to their soldierly honour – this always produced results. In return, on our side we always wore uniform and made every attempt to impress the Germans with our power and authority. Sergeant Grønnebæk and I managed to rent some horses, which we rode when we went to see the Germans who were impressed at what they thought were our service horses. By far the hardest part of negotiations focused on solving accommodation problems. This issue, which was of such importance for the population, often gave rise to discussions in which all means were used to prevent private properties being used for this purpose. Preferably, of course, we used hotels, community centres and the like, and then came schools and colleges. A great help was that just west of Odder was located the Manor Rathlousdal main building, which stood empty. This was used always in the first place and offered the advantage that it meant there were no Germans in the middle of the city.

He clearly understood the ambiguity of his role and the way it could be viewed as a form of 'collaboration', and was always keen to avoid it being seen in that way by his fellow Danes.

> *A great consolation during this unpleasant and difficult work was knowing that an overwhelming majority of people understood our position ... and refrained from wanton demonstrations at the beginning of the occupation, which could only have led to stronger measures from the German side. This is not to say that kindness was shown to the Germans. Fraternization on a large scale was unknown, people regarded them as a necessary evil.*[6]

In the middle of all of this, in March 1943, a very strange thing in Nazi-occupied Europe occurred in Denmark – a free democratic general election was held to vote in a new government. Yes, that actually happened – the Nazis allowed a people they had conquered to do what even their own population was unable to do – vote freely for a political party of their choice. The result was a clear victory for the democratic parties, and humiliation for Clausen and the DNSAP who had hoped for a huge upsurge that would carry them into power. The Germans were stunned and unsure how to react, and then when the Danish people began to go on strike and take to the streets in peaceful protest the Nazis fell back on their preferred option of oppression. The Germans ordered the Danish government to impose the death penalty for saboteurs – a directive the Danes not-so-politely refused. That was that, the Nazis had had enough and on 29 August 1943 co-operation between Germany and the Danish government officially ended and Germany declared Denmark to be in a State of Emergency – four Danish soldiers ended up being killed when the government was dissolved by the Germans[7] – although the Danish police weren't completely disbanded and continued to co-operate with their German counterparts.

Back in Russia, not all Scandinavian Waffen-SS volunteers were involved in the titanic battles that characterised much of the fighting in the Soviet Union in 1943. Many had enlisted specifically to help their Finnish brethren in the far north, where most of the combat was characterised by long patrols, small unit ambushes and the ever-present threat of mines. One such veteran involved in that arena of endless forests, swamps, rivers and winter snow was the Norwegian former SS-Schütze, Asbjørn Narmo.

Born in 1921, Narmo was just 19 when the Germans invaded his country. I interviewed him when he was 96 years old, in what became one of the most unsettling sessions I have had with any veteran.

The setting was so much a carbon copy of so many others across Scandinavia that I was in danger of becoming blasé about it. Narmo lived in a light, airy and modern apartment on the third floor of a well-kept block. Furniture and personal trappings were fairly minimal in a Scandinavian way, but there were tapestries on most of the walls depicting medieval scenes of hunting and the like (I discovered later that they had all been handmade by his late wife), and he obviously liked his technology with a very big flat-screen TV showing the tennis and lots and lots of related electronic gismos; DVD players, disc contraptions and so on.

Narmo himself was sitting in a large, comfortable chair in shorts and slippers – the day was sunny and warm – with a grey casual shirt emblazoned with the logo of 'Narmo Concrete' – his own business. So far so good, except the man inside the clothes looked terrible. He was covered in dark blue and black bruises – which were interspersed on his bald scalp with fresh scabs. Other cuts were all over his legs and arms, most covered by plasters, and there was a huge bandage on his left leg that had tubes coming out of it that were plugged into a machine of some sort. Like so many other men of his age I had met, the flesh had seemed to have melted off him, leaving only bone and paper-thin skin, although even this couldn't hide that he had clearly been a very strong man once – his oversized hands and forearms perched on the arms of his black leather chair. Looking at him, his blue eyes were unfocused and seemingly distracted across the room, and I found myself staring at him, lost for words.

It seemed like an age, but it was only a matter of moments, and then I composed myself and went through my standard routine, explaining why I wanted to interview him, what the book would be about, and confirming his permission for me to both record and publish anything and everything he said or showed me. He nodded his assent and I launched into my first question. It was a typical starter: 'Why did you volunteer for the Waffen-SS?' but his reaction to it was anything but typical, and I will always remember it – Narmo began to cry, the tears rolling down his cheeks as he moaned loudly and his whole body began to shake. I was totally dumbfounded. This wasn't what I had expected, nor what I had intended – I wasn't there to cause a nonagenarian severe distress, to make him recall events and decisions he made more than 70 years ago so that he could relive the horror and angst of it all – no, it was time for me to leave. I turned to his grandson Peter and apologised and said I would go and leave his grandfather in peace, but Peter motioned me to sit down and poured me a cup of coffee.

Don't worry, you haven't upset him, not at all. He has had a couple of small strokes recently, on top of everything else in terms of his health problems, and the result is he can't control his emotions and bursts into tears all the time. In fact, he has been looking forward to meeting you and speaking to you, so don't worry about it, just carry on and keep on with your questions.

What else could I do but crack on. Narmo recovered himself, nodding at Peter's explanation, and motioned me to begin again – so I asked my question a second time.

AN: I was a member of the NS and wanted to help Finland, so, I joined the SS-Schijäger in October 1942. They were formed to help the Finns so I decided that was the unit for me.

I was trained in Sennheim first of all. The training wasn't too hard. I was physically strong at the time as I had been working outdoors for a long time, so that wasn't a problem. I found the language issue more difficult as they taught us in German and I didn't understand a lot of it, particularly at first. I got used to it after a while though.

There were about 120 of us in the unit, almost all of us were Norwegians, but we had three Germans too. The Germans treated us with respect and we had good relations with the German officers, even though they didn't speak much Norwegian. After we finished our training we were sent north – the far north – and we were based up there near Murmansk, my commander was called Jonassen.[8] *When I was there I was on patrol more or less every day I was at the front. Sometimes we used to meet Russian civilians, out in the forest, they'd be collecting firewood, or something like that, but we never fired at them, or hurt them at all, we just wouldn't have done that. We also met Russian soldiers of course, and we thought they weren't very good as individual soldiers or when they were in small groups, but when there was a lot of them they were good. We tried to avoid fights if we could as we were there to patrol and find out information – for reconnaissance and intelligence gathering you know – rather than to fight all the time.*

I remember one fight though, when we attacked a Russian column. We killed the Russian officer in charge and almost all of his men, but we took one prisoner – a Russian. We kept him and used to make him look after the fire during the night – keep it going you know – he became our helper, our Hiwi.[9] *Everyone was asleep when he was doing that, he could have done anything to us – killed us, stolen our weapons, or even escaped, but he didn't, he stayed with us. We got rations for him and gave him some uniform too, he was a good guy.*

Asbjørn wasn't as complimentary about all Russians though.

AN: It was strictly forbidden for us to modify our ammunition, you know, to make dum-dum bullets, but I think some other soldiers did do that, but I'm not sure. The Russians definitely did. Some of the wounds our soldiers got were terrible, just terrible.[10] *But mines were just as bad, in fact they were worse. I was only about a metre away when my commander – Gust Jonassen – was killed by a mine. He stepped on it and off it went. I liked Jonassen a lot, he was a good officer and he really looked after us. Losing him was a big blow to us all.*

Jonassen was killed on 26 May 1943 while returning from a patrol with Asbjørn and his comrades. The unit he had founded had been in action less than three months.

AN: The next week we were out on patrol again and found ourselves in another minefield, it was very scary, and I was lucky to survive. A mine went off behind me – I was on the other side of a small river at the time – and this time it was a German pioneer[11] *who had trodden on a mine.*

Although Jonassen was replaced pretty much immediately by Otto-Andreas Holmen – a popular former member of the Norwegian Royal Guard, graduate of Bad Tölz and an NS member like most of his men – the Company's morale suffered a crisis of confidence and as a result they were all sent home on leave in July to recover. The furlough also signalled the end of the majority of the volunteers' enlistments, which had only been for one year. The Company had been a success though, and the SS authorities committed to reconstituting the unit if enough volunteers could be found – Asbjørn was one.

AN: I signed up again, and was then sent to Poland to do a veterinary assistant's course. There were two other Norwegians on the same course and we all got on very well. It was good to have other Norwegians there, especially to help with the language as it was quite technical and all in German of course. When the course finished I went back to the front and stayed there until June 1944 when I was sent back home to Norway with some of my comrades, where they were discharged and I went to work in the offices of the Germanske SS.[12]

As Asbjørn went home, so Jostein Berge went north to replace him in the ski troops:

JB: It was the winter of 1942–43 and I was away with the Germanische Landdienst – I was with them until 1944 – and when I got back I enlisted in the Ski Battalion to go to Finland, partly to get away from those people who were treating us so badly at home because we were NS, and also because I wanted to help Finland.

It wasn't a particularly strange thing to do, to volunteer to serve with the Germans, lots of Norwegians did it, and not just with the Waffen-SS either. There were also Norwegian volunteers in the Kriegsmarine [Author: the Third Reich's navy] serving in the Baltic Sea on board the Nürnberg.[13] *Later on during the war – towards the end – the* Nürnberg *was ordered into the North Sea, but the Norwegians didn't want to stay on her as they had volunteered to fight the Russians and not the British. The Germans tried to send them to the Waffen-SS, but they hadn't enlisted for that either. One of them, a doctor, deserted and escaped to Sweden. That was a dangerous thing to do, because if you deserted and were caught you were shot. I knew a man, another volunteer in my unit, he was called Dahl, and he deserted. He was caught, brought back and shot. It was stupid, the war was just about over. About two or three men from the unit were ordered to go and watch the execution – luckily I wasn't one of them, so I didn't have to watch.*

Hundreds of miles south of Jostein and Asbjørn's patrol base in Finnish Karelia, Ivar Corneliussen was adjusting to life as a one-eyed infantryman.

IC: I was in the field hospital for a few days, and then for some reason I was flown in a Ju52 to the SS hospital in Dnepropetrovsk. I arrived there on 27th July 1943. A couple of days later, the senior doctor – an Oberstabsartz – showed up, he was the same surgeon who'd done my operation – and he asked me to pour a glass of water from the carafe that was on the little table next to my bed. I picked it up and tried to pour it and the water went all over the place! It was what he expected, he told me that now I had just one eye I couldn't judge distance accurately and it would take me a while to learn how to do it with just my right eye – he was right, it took some time but I learnt.

While I was recovering, Kobe Martinsen came to see me and asked me if I would be willing to go back to Denmark and work with him, but I said no, I wanted to get back to the front, I didn't want to let my comrades down. The doctor agreed with me, saying that as I aimed a weapon with my right eye it was fine and I would be OK to fight again when I'd recovered.

From Dnepropetrovsk I was sent to Breslau [Author: modern-day Wroclaw in Poland], west of Warsaw, where I was fitted with a glass eye and sent to the SS-Panzer-Grenadier Ausbildung und Ersatz battalion 5 [Author: the Wiking's training and replacement battalion] at a barracks in Swabia, I can't remember the name. It was full of Waffen-SS soldiers who had been wounded and were recovering. Some of them had been very badly injured; they were missing an arm or a leg. Ah, I remember now, it was Ellwangen.[14]

I didn't live in the actual barracks there, but in a former chocolate factory together with many other wounded soldiers. Those of us that could perform some duties were used as overseers at exercise time, and we did courier service, things like that.

I was lucky too – I got ten days special leave to the San Martino di Castrozza resort in the Dolomites in Italy – the Waffen-SS used to go there for skiing trips so it was all set up to look after guys like me. I spent some wonderful days there in a very nice hotel and did many walks in the area. After returning to Ellwangen I requested one week's leave to go to Denmark, and it was granted, in fact they gave me another ten days, this was in August 1943, which was a very turbulent time here in Denmark. I went home by train and it was on that journey I met Gunter – Unteroffizier

Gunter Lang – and we became friends. In civilian life Gunter had been a carpenter in Solingen in Germany and had just been back on leave there, now he was in the Luftwaffe and was returning to his base in Odense – my home city, of course – where he worked on a GEIGE 52 site.[15] *Gunter and I agreed to meet up in Odense, but first I had to go to Copenhagen – to the Shellhus*[16] *which was Gestapo HQ – to get the necessary paperwork so I could get back to Ellwangen after my leave.*

At this point I remembered what the Danish author and newspaper editor Bo Lidegaard had written about what the people back home in Denmark had thought of the volunteers: 'The relationship between the population and the *Frikorps* was freezing cold, and legionnaires on leave time and again got into fights with civilians, who treated the Korps' volunteers with massive contempt.'[17]

That seemed pretty clear-cut then. So, I asked Ivar about his personal experiences back in Denmark as he wandered around in his Waffen-SS uniform; how did people on the street treat him, was he ever afraid, did people attack him? I'd asked Magnus the same question about when he went home, but he lived down near the German border of course, and many of his neighbours were ethnic Germans like Andreas Fleischer and his family, with boys already serving in the Wehrmacht or the Waffen-SS, so it wasn't a surprise there was no animosity there. But what was it like in Copenhagen, in Odense – after all, the latter city was Denmark's third largest and a long way from south Jutland. Ivar's response was instructive to say the least.

IC: I never had any problems. I got my papers in Copenhagen, and people were all over the city, shopping, going to work and so on, and nothing – no one gave me any trouble or said anything bad to me. I then went to see my mum and stepdad in Odense – Thorsgade 66, 2nd floor. My mum was always pretty pragmatic and just said when I knocked on the door; 'So there you are, nice to see you are still alive.' The first thing I did after that was to take my uniform off and find some of my civilian clothes, but they didn't fit anymore, so I had to borrow some from my stepdad. I wasn't worried about wearing my uniform, but I felt more comfortable in civilian clothes, and I could walk around without drawing attention and just blend in with everyone else.

Anyway, I met Gunter in town as planned and took him home to meet my mum, and then I took him to meet my cousin Johannes Hansen. We had been in the Boy Scouts together, Johannes and I, and were pretty close. He'd become a Second Lieutenant in the Danish Army and lived at his parents' place in Vesterbro. He had gathered together a bunch of our old Scout comrades to see me and it was a merry reunion – lots to drink! We were all chatting and laughing and telling stories, and I quickly realised they were all into Resistance work, and they didn't hide it either – in fact when I asked Johannes he told Gunter and I straight out that not only were they all in the Resistance, but that they kept their explosives in the very box that we were sitting on in the kitchen. I said OK, and Gunter and I both stood up and lifted the lid of the box and there it was – the explosives. But we both thought it was none of our business, so we just closed the lid, sat back down and had another drink.

No one seemed worried, but after that we didn't talk at all about me being a soldier in the Waffen-SS, even though everyone knew I was.

I never reported Johannes – he was my cousin – but I heard later on that he had been arrested by the Gestapo and sent to Dachau in December 1944 – he survived and ended up going to Sweden on a 'Count Bernadotte white bus.'[18] *After the war Johannes became such good friends with Gunter that they and their wives went on holiday together – they have photos of those holidays in their houses. Funny really, a Resistance man and a German Luftwaffe man becoming such good friends. Unfortunately, Johannes became an alcoholic later on, it was very sad.*

A few days after that I went back to Ellwangen, and was then promoted to Rottenführer.

Denmark may have seemed an oasis of peace after the Russian front, but the reach of the war could now be felt everywhere, as Ivar was about to see for himself.

IC: It was September of 1943 by then and I was still on light duties. I was given an assignment to escort another Danish Waffen-SS volunteer from Ellwangen to the Waffen-SS administration centre at the Lützowplatz, not far from the Admiral-von-Schröder Strasse[19] *in Berlin. This guy had had a mental breakdown at the front and wasn't allowed to travel alone. During our train ride together we spoke a lot and it was my job to see we got something to eat and drink too when we stopped at stations. He was happy he was going to undergo treatment in Berlin and was hoping to be deemed unfit for further service and so would be discharged and sent home.*

Shortly after we arrived at the Anhalter Bahnhof in Berlin the air raid alarm sounded off and we ran for cover in the nearest shelter, which was in the basement of a large apartment block, but in the chaos I got separated from my comrade. The bombs wrecked the entrance to the shelter so we were buried alive. At this time I was only thinking about myself and how I could get through this Armageddon. It took us two days of digging to break through many walls into a neighbouring basement and finally find a way out. When we came out above ground it was a total mess. There was rubble everywhere, so many houses had collapsed, the asphalt on the roads had melted in the heat of the fires and they were still digging dead bodies out. I was in shock, and fear of the bombs was still lodged in my mind as I could remember the whistling sounds as they fell. I was also hungry and very thirsty, but couldn't get my bearings in the middle of all the destruction. I thought; 'Where should I go?' So, I followed other survivors from the basement and saw a sign that said 'Anhalter Bahnhof'. I set off. Entire neighbourhoods were demolished, but I had survived. My only thought was to get out of this hellhole and find the nearest Red Cross station to get something to eat and drink. After that I found a military post and was issued new papers so I could return to Ellwangen.[20]

When I got back to Ellwangen the quarters we had lived in before had been shut down, so me and some other fellows were sent to Guebwiller in Alsace, high in the Vosges Mountains, not far from Mulhouse and about 20 kilometres from Basel. In clear weather we could see the snowclad mountains of Switzerland, and just like in Ellwangen it was a place of rehabilitation for men that could perform light duties like office work, driving, supervision and so on. I stayed there between Christmas and New Year of 1943/44 and every now and then we went to Mulhouse and played 'civilians'. It was a pretty boring and repetitive life, so in January of 1944 I had had enough of it and requested to be transferred back to my regiment – I should have had my head examined at such an idea! I went to an elderly doctor who told me 'well you have been lucky my boy, it's the left eye that got hurt, or else we would have to train you to be a left-handed shooter!'

> *So, I got my papers and started on a long journey through Germany, Poland and to the Ukraine – the whole journey took several days with many stops on the way. Finally, I reached my old unit in Russia, back with the Westland. The Germans were retreating at the time in Russia, and that's when I went to Cherkassy.*

I remember that moment. The moment Ivar said the word 'Cherkassy'. His English was OK – as was his German – but most of the time he spoke in Danish of course, but there was no language issue with that word – he'd said 'Cherkassy'. I looked up from my notes, startled, my pen frozen and unmoving in my hand. Ivar himself was staring with his one eye down at his coffee table, his mottled hands on the knees of his blue jeans. After a moment he looked up at me and smiled faintly, the skin stretched taut across his face, bi-focal glasses on his nose, hearing aids in both ears – his open-necked checked shirt and brown slippers making him look more like a retired lumberjack rather than an ex-Waffen-SS panzergrenadier and merchant sailor.

Why was I taken aback? What was it about that one simple word that grabbed my attention – there was an easy answer to that. I'd never interviewed a veteran of that particular battle before – and Cherkassy was a battle that seemed made for eyewitness descriptions. If readers want to know more about it I would suggest reading Douglas Nash's superb *Hell's Gate*, a wonderful piece of writing, but in short it was a battle fought at the beginning of 1944, when the advancing Red Army cut off and encircled around 60,000 Axis soldiers, including the 5th SS-Panzer Division Wiking and its Belgian Walloon running mate, the 5th SS-Sturmbrigade Wallonien. Given the order to break out, the trapped troops surged west only to have to run a gauntlet of Soviet forces that decimated them – casualties were horrific, including the Pocket commander, General Stemmermann. It was fought in the snow and cold of a Soviet winter, a bitter struggle that ended with hundreds of desperate would-be escapers cut down by marauding Cossacks or drowned in an icy stream no more than 30 feet across as they struggled to reach the safety of its western bank.

It seemed a world away from Ivar's modern red-brick bungalow, tucked away in a small village south of the motorway. I'd seen the odd car or truck on the way there, doing battle with farmers' tractors to break the peace and quiet, apart from that, it was fields, barns and sky.

And then here I was, in a living room with rugs all over the floor, a big tapestry depicting a bird of paradise on the wall, and the thermostat turned up way too high so I could feel the sweat running down my back and pooling above my belt – I shivered.

IC: Cherkassy.... I was there, you know, it was dreadful, really dreadful, total shit. I don't remember much of it now, I think my mind has blocked it out after all these years, and I don't want to remember it to be honest. But one thing I do remember is that during the break-out – towards the end – we had to get over this river, it was freezing and flowing very fast [Author: the Gniloy Tikich], and we formed a column, a human chain to get across, and there, right at the front, holding a K98 rifle above his head and with water right up to his armpits was Herbert Gille – our general.[21] I will never forget that sight, he was right there, leading us out of the 'kessel' [Author: 'cauldron']. We all liked Gille, he was well-respected. He used to turn up in his armoured car and he'd be standing upright so we could see him all the time. We liked all our officers, but Gille was one of the best.

Even now I don't know how we got out of there – a lot of luck I think.

Ivar wasn't the only Scandinavian Waffen-SS volunteer experiencing the 'pleasures' of the Eastern Front around that time. Bjørn Lindstad, still only 18 years old, was there too.

BL: We left Bosnia and went to Leningrad around the 10th of December 1943. Lots of snow and trenches, we had three infantry companies up front and my company – the heavy weapons company – behind them. Around Christmas Eve we sent out patrols to take prisoners to get information, such as what units we were facing. When the job was done they had to fire a flare into the sky as a signal to our own side so they could be covered as they moved back to our own lines. They never got that far though. We were attacked at the same time and that was when the first Norwegians got killed. I watched it all. We were hit by artillery. Then after New Year I was sent home on leave as I had been in service for a year by then, and that was the rule – after one year you got home leave – so I went home. Also, after a year, you became a Sturmmann, and a Rottenführer after two – usually, but not always. Anyway, I travelled by train to Denmark and then by boat from there. It was good to be home. I met up with my old friends, and everything was pretty normal, they were still friendly, but some people reacted badly to seeing me. I had two weeks at home plus travel time, and then it was back to the front around the end of February, beginning of March time. The big Russian attack had come in on 14 January and I'd already left by then.[22]

So, I didn't go back to Leningrad, I went to Narva as that was where we'd retreated to. Some of my friends had already been killed in the fighting. One of the companies we had been covering

> *at Leningrad was completely destroyed – the 7th. Only the company commander had escaped because he had skis. He had left the company to see what was going on and when he tried to get back to the company the Russians were between him and them. He got away but was charged by the Germans with leaving his men. He was Norwegian – Prytz was his name.*[23] *I didn't know anything about this, of course, as I was on leave at the time. Another Norwegian took over – Arne Hanssen – he was then accidentally shot by the Germans as he tried to cross a river as they thought he was a Russian. He died of his wounds.*[24]

Narva – there was that word again – the so-called 'Battle of the European SS', although it most definitely was not the romanticised zenith of the pan-European anti-Bolshevik crusade that it has been built up into since the war. Yes, there were lots – thousands – of non-German Waffen-SS volunteers there; Estonians (it was their country after all), Dutch, Norwegians, Danes and Flemings (even a few Swedes) – but they were always far outnumbered by the Germans in the trenches next to them. It also wasn't a battle as we perhaps think of one in the popular imagination, something where opposing armies meet and fight it out over the course of a few days or weeks at the most and then there's a decisive point that decides who is the winner and who is the loser. Narva wasn't like that at all. Firstly, it went on for months – depending on how you calculate it six or seven-ish – and it ebbed and flowed with weeks of bitter fighting followed by relative calm, and then more fighting and so on. There was no podium finish either; the Red Army didn't win because it failed to break through, while the Ostheer didn't win either despite standing its ground, as it lost thousands of men and was totally exhausted at the end.

Yet – and yet – the fact remains that the battle has a mystique, an aura – call it what you will – that casts a spell over those who fought there and those, like me, who write about such things, and that makes the opportunity to sit across a coffee table from someone who was actually there and hear their story a remarkable thing indeed.

BL: I went back to my regiment after my leave, back to the Norge, and do you know what I took for my comrades? A backpack full of boxes of matches! You know why? No one could get hold of them at the front, crazy but true, and it was easy to get hold of matches at home so I took back lots and lots and gave all my friends who were still alive and with the regiment a box each – that was a great moment when I could hand them out as presents, I really felt I had done something useful.

By the 26th of February the whole Nordland Division was there, in position, at Narva, and the Norge was part of the Nordland of course. Narva was a city, but it was also a river and the Russians were attacking across the river and trying to attack us from the sea, from the Baltic, We had Estonians from the 20th Waffen-SS division[25] on our flank, they were between us and the sea and had to hold the Russians so they couldn't get behind us. We were all in the III SS Panzer Corps, us and the Estonians.

The fighting was hard – it was a delightful return to the front for me! I was an observer, and our job was to figure out where to put down fire from our cannons. As Waffen-SS we had jackets that were white on one side and camouflage on the other, which was great for me because on the ground with the snow I could wear the jacket one way, and then when I was climbing a tree to see the enemy I wore it the other way. I spent nine months at the front, during that time and four of those months I was sitting in a tree! I used to sit at the back of the trees with my scissor binoculars tied to the tree so I wasn't seen, as the leaves and branches on the front – that is facing the Russians – had been shot off. I had a platform I could sit on, but I used to climb higher than the platform all the time so I could get a better view and see further. My commander at the time was called Abels, and the way we worked was that the cannon would fire one shot and I would see where it landed and then I would call through on the field telephone with the adjustments to bring it onto target, you know, left or right, range and so on. We usually did it in the evenings when we could see their camp fires. We would shoot at the fires to hit them, but if we shot at them during the day it was usually in the morning when we could see their infantry moving around. It was funny about their camp fires, they used to have them all the time. They all had long coats with small burn holes in them from those fires they stood around.

Anyway, our main problem was with communications back to the cannons. At first, we tried to use the radio but there was too much interference so we didn't use it, and so we used to use a telephone line to call back to the cannons, but the line was always getting cut, usually by Russian artillery fire, but sometimes by our own vehicles driving over it – tracked vehicles were the worst and did the most damage. We only knew about it when we tried the line and it didn't work, and then it was the job of my two Volksdeutsche comrades to find the break and fix it. One would go from the end of the line by the guns, and the other would go from where I was, until they found the break. Mind you, after a while we found it easier to just roll it up from one end, fix it and then re-lay it afterwards.

The fighting was going on all the time, but a lot of the time it was just artillery or air attacks or patrols, then in March 1944 the Russians attacked in strength. They were very good soldiers, the Russians, and they did very well, especially as a lot of their equipment wasn't very good. When the Russians attacked, their officers were usually behind them; so we could confuse them if we reacted fast. If you counter-attacked quickly, they didn't know what to do and you could push them back. We used to react differently to them to being attacked – we would splinter apart and all go off in different directions, this confused the Russians – while they would all gather together and that meant we could destroy or capture them pretty quickly. As they attacked, we had cross-fire from our machine-guns – MG42s – lots of them, and we managed to stop the Russians, to cut off the spearhead of their attack – about 10,000 of them were cut off like that. Some surrendered, and the rest were killed. The bodies were left on the battlefield.

The spring thaw – in Russia it is called the *rasputitsa,* which is only very roughly translated as 'the time without roads' – effectively closed down the majority of large-scale operations by both sides, and gave a breathing space to Bjørn and his comrades, as well as the Soviets. Not that this meant the killing stopped, it just meant it died down a lot. German High Command – the *Oberkommando der Wehrmacht* (OKW) – calculated that a standard-sized German infantry corps engaged in passive trench warfare, such as at Narva, would lose between five and 10 men killed and between 15 and 25 wounded *per day* due to Soviet snipers, artillery fire and air attacks – so much for peace and quiet. Meanwhile, the arrival of summer and the subsequent drying out of the roads and tracks meant the armies needed to move men, equipment and supplies, and always meant that more fighting was on the way.

BL: We stayed in our positions until that July. At that time the Russians cut down lots of trees to build a corduroy road across the swamp to get to Narva from their bridgehead. I was watching them, there was so much activity, lots of Russians in brown uniforms, and some in green uniforms, all moving into assembly areas, and looking in my direction, like they were looking directly at me! I knew then that there was trouble coming, but it was also a great target.

But I could also see German planes behind us bombing Russians, so I knew that somehow the Russians had got behind us and we were in danger of being surrounded. I called my commander on the telephone and he told me to grab my kit and get back to the cannons as fast as I could. By the time I reached our bunker everyone had already packed up. Everything we couldn't carry was piled up and we destroyed it all so the Russians couldn't have it. The bunker was near a house and in the house was a piano. I heard a lot of noise coming from that house and I went up to the door and saw my two Volksdeutsche comrades in there breaking up the piano!

We had half-tracks to pull the cannons and so we drove off to the railroad tracks that went all the way back to Tallinn. The tracks were up on an embankment and we were on one side of them and there was a battle going on over on the other side; we could hear it but we couldn't see it. I met some Estonian Waffen-SS men then, they had their national flag on the arm of their uniforms. They were fighting for their country, and that was the first time – the very first time – that I really felt that volunteering was the right thing to have done. Up until then I wasn't sure, but that made my mind up.

Anyway, we were driving along when a Russian plane came over, dropped a bomb and blew the road away. The Estonians could walk round the crater, but we couldn't drive the half-track and the cannon through it – the hole was too big. Then one of our officers – Riedel – appeared and shouted at us that either we filled in the hole as quickly as possible and drove over it, or we would become infantry and could get marching! So, we threw everything we had and didn't really need into that hole, even the Army bread – those loaves were so hard! As we were throwing them in though, the Estonians were grabbing some of the loaves and eating them! It wasn't enough, we needed more things to fill the hole, and luckily there were some panzers – including a Tiger – near us,[26] *and they were firing at the Russians and throwing the empty shell cases out onto the ground so we could use them to help fill the hole too.*

A Volkswagen jeep with an Army Colonel arrived, and he left his VW on the side of the hole, walked round it and got into another one on the other side and drove off. Before he went he set fire to the VW he was abandoning, and we then pushed it into the hole as well, along with the radio he was using – we literally threw everything into that damned hole, and eventually we filled it enough to be able to drive over it! We then drove past the Estonians who were still eating our bread!

In the end we managed to escape, but the Regiment Seyffardt – they were Dutch – they didn't get out and were destroyed. One of their officers – Obersturmbannführer Benner – had been in Finland with the Norwegians, during the fighting for the Kaprolat and Hasselmann Hills, then he was sent over to the Dutch – he was unlucky that officer.[27]

We were told to fire all the heavy weapons we had to try and keep the Russians at bay, and we then had to move forward, towards Orphanage Hill and Grenadier Hill. The Russians were well dug-in but we knew we had to get closer. Over twenty Russian aircraft with cannons were attacking us, maybe 27 or 29, I can't remember exactly but I counted them at the time – they had so much air cover – while there weren't many German aircraft at all. There were some Stukas I saw attacking the Russians, and I watched as they tried to get through the Russian fire. The Russians had half of Orphanage Hill and they could see our cannons so we had to move them. Our 2nd Battalion was sent to recapture the hill, and we had to figure out where the Russians were on the hill so we could support the 2nd Battalion with our guns. But the Russians attacked before we could attack them. The firing was terrible. We had each dug a hole to hide in, and I had my scissor binoculars and their stand in with me. I also had a quarter of a tent – four of us could then make a whole tent, or you could use it to protect your weapons, to keep them clean, and you could use it as a raincoat – anyway, I was lying on my back in my hole and I began to worry that so much dirt was coming in from the explosions that I would be buried alive as the firing was so bad. We had to go. We had a rule that we never left our wounded behind, but there was no way we could take anyone with us at that point, but luckily all four of my team managed to get away, but when we reached our rear trenches we found the infantry had already got into them, so we had to squeeze in with them.

A couple of days later Schrijnen saved the day!

At that point we all laughed – it was something of a running joke between us all given that I have written two books on the Flemish Waffen-SS, and Remy Schrijnen was the most famous Fleming at Narva and won his Knight's Cross there.

BL: The fighting at Narva went on for months. One hundred and sixty thousand men died at Narva all together, and 50,000 during those two weeks in July.[28] *The fighting for the hills was the worst, the hardest, of all the months that I was there.*

Three weeks later we were relieved and all we wanted was fresh air, to get away from the smell of all those dead bodies. Our 1st and 2nd Battalions were reunited and one man from each company was sent back to bury or burn our own dead – the Russian dead were left to rot over the summer. The rest of us were sent back to the positions we'd held back in March, and the smell there was really bad as the bodies had had several months to decompose. Where it was dry, the bodies had been eaten by animals, and in the swamp, the water and insects had done their worst. There were also lots of dead bodies in shell craters, which had filled up with water, and then when another shell or bomb hit a crater the bodies were blown into pieces and bits went everywhere – it was horrible and it stank, I'll never forget it.

Notes to Chapter Five

1. Willmott, H. P., *The Great Crusade: A New Complete History of the Second World War*, Pimlico.
2. Adolf Hitler to General Heinz Guderian, 14 May 1943.
3. The German *Panzerschreck* ('tank fright') was the popular name for the *Raketenpanzerbüchse* (abbreviated to RPzB), an 88mm calibre reusable anti-tank rocket launcher developed by Nazi Germany in World War II. Another popular nickname for it was *Ofenrohr* ('stove pipe'). Designed as a lightweight infantry anti-tank weapon, it was an enlarged copy of the American bazooka. The weapon was shoulder-launched and fired a fin-stabilized rocket with a shaped-charge warhead.
4. Ivar received a military disability pension from the German government, and twice a year travelled to Germany for medical check-ups and to have his false eye properly cleaned and/or replaced.

5. Odder is a town in the Odder municipality, just south of Aarhus, in the Midtjylland region. As of 1 January 2014, the town had a population of 11,404. The town is affectionately described by its inhabitants as 'the heart of Denmark'. Odder and the surrounding areas have for centuries been amongst the richest farmlands in Denmark and still today, the area is home to a great selection of manors and castles of the wealthy nobility who used to rule the area.
6. This account was written in 1949 and filed in the Odder local archive.
7. These four added to the 19 Danish soldiers killed, and 23 who were wounded, during the 1940 invasion of Denmark.
8. Trigg, Jonathan, *Hitler's Vikings*, The History Press. A Danish-born skiing expert and Professor of Physical Education, Gust Jonassen was the NSUF's Sports Leader and a subordinate and close friend of Bjørn Østring, who rather than join the DNL proposed instead to form and lead a group of ski specialists to fight in the trackless forests of Finnish Karelia. The intent was for a purely Norwegian unit that would be engaged in long-range patrolling, deliberate ambushes (i.e. planned long-term ambushes, perhaps lasting for days), and behind-the-lines attacks. The Germans acquiesced to the plan to smooth ruffled Norwegian feathers after the DNL was sent to Leningrad and not Finland, and in no time at all some 120 eager volunteers (including Narmo) were training at Sennheim in the Alsace. Jonassen himself was sent to Bad Tölz to earn his rank of SS-Obersturmführer, while his men ended up being put through their paces by a team of instructors led by Jouko Itälä, a Finnish SS-Wiking veteran. Itälä ignored the order from the Finnish government to return home and would serve in the Waffen-SS till the end of the war. The Italian SS volunteer, Giovanni 'Nino' Niquille, was assigned from the Nord as the new unit's war correspondent. Like Jonas Lie's men, Jonassen's were officially classed as SS-Police rather than full Waffen-SS members, and so after Sennheim they finished off their

training in Hallertau near Dresden at the German Police Instructional School. Christened the SS-Police Ski Company, it would become in time the *SS-Ski Battalion Norge* (*SS-Schijäger-Bataillon Norwegen* in German). Highly rated by the powers-that-be, the Company joined the SS-Nord division in Karelia during March of 1943, where they quickly gained an enviable reputation for combat effectiveness. Organised into three platoons of three sections each, they travelled on foot, or on skis when there was snow. They were armed with a preponderance of automatic weapons including one machine-gun per section and every other man had a submachine-gun, and, uniquely, they had two snipers per section. They also had a section of mortars as 'mobile artillery'.

9. A Hiwi was a foreigner – specifically from the territories of the Soviet Union – who volunteered to serve in the Wehrmacht during World War II. Hiwi is a German abbreviation of the term *Hilfswilliger*, meaning 'willing helper'. Hiwis typically filled roles such as drivers, cooks, hospital attendants, ammunition carriers, messengers etc. By the end of 1942 Hiwis constituted as much as 10 percent of total Wehrmacht strength on the Eastern Front.
10. Expanding bullets, also known as *dumdum* bullets, are projectiles designed to expand on impact, increasing in diameter to limit penetration and/or produce a larger diameter wound for faster incapacitation. Therefore, they are used for hunting and by police in certain countries, but are generally prohibited for use in war. Two typical designs are the hollow-point bullet and the soft-point bullet. Expanding bullets were given the name *dumdum* after an early British example produced in the Dum Dum Arsenal, near Calcutta, India, by Captain Neville Bertie-Clay. An improvised version can be made by cutting an X across the nose of a bullet with a knife so that it will fan out on hitting a target – the resulting injuries can be horrific.

11. German pioneers (German: *Pionieretruppen*) were what Anglo-American armies would call combat engineers. They would typically carry out assault tasks such as attacking fortified positions with demolitions, flamethrowers etc., as well as specialist engineer jobs such as laying minefields, erecting obstacles and crossing water courses.
12. The *Germanske SS Norge* (GSSN, Germanic SS Norway) was a paramilitary organisation established in Norway in July 1942 as the Norwegian branch of the Germanic-SS. The leader of the GSSN was Jonas Lie, and second-in-command was Sverre Riisnæs. The number of members reached a maximum of about 1,300 in 1944. Many of the members were recruited from the police, and about 50 percent served on the Eastern Front. Dahl; Hjeltnes; Nøkleby; Ringdal; Sørensen. *Norsk krigsleksikon 1940–1945*, Cappelen.
13. The *Nürnberg* was a German light cruiser named after the city of Nuremburg – her sister ship was the *Leipzig*. *Nürnberg* was the longest-serving major warship of the Kriegsmarine, and the only one to see active service after the end of the war, though not in the German navy. In January 1945 she was assigned to mine-laying duties in the Skaggerak, but severe fuel shortages permitted only one such operation. After the end of the war, *Nürnberg* was seized by the Royal Navy and awarded to the Soviets as war reparations. In December 1945, a Soviet crew took over the ship, and the following month took her to Tallinn where she was renamed the *Admiral Makarov*. By 1960 she had been broken up for scrap.
14. Ellwangen an der Jagst is a town in the east of the Baden-Württemberg region in Germany. The barracks at Ellwangen were a school for German panzer troops during the war, and the town was also a convalescent centre for wounded and sick Waffen-SS men. The US Army took the town in April 1945 and occupied it until 1946. After the war several members of the 17th SS Panzergrenadier Division

were convicted of a number of war crimes involving the shooting of foreign concentration camp prisoners in Ellwangen. From 1946 until 1951 the International Refugee Organisation (IRO) used the barracks as a Displaced Persons (DP) Camp for 3,000 Ukrainian refugees.

15. *Stoer Sende Stelle GEIGE 52* – special sites run by the Luftwaffe as part of the Nazis' mainland Europe defences against Allied air raids. Their specific purpose was to try to jam the navigational transmissions for Allied aircraft.
16. The Shellhus was the Gestapo HQ in Copenhagen and was used for the storage of dossiers and the torture of Danish citizens during interrogations. The Danish Resistance repeatedly asked the British to conduct a raid against this site and finally, on 21 March 1945, the RAF conducted Operation Carthage to bomb it. The building was destroyed, 18 prisoners escaped, and anti-resistance Nazi activities were severely disrupted. Fifty-five German soldiers, 47 Danish employees of the Gestapo, and eight prisoners died in the attack. Four Mosquito bombers and two USAAF Mustang fighter escorts were lost, and nine Allied airmen died. As the RAF had feared, there were significant civilian casualties too. A nearby Catholic school was also hit and 125 civilians (including 86 schoolchildren and 18 adults – mainly nuns) were killed. A similar raid against the Gestapo headquarters in Aarhus, on 31 October 1944, was also successful with fewer civilian losses. The raid was one of several carried out by the Allies against important Gestapo buildings in occupied Europe during the war, including the Victoria Terrasse building (Gestapo HQ) in Oslo, Norway on 25 September 1942. The Oslo raid was intended to be a 'morale booster' for the Norwegian people and was scheduled to coincide with one of Quisling's NS rallies in the city.
17. Lidegaard, Bo, *Dansk udenrigspolitiks historie. Overleveren – 1914–1945*. Danmarks Nationalleksikon.

18. The 'White Buses' were an operation undertaken by the Swedish Red Cross and the Danish government in the spring of 1945 to rescue concentration camp inmates in areas under Nazi control and transport them to safety in neutral Sweden. Although the operation was initially targeted at just saving citizens of Scandinavian countries, it rapidly expanded to include citizens of other countries. All told, the operation brought out 15,345 prisoners; of these 7,795 were Scandinavian and 7,550 were non-Scandinavian (Polish, French, etc.). In particular, 423 Danish Jews were saved from the Theresienstadt concentration camp inside German-occupied Czechoslovakia. The term 'white buses' originates from the buses having been painted white with red crosses, to avoid confusion with military vehicles.
19. This street had been the *Königin Augustin Strasse*, but had been renamed in 1935 as part of the Nazi programme to replace monarchical street names with military ones.
20. There is no official record of a large-scale bombing raid on Berlin in September 1943, so Ivar in all likelihood has just got his dates mixed up and is actually describing the massive RAF bombing raid of the night of 22/23 November 1943 that so badly affected the station. This could be viewed as divine retribution given that the Anhalter was one of three stations used to deport some 55,000 Berlin Jews between 1941 and 1945, about a third of the city's entire Jewish population. From the Anhalter alone 9,600 left, in groups of 50 to 100 at a time, using 116 trains. In contrast to other deportations using freight wagons, here the Jews were taken away in ordinary passenger coaches, which were coupled up to regular trains departing according to the normal timetable. All deportations went to Theresienstadt, and from there to other concentration camps. The raid that hit the Anhalter was the second major raid of the Battle of Berlin, and was the most effective raid by the RAF on Berlin. It

caused extensive damage to the residential areas west of the centre, Tiergarten and Charlottenburg, Schöneberg and Spandau. Because of the dry weather conditions, several firestorms ignited. The Kaiser Wilhelm Memorial Church was destroyed. Several other buildings of note were either damaged or destroyed, including the British, French, Italian and Japanese embassies, Charlottenburg Palace and Berlin Zoo, as were the Ministry of Munitions, the Waffen-SS Administrative College, the barracks of the Imperial Guard at Spandau and several arms factories. The Anhalter was finally closed in 1952.

21. SS Obergruppenführer Herbert Otto Gille, the Wiking divisional commander at the time and the most highly decorated Waffen-SS officer of the war.
22. The Leningrad–Novgorod strategic offensive was launched by the Red Army on 14 January 1944 with an attack on the Germans Army Group North by the Soviet Volkhov and Leningrad fronts, along with part of the 2nd Baltic Front, with the goal of fully lifting the siege of Leningrad. Approximately two weeks later, the Red Army regained control of the Moscow–Leningrad railway, and on 26 January 1944, Joseph Stalin declared that the siege was finally lifted. The ending of the 900-day-long blockade was celebrated in Leningrad on that day with a 324-gun salute. The strategic offensive ended a month later on 1 March, when the STAVKA ordered the troops of the Leningrad Front to mount a follow-on operation across the Narva River. The Germans had suffered nearly 72,000 casualties, lost 85 artillery pieces and were pushed back between 60 and 100 kilometres from Leningrad to the Luga River. The SS Danmark Regiment, in particular, suffered very heavy casualties.
23. There were two Norwegian Waffen-SS officers with the surname Prytz; this officer was Kristian Peder Prytz, born on 16 August 1910 in Salangen, he was later killed by a shell splinter to the head

in Estonia after being cleared of any charges and reinstated as the commander of the 7th Company. The other 'Prytz' was Trond Prytz, born on 23 July 1921 in Bangsund.

24. Arne Einar Olav Hanssen – born on 18 August 1917 in Sandefjord, and Killed in Action on 10 February 1944.
25. The 20th Waffen-Grenadier-Division der SS (estnische Nr.1).
26. This was probably Major Schwaner's *schwere Panzer-Abteilung 502* – Heavy Panzer Battalion 502 – an Army unit in the area at the time that was equipped with Tiger I tanks.
27. The SS-Freiwilligen-Panzergrenadier-Regiment 48 'General Seyffardt' was part of the Dutch 4th SS-Panzergrenadier Brigade 'Nederland'. The entire regiment was annihilated in the chaotic attempted retreat from its defensive position on the night of 26 July 1944. Barely 20 percent of the unit managed to reach the safety of German lines, Richard Benner had previously served in the 6th SS-Gebirgsjäger-Division 'Nord' in Finland as a battalion commander and had been in command of the Norwegians involved in the June 1944 fighting – see Trigg, Jonathan, *Hitler's Vikings*, The History Press.
28. Laar, Mart, *Sinimäed 1944: II maailmasõja lahingud Kirde-Eestis (Sinimäed Hills 1944: Battles of World War II in Northeast Estonia)*, Varrak. During the Soviet era, their losses at the Battle of Narva were not released by the Soviets. In recent years, Russian authors have published some figures but not for the whole course of the battle. The number of Soviet casualties can therefore only be indirectly estimated. According to STAVKA data, the total casualties of the Leningrad Front in 1944 were 665,827 men, with 145,102 of those being dead or missing. The share of the battles around Narva is unknown but considering the length of the operation, Laar counts roughly half of the documented 56,564 dead or missing and the 170,876 wounded or sick in the Leningrad-Novgorod Offensive for the Battle of Narva. This is in accordance with the estimation of F. Paulman, stating in

his *Ot Narvy do Syrve* that the Soviet 2nd Shock Army lost over 30,000 troops at the Narva bridgeheads during February. Deducting the losses in the operations of the Leningrad-Novgorod Offensive conducted elsewhere, the casualties in the battles in Finland and in the Baltic Offensive, Laar totals the numbers of Soviet losses in the Battle of Narva at approximately 100,000 dead or missing and 380,000 wounded or sick. On the Axis side, the Army Detachment 'Narwa' lost 23,963 personnel as dead, wounded and missing in action in February 1944. During the following months through to 30 July 1944, an additional 34,159 Axis personnel were lost; 5,748 of them dead and 1,179 missing in action. The total Axis casualties during the initial phase of the campaign was approximately 58,000 men, 12,000 of them dead or missing in action. From 24 July to 10 August 1944, German forces buried 1,709 men in Estonia. Adding the troops missing in action, the number of dead in the period is estimated at approximately 2,500. Accounting the standard ratio of one quarter of the wounded as irrecoverable losses, the number of Axis casualties in the later period of the battle was approximately 10,000. Total German casualties during the Battle of Narva is estimated at 14,000 dead or missing and 54,000 wounded or sick. Therefore, Bjørn's statement of 160,000 men killed at Narva doesn't seem that far off, but the 50,000 in the last two weeks of July alone looks high.

6

THE END OF THE WAR

As the war in Europe entered its fifth year in 1944 (for China and Japan it was their seventh), Nazi Germany still looked a mighty power – true, by then the Wehrmacht had taken casualties of 3.5 million men and they had been thrown out of North Africa and Sicily, and mainland Italy was in the process of being liberated from the 28 German divisions occupying it (if Italy had stayed in the Axis it would have been 'invasion' rather than 'liberation') – but the Ostheer was still deep in Russia with 193 divisions, and a further 59 were across the English Channel in France and the Low Countries.[1] Hitler's manpower reserve was seemingly so deep that he could even afford to garrison Norway and Denmark with no fewer than eighteen divisions. This huge *Westheer* was set to face the threat of an Anglo-American invasion that Berlin had been expecting for more than a year.

Their enemy would be the British and Canadians, some Free French, and 20 American divisions in southern Britain – with another 37 en route from the States. Added to this was George Patton's non-existent 150,000-strong US 1st Army Group based in the south-east of England and all ready to hit the Pas de Calais, and another force of eight divisions in Scotland – also non-existent – set to land in Norway in conjunction with an offensive by the Red Army. Those American units – the real ones anyway – were lavishly equipped, well-fed (ask any British civilian of the day clutching a ration book as they gawked and slavered at the mountains of meat, white bread, chocolate, coffee and fresh eggs the GIs brought with them) and, according to the US War Department, 'the world's best paid soldiers', with an American private earning an astonishing $50 a month – three times what was paid to his impoverished British or German counterpart – and a Yankee staff sergeant banking the same as a British or German captain, no less. For once, however, American brashness was tempered by an element of local sensitivity, and so the US government paid its soldiers in the UK twice a month rather than once to make it look less to the local populace than it actually was.[2]

But all was not what it seemed on the swastika side of the line; true, German factories were churning out more aircraft, guns and panzers than ever before, but as the Reich's fuel reserves dwindled, so buses, cars and trucks were being converted to burn wood to keep them moving. The number of Wehrmacht divisions may have still looked high, but most were a lot smaller than they had been in the heyday of 1940; General Max Horn's 214th Infantry Division for example – raised in 1939 from the Frankfurt-am-Main area in Hesse, and stationed in Norway since the 1940 invasion – had lost its entire third rifle regiment to reinforce a coastal defence division over in Finland.[3] Not only that, but those regiments themselves were increasingly manned by callow teenagers, overweight middle-aged men and those previously deemed unfit for service, mainly due to medical problems – a standing joke at the time in the frontline was that these men had to be put on sentry duty three at a time; one to see the enemy, one to hear the enemy and, if all else fails, one to smell them – the well-trained, fit and aggressive *landsers* (German Army slang equivalent of Britain's *Tommy*, or the Red Army's *Ivan*) of yesteryear were long gone, mostly buried somewhere out on the steppe.

The facade of Hitler's Fortress Europe finally cracked wide open in June when the Anglo-American forces hit the Normandy beaches on D-Day, and the Red Army annihilated a staggering 35 of Army Group Centre's divisions in Operation Bagration.

As autumn turned to winter, France and Belgium had been liberated, as had the Ukraine, Belarus and Estonia (although it was debatable whether the majority of Estonians felt 'liberated' by the Soviets), and Germany's position in the Balkans and south-east Europe was looking grim as her erstwhile allies abandoned the visibly sinking ship.

Back in occupied Scandinavia, life went on, getting a bit harder, people getting hungrier, more and more just yearning for an end to the war. In Odder, Assistant Police Chief E. Lemvigh-Müller was still trying to keep the peace with the Germans:

> *In the summer of 1944 a Colonel Zimmermann arrived and demanded accommodation for 2,000 men. Maximum accommodation in the city hotels and schools was for circa 1,200 men. I tried to make him understand that the rest had to be placed in community centres in Hou, Gylling or other villages, but this was rejected. We went all around town and still he demanded private accommodation. This I refused to go along with, and when he was tired of the trip, I suggested that we ate lunch together at a central hotel. After several schnapps, he abandoned the claim, and only circa 1,000 men were accommodated in Odder, the rest were directed to Aarhus.*

That same summer Lemvigh-Müller watched as the Gestapo broke up the small local Resistance network in the district by arresting several of its leaders – mainly Lemvigh-Müller's fellow police officers – who were then sent to Buchenwald concentration camp. Thankfully, all survived and returned home safely after the war. Having said that, the point must be made that even when they were still active in the district, the local Resistance were pretty somnolent – and I mean no disrespect in that comment, it is simply a statement of fact. One former Odder Resistance member, the local accountant Poul Louring-Andersen, wrote about his experiences almost 50 years after the liberation, and placed them in the local archive:

> *My nephew, Ejgil Brauer, has urged me to write something about my participation in the resistance movement in Odder. My name is Poul Louring-Andersen, born in Odder April 10, 1923 as the son of a typographer Marinus Andersen and wife Kristine Andersen, born Louring. I was actually christened Poul Louring Sand Andersen, but after my youngest son's birth in 1948, I got permission to keep the name Louring-Andersen. The reason for this was that there were hardly any males in my mother's family, so there was a risk that the name Louring would become extinct. I thought it was important to preserve the old family name. On 16 September 1939, I was employed in the municipal engineer's office in Odder and worked for the municipality up until March 1947. As for so many others, for me the German occupation of our country was a crippling blow. I hated Nazism – a political system that I had come to despise in the 1930s because of its actions against dissidents – and my whole family felt the same. At the beginning of the occupation, organised resistance was quite small. It was more a case of 'the cold shoulder' towards the occupiers.*

But gradually it became a real resistance movement. It began with illegal pamphlets, which several of us distributed – the stonemason H. Holm and the foreman Hans Ravn among others. In addition, I attended a few meetings in the home of the tobacconist Soren Petersen. They probably weren't really 'illegal meetings', but more just 'hush-hush'. Speakers were invited to talk about everything that the newspapers couldn't write about. Then, gradually, explosives and weapons began to arrive from England and armed groups could be formed. In 1944, I was a member of the Odder Gymnastikforening (an athletics club) and one of the other members was the draper, P.W. Christensen. On one occasion he asked me about my attitude toward the Resistance. I was positive about them and he asked me to contact Thorvald Knudsen, who as it turned out had been tasked to form a so-called 'Military Group' (M-group). As the group was forming each of us nominated people we could trust to be approached, and soon the group consisted of the following members as well as myself:

– Thorvald Knudsen, skotøjshandler, Rosensgade, (group leader)
– Hans Christian Andersen, a joiner, (later married to Rita Sorensen, daughter of master builder Axel Sørensen)
– Kaj Jensen, grocery, Colonial Warehouse, Rosensgade,
– Carlo Sloth, joiner, (later married to my sister Inge)
– Niels Smidt, farmer, Snærild Vestergaard,
– Søren Aagaard, engineer, later mayor of Odder.

At some point in the autumn of 1944, Søren Aagaard and I were called up for weapons training along with Thorvald Knudsen. The instruction was to take place in a barn near the Vejle woods. After our first session was cancelled, we ended up in the attic above the chapel at the new cemetery. The weapons were stored in a specially-

built concrete pipe in an abandoned tomb and consisted of a machine-gun, a submachine gun and a US carbine. In the middle of the lesson there was a knock on the side door of the chapel. Who was it? Was it the Germans? PW said, 'Stay here and keep quiet.' We heard him speak with someone and then he came back up. It was the architect H.P. Nielsen, who was living on School Street, diagonally across from the cemetery. He had noticed light shining between the tiles so we got some newspapers, blocked up the gaps and carried on with our weapons lesson.

Extremely brave though any form of resistance undoubtedly was, this was hardly popular insurrection, and definitely not in the same league as the propaganda films being made in Britain and the USA to showcase Scandinavian resistance to the invader. Interestingly, these were almost all about Norway, not Denmark, and included the likes of the 1942 movie *Commandos Strike at Dawn* – depicting a Norwegian resistance fighter leading British commandos on a raid to destroy a 'secret' Nazi air base – and Errol Flynn's *Edge of Darkness* about a small Norwegian fishing village that rises up against its Nazi occupiers and wipes out the German garrison. Both films don't shy away from the issue of collaboration, with the hero in the former film drowning a local informer, and another collaborator shot for treachery in the latter.

At the front, the remaining Scandinavian Waffen-SS volunteers battled to survive against the lengthening odds.

IC: We got the order to retake Kovel. But before we could do this we had to confiscate weapons and equipment from the Wehrmacht – from the Army guys – because we didn't have enough, we'd lost so many at Cherkassy – anyway, it was something the Army guys were really, really unhappy about. In fact, years later in 1962, I was at a party in Stadtlohn near the Dutch border – my wife Ursula was from the city – and I got talking to this guy who it turns out had been a company commander in the Wehrmacht during the war. Anyway, we got to talking about the war and the city of Kovel was mentioned. When I told him I was at Kovel too, and that back then we had taken weapons and gear from the Wehrmacht so that we could retake the city, his face went white and he shouted; 'so you were one of them, you bastard, I will not sit in the same room as you,' and with that he upped and left the party. Everyone was speechless! For him it had been a great humiliation to have to hand over his weapons and equipment to the SS – it was something he apparently never got over, but it could have been trauma too that caused his reaction I suppose.

Anyway, after having retaken Kovel we were drawn back east of Warsaw between the rivers Bug and Weichsel [Author: Vistula]. We knew the Russians were preparing a major offensive, and at this point in time we had had so many losses that we were given replacements from all over; from the Kriegsmarine, the Luftwaffe and the Hitler Youth – young boys of 16 to17 years old. These young guys were totally inexperienced and most of them only survived for a few days. I still wonder, to this day, so many years later, if I did enough to help those young lads ... we were all under pressure and each man was thinking of himself and if he could survive, and there was little time to care for others, but even so. I remember one day we got more of these replacements and there was this young kid – 17 years old, just 17 – his surname was Bauch, I can't remember his first name. He had grown up in Ellwangen, of all places, who'd have thought, and when he got drafted he was originally sent to the cavalry, before being sent to

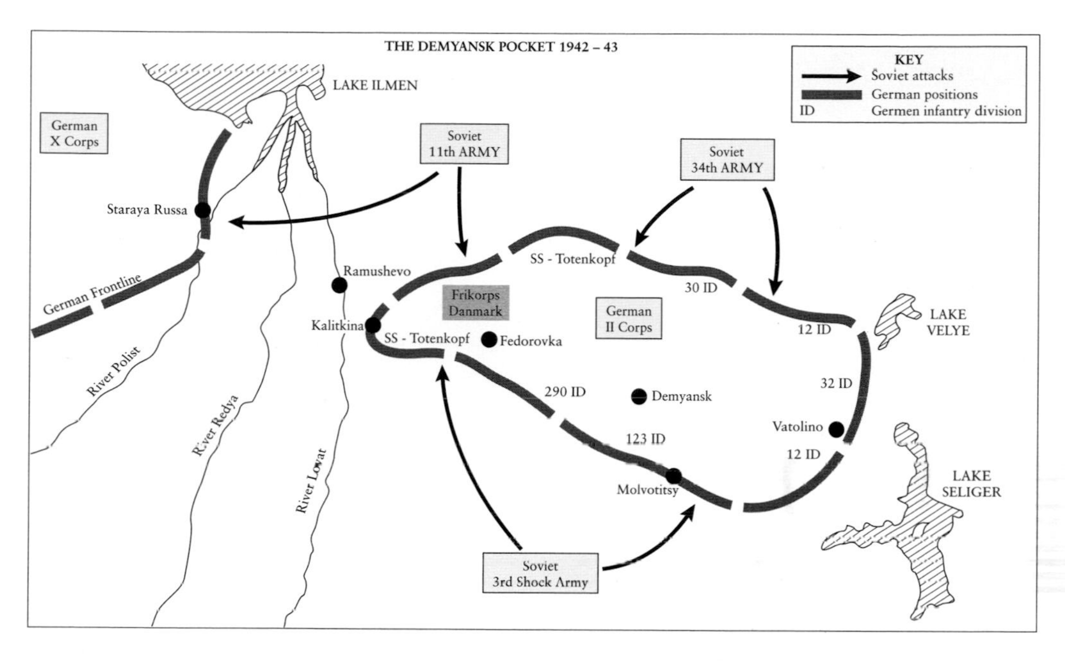
THE DEMYANSK POCKET 1942 – 43
KEY
Soviet attacks
German positions
ID
Germen infantry division
LAKE ILMEN
German
X Corps
Soviet
11th ARMY
Soviet
34th ARMY
Staraya Russa
SS - Totenkopf
German Frontline
Ramushevo
30 ID
Frikorps
Danmark
German
II Corps
Kalitkina
SS - Totenkopf
Fedorovka
12 ID
LAKE
VELYE
River Polist
290 ID
Demyansk
32 ID
River Redya
Vatolino
123 ID
12 ID
River Lovat
Molvotitsy
LAKE
SELIGER
Soviet
3rd Shock Army

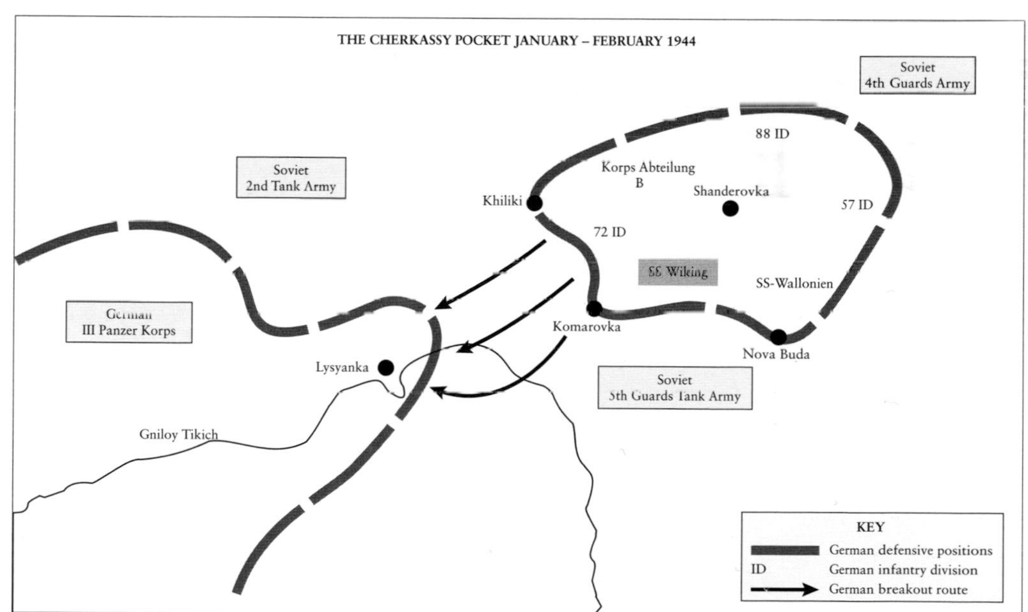
THE CHERKASSY POCKET JANUARY – FEBRUARY 1944
Soviet
4th Guards Army
88 ID
Soviet
2nd Tank Army
Korps Abteilung
B
Shanderovka
Khiliki
57 ID
72 ID
SS Wiking
SS-Wallonien
German
III Panzer Korps
Komarovka
Nova Buda
Lysyanka
Soviet
5th Guards Tank Army
Gniloy Tikich
KEY
German defensive positions
ID
German infantry division
German breakout route

Above: *Danish volunteers of the Frikorps Danmark in training at the Treskau camp in German-occupied Poland in early 1942. (Courtesy of Lars Larsen)*

Left: *The Danish Frikorps Danmark volunteer, Magnus Møller, in his Waffen-SS uniform – note the trifos (three-legged swastika) collar patch, which was worn by many volunteers who transferred from the original SS-Freiwilligen-Standarte Nordwest. (Courtesy of Lars Larsen)*

Magnus Møller with other members of the stable staff who looked after the officers' horses in the Frikorps. Most would later be trained as drivers. Magnus is second from the left. (Courtesy of Magnus Møller)

The Danish Waffen-SS volunteer, Magnus Møller, in 2017. (Author's private collection)

Norwegian volunteers for the Germanic Land Service on their way via ferry to their service in German-occupied Poland. Among them is Karin Matre, front row seated, far right. (Courtesy of Karin Matre)

The Norwegian Land Service and German Red Cross volunteer, Karin Matre, in 2017. (Author's private collection)

Right: *The Danish SS-Wiking volunteer, Ivar Corneliussen. He would lose his left eye to a Soviet tank shell. (Courtesy of Ivar Corneliussen)*

Below: *Ivar Corneliussen's childhood home in Barmose in the Davinde forest in Denmark. (Courtesy of Ivar Corneliussen)*

The ex-SS-Westland Regiment volunteer, Ivar Corneliussen, in his post-war career as a third engineer on a Norwegian tanker. (Courtesy of Ivar Corneliussen)

1943: Ivar Corneliussen on the right, with his friend Unteroffizier Gunter Lang of the Luftwaffe. (Courtesy of Ivar Corneliussen)

The Danish Waffen-SS volunteer, Ivar Corneliussen, in 2017. (Author's private collection)

Frikorps Danmark officers enjoy a meal during training at Treskau. The Frikorps's Russian-born commander, Christian Frederik von Schalburg, is looking at the camera, to his right is his friend, Knud Børge Martinsen, who would succeed him as commander following his death in action. (Courtesy of Lars Larsen)

Right: *A Frikorps Danmark volunteer stands sentry under the Danish flag, flanked on the wall by recruiting posters for the Frikorps. (Courtesy of Lars Larsen.)*

Below: *A Frikorps Danmark platoon pose for a photo during field training at Treskau. (Courtesy of Lars Larsen)*

A Frikorps Danmark volunteer welcomes a visiting dignitary from Denmark to the Treskau training area. (Courtesy of Lars Larsen)

The Demyansk Pocket 1942 – the figure with the moustache is the Danish war reporter, Flemming Helweg Larsen, who initially tried to enlist in the British Army to fight the Germans, before joining the Waffen-SS. The man with the microphone is SS-Untersturmführer Christian von Eggers. This photo was taken during a transmission on Radio Denmark. (Courtesy of Lars Larsen)

Life in the Demyansk Pocket was very hard for the Frikorps Danmark, but a bottle of champagne was always something to celebrate! Standing pleased with his prize is the Danish volunteer, SS-Unterscharführer Jens A. Kristensen. Kristensen won the Iron Cross while serving with the Danmark Regiment in Croatia in the autumn of 1943, and was then subsequently killed in action on 5 March 1944 in Siivertsi during the Narva fighting. (Courtesy of Lars Larsen)

No road, just a sea of mud – this photo perfectly illustrates the appalling transport conditions in the Demyansk Pocket that did so much to hamper military operations. (Courtesy of Lars Larsen)

Danish Waffen-SS volunteers in Demyansk – in the centre, in profile, is the former Danish Army officer, Per Sørensen, who would go on to eventually command the SS-Regiment Danmark before being shot and killed by a Red Army sniper in the ruins of Berlin in May 1945. (Courtesy of Lars Larsen)

A Frikorps Danmark volunteer poses for a photo on a destroyed Soviet T26 light tank. The Soviets produced more than 11,000 of these thinly-armoured and poorly armed vehicles, which were obsolete by 1942. (Courtesy of Lars Larsen)

An eight-wheeled Sd.Kfz.232 heavy armoured car sitting camouflaged in the Demyansk Pocket. (Courtesy of Lars Larsen)

German 105mm horse-drawn artillery move into the Demyansk Pocket to support the Frikorps Danmark. (Courtesy of Lars Larsen)

The Demyansk Pocket – with mud the constant enemy, often the only way to get around was on so-called corduroy roads such as these made from laying tens of thousands of tree-trunks side by side. (Courtesy of Lars Larsen)

A Frikorps Danmark volunteer poses next to an abandoned Red Army T34 tank. The holes made by the anti-tank shells that destroyed it can clearly be seen in the turret next to the Dane. (Courtesy of Lars Larsen)

A Danish Frikorps Danmark volunteer poses for a photo with a local Russian family in the Demyansk Pocket. Relations between the local populace and the Danes were usually good. (Courtesy of Lars Larsen)

Summer 1942, and three Frikorps Denmark soldiers relax in the sun outside a bunker in the Demyansk Pocket. SS-Unterscharführer Jens A. Kristensen is in the middle. On the right is SS-Untersturmführer Poul Vindekilde Hansen. Hansen had previously volunteered to fight the Soviets during the Finnish War. He was later killed in action on 9 January 1944 leading a patrol at Florowitzy in the Oranienbaum fighting. (Courtesy of Lars Larsen)

Given the horrendous road conditions on the Eastern Front, horses were often the best way to get around, but even they struggled in the Demyansk mud. (Courtesy of Lars Larsen)

Spring 1942 in the Demyansk Pocket with the Frikorps Danmark. The Danish volunteer on the far left with the pipe is N. K. Jensen. Jensen volunteered in July 1941 and was in the Frikorps's 2nd Company when he was awarded the Iron Cross in May 1942. Trained as a pioneer, he was badly wounded by Soviet fire on 11 July 1942 while re-laying a bomb-damaged minefield. He later died of his injuries. (Courtesy of Lars Larsen)

Above: *A Frikorps Danmark motorcycle and sidecar combination cross a sunken road in the Demyansk Pocket. (Courtesy of Lars Larsen)*

Right: *Danish Frikorps Danmark volunteers pause for reflection at a cemetery for their dead in the Demyansk Pocket. (Courtesy of Lars Larsen)*

The Danish Frikorps Danmark volunteer, Werner Bircow Lassen, with a skull. Supposedly the skull of a Red Army officer, Lassen kept it as his 'good luck charm' throughout the war. The Dane on the left is carrying a Soviet SVT-40 Tokarev semi-automatic rifle. (Courtesy of Lars Larsen)

Spring 1942, and the Danes of the Frikorps prepare for another operation amidst the mud and squalor of the Demyansk Pocket. (Courtesy of Lars Larsen)

Soviet Red Army POWs – guarded by Danish Frikorps volunteers – are used as labour to build a corduroy road in the Demjansk Pocket. (Courtesy of Lars Larsen)

A wrecked German SdKfz 2, better known as the Kettenkrad, was used as a light tractor, mainly for pulling guns. It was designed to be delivered by Junkers Ju 52 aircraft, and this is how this one was sent into the Frikorps Danmark before its destruction in the Demjansk Pocket. (Courtesy of Lars Larsen)

The interior of a Junkers Ju 52 aircraft on its way into the Demjansk Pocket, packed with supplies for the Frikorps Danmark. Its relatively low lift capacity – just 4,010lb – was a major weakness, severely limiting the Luftwaffe's ability to supply large numbers of troops with everything they needed to survive and fight. (Courtesy of Lars Larsen)

The ruins of Demjansk town. Soviet strategy to destroy the Pocket called for the deliberate destruction of all buildings to deny shelter to the Frikorps Danmark and the other encircled units. (Courtesy of Lars Larsen)

During a break in the Demjansk fighting, the Frikorps's commander – Knud Børge Martinsen (right) – sits down with the Danish war reporter, Flemming Helweg Larsen (left). (Courtesy of Lars Larsen)

Above: *Propaganda poster for the Norwegian Nasjonal Samling party. (Author's private collection)*

Right: *Vidkun Quisling's gravestone in Gjerpen cemetery in Skien. (Author's private collection)*

The Norwegian DNL officer, Bjørn Østring, on the Leningrad Front. (Courtesy of Bergljot Østring)

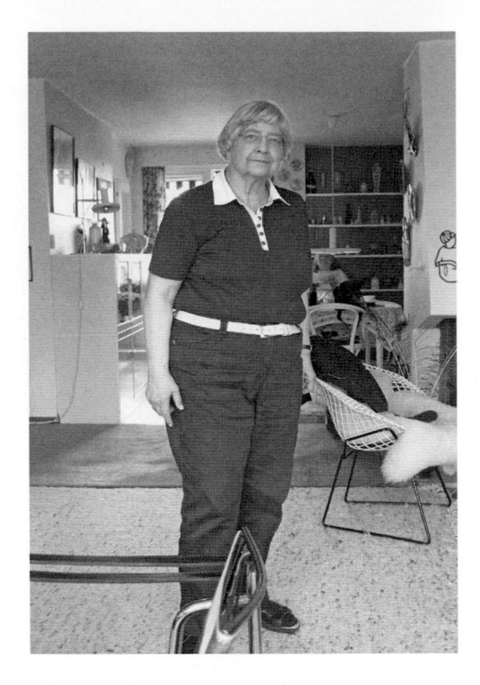

Above left: Bjørn Østring, who in later life became something of an unofficial spokesperson for the former Norwegian frontfighters. (Courtesy of Bergljot Østring)

Above right: Bergljot Østring, the widow of the former Norwegian Waffen-SS veteran Bjørn Østring, in 2017. (Author's private collection)

Below: A Norwegian volunteer from Den Norske Legion near Krasnoye Selo during the siege of Leningrad, 1942. The Norwegians were no slaves to uniform regulations and this man's non-issue scarf is typical of that attitude.

Above: *The sun cross – a cross inside a circle – is one of the oldest Nordic mythic symbols. The Nazis used a swastika variant of the sun cross as the Wiking division insignia – right. The left picture is the same symbol and uses figures and scenes from Norse mythology to draw parallels with the Wiking volunteers themselves. (Courtesy of Willtron)*

Left: *The Norwegian SS-Germania Regiment volunteer, Ørnulf Bjørnstadt. Bjørnstadt fought in the Caucasus before returning home in 1943. (Courtesy of Geir Brenden and Tommy Natedal)*

Below: *Propaganda photo of suitably Aryan-looking Scandinavian volunteers in the 5th SS-Panzer Division Wiking in 1943 – the Finnish flag can be seen flying in the background.*

The Ostheer made extensive use of captured Red Army hardware, including here a T34 tank painted with German crosses and manned by SS-Wiking division troopers.

An SS-Wiking panzer company rests up in a balka on the endless Russian steppe. The company is equipped with Panzer IIIs, which were the workhorse of the German panzerwaffe in the early years of the war but were obsolete by 1942.

Norwegian officers from the Wiking Division wearing the autumn/winter reversible camouflage uniforms in the autumn of 1943. In the middle (fourth from the left) is the renowned artist, Olav Wendelboe Jøntvedt. After surviving the war he joined the French Foreign Legion before settling down in Porsgrunn, Norway, where he passed away in 1980.

Winter 1944 – A 5th SS-Panzer Division Wiking Panther moves cautiously along the railway towards Kovel after the Cherkassy Pocket break-out.

Left: *Elizabeth and Ørnulf Kvaal. Both members of the NS party, Ørnulf would volunteer for the German Army and end up in a Soviet POW camp. (Courtesy of Elizabeth Kvaal)*

Below: *Elizabeth Kvaal, former NS member and widow of the Germany Army veteran Ørnulf Kvaal, in 2017. (Author's private collection)*

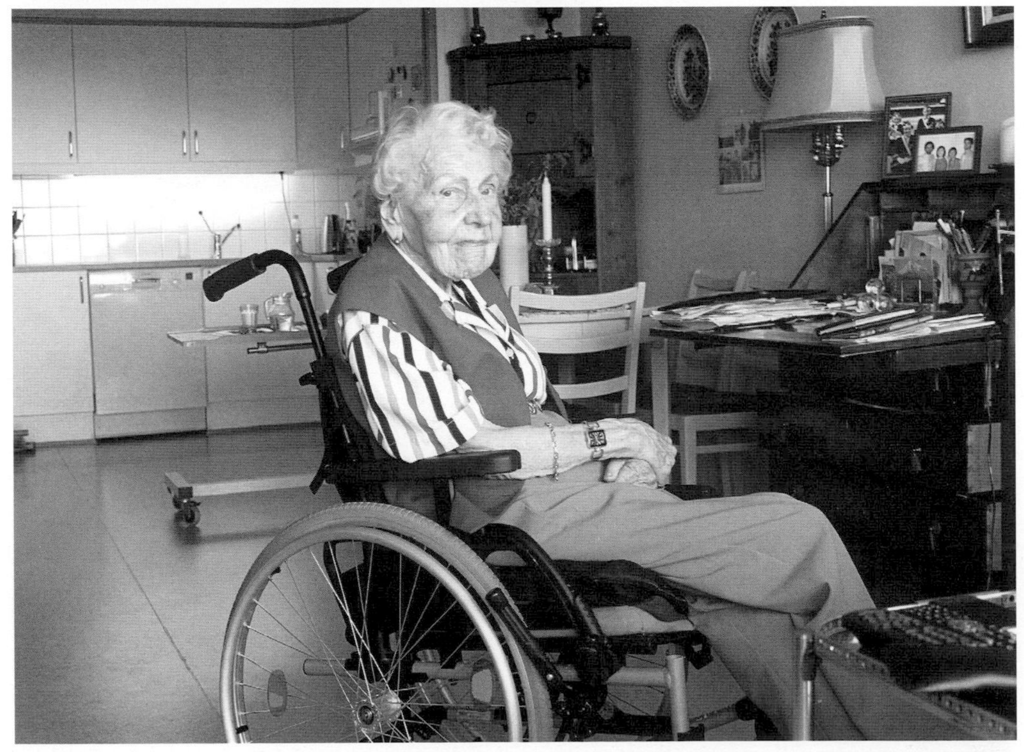

Above left: *Andreas Fleischer in his Waffen-SS uniform. Despite being Danish, Fleischer never served with a Danish Waffen-SS unit, and instead spent the war in the 3rd SS Panzer Division Totenkopf. (Courtesy of Andreas Fleischer)*

Above right: *After the war, Andreas Fleischer ended up as a sergeant in the Danish Army. (Courtesy of Andreas Fleischer)*

Below: *The North Schleswig SS-veteran, Andreas Fleischer, in 2017. (Author's private collection)*

Above: Norwegian volunteers in the first SS-Schikompanie Norwegen at the Karelia front in northern Finland. Kneeling at front; unknown, front row standing from left; Aleksander Herseth, Egil Kyllo and Martin Løvlien. Rear row standing from left; Olaf Weberg, Marius Sagbakken, Ove Eriksen and Asbjørn Narmo. (Courtesy of Geir Brenden and Tommy Natedal)

Below left: *The Norwegian Waffen-SS veteran Asbjørn Narmo in 2017, holding his signed frontfighter certificate. (Author's private collection)*

Below right: *The frontfighter certificate of the Norwegian Waffen-SS veteran Asbjørn Narmo, duly signed by Vidkun Quisling. Constantly refused work after the war, Narmo founded his own company. (Author's private collection)*

FRONTKJEMPER

Herved tildeler jeg

Asbjörn Narmo

FRONTKJEMPERMERKET

for innsats i kampen mot bolsjevismen.

Oslo, den 13/7 1944.

Quisling

Bjørn Østvedt

Kansellisjef.

The Danish-born Norwegian leader of the NSUF's sports section, SS-Obersturmführer Gust Jonassen in Karelia shortly before his death in a minefield. (Courtesy of Geir Brenden and Tommy Natedal)

The ex-Norwegian Land Service and Waffen-SS veteran, Jostein Berge, in 2017. (Author's private collection)

Above: *Norwegian members of the SS-Polizei-Schijaeger-Bataillon 506 (mot.) in Oslo. From the left; former DNL member Magne Ødegard, ex-SS-Nordland veteran Bjørn Lindstad, unknown, and SS-Wiking veteran SS-Unterscharführer Reidar Bjørgan. (Courtesy of Geir Brenden and Tommy Natedal)*

Below left: *On the right is the Norwegian Waffen-SS frontfighter, Bjørn Lindstad. (Courtesy of Bjørn Lindstad)*

Below right: *The Norwegian frontfighter Gustav Svalland, who deserted in the last days of the war alongside Bjørn Lindstad. (Courtesy of Bjørn Lindstad)*

Above left: *The Norwegian frontfighter Bjørn Lindstad who fought in Croatia, at Narva and in the Courland Pocket before being wounded and evacuated back to Germany as the war drew to a conclusion. (Courtesy of Bjørn Lindstad)*

Above right: *Bjørn Lindstad sporting his Wound Badge in Silver, Iron Cross ribbon and frontfighter award. (Courtesy of Bjørn Lindstad)*

Below right: *The Norwegian Waffen-SS veteran, Bjørn Lindstad, in 2017. (Author's collection)*

Aage J Sørensen's machine shop in Copenhagen, blown up by the Danish Resistance in May 1944. (Courtesy of the Danish Freedom Museum Archives)

The Danish police officer, E. Lemvigh-Müller, and the German Army's Major Erdmann salute each other in Odder high street just before they negotiate the latter's withdrawal from the town as the Third Reich finally surrenders in 1945. (Courtesy of the Danish Odder Archives)

The Norwegian ex-SS-Wiking veteran, Olav Tuff – the only frontfighter to publicly admit his involvement in a war crime in Russia. (Author's collection)

Right: The Norwegian frontfighter, Olav Tuff in 1941 in his Waffen-SS uniform. (Author's collection)

Above: *The ID card of Rachel Feinberg – the letter 'J', stamped on it in red, identified her to the Nazis as Jewish and condemned her to death in one of Auschwitz's gas chambers. (Courtesy of the Danish Freedom Museum Archives)*

9091 (Foto). 1438 J.

Etternavn: Feinberg

Fornavn: Rachel

Fødested: Oslo

Født: 6 juni 1923

Statsborgerlige forhold: Norsk

Nr. 121118

J

Right: *The once-destroyed stone monument to the Norwegian frontfighters and frontsisters, as the Red Cross nurses are called, now rebuilt by the veterans and their families, nestling in the hills in southern Norway. (Author's private collection)*

Below: *Two Danish Frikorps Danmark members somehow find something to smile about in the Demyansk Pocket. (Courtesy of Lars Larsen)*

us. He showed up wearing riding trousers and high boots – riding trousers for goodness sake, madness! Oh, and with no military training. He knew nothing, nothing at all, he was dirty and we had to teach him the most basic stuff, like how to wash himself in the field and brush his teeth, stuff like that. Then one night he was sent to a forward position – out in front of the frontline – so he could raise the alarm if the Russians attacked – I don't know who thought that was a good idea, whoever it was was a fool. Every now and then the Russians shelled our positions, and the forward post too, and they did that again the night when Bauch was on guard, with mortars. After the mortar attack I wanted to check out if everything was OK in the forward position, I was an experienced guy by then, you know, and that's what we old hands did ... when I got there I found Bauch standing and looking out across no-mans' land. I smiled and thought it was OK, so I spoke to him, but there was no reaction. When I got closer, I realised why he hadn't replied – he had been hit in the head by shrapnel and killed on the spot – still leaning on the side of trench. We old-timers knew the sound of a mortar shell and so had a chance to take cover if the shell didn't hit us directly... but Bauch didn't have this experience and so he must have stayed standing up as the mortar shells exploded – and that was that, he got hit and died. I went back to the HKL[4] and I didn't take his ID disc, or have anybody go out to pick him up and bury him – I just left him standing there, dead.

A short time later the expected Russian assault started, and I had enough to think about with the fighting and forgot all about Bauch – it pains me to this day! I still feel that I let this kid down. I should have cared for him and at least seen to it that his family got notice of his death and that he was properly buried – the bloody war!

Ivar walked out unscathed from Cherkassy and Kovel, but his comrade Andreas was not so lucky.

> *AF: I was wounded for the first time in the summer of '44. I got hit by shrapnel in my left arm – in the shoulder – from an explosion during a counter-attack we made with some panzers. They set it in a cast, and they used a piece of wood to hold it out at an angle – [Author: at this point Andreas demonstrated the position, with his left arm sticking out like a wing] – and so I called it my 'Stuka arm', (in German Army slang it was a Stukaverband) because it looked like a Stuka's wing!*

Andreas laughed – he did a lot of that.

> *AF: I was sent to a hospital in Breslau, and then up into the mountains to another hospital, a convalescent home for wounded soldiers, up in Bad Kudowa [Author: modern-day Kudowa-Zdrój in Poland].[5] I used to walk around the place fine, but I couldn't get my jacket on because of my arm, and I got fed up with it and couldn't take it anymore. So, I went to the office where the nuns and nurses were and said they had to take it off me, and they asked why and I said, 'Because I have lice and it itches like crazy!'*

Andreas laughed again for maybe the fifth or sixth time since I arrived to interview him.

> *AF: It was a lie of course! Anyway, they said no, so I just ripped the thing off myself anyway, damn them!*

Andreas carried on chuckling, and then said he was making more coffee and went off to the kitchen. While he was away I used the time to look around his flat as I always did when interviewing a veteran – yes, I am a nosey bugger.

From the outside, his third-floor flat in a modernish three-storey block, looked a bit like him; clean, well-tended, not run down or vandalised, it sort of matched Andreas himself in his pressed jeans, open-necked blue and white striped shirt, Burgundy V-neck jumper and polished brown shoes – looked after but not showy. There was no lift in the building, and I could imagine him taking the stairs every day without much of a problem at all – even revelling in it as other elderly residents huffed and puffed up the concrete steps as he marched past them smiling. He wasn't a tall man, but he was still square-shouldered and solid looking with strong, powerful hands, no glasses for his bluey-green eyes, white hair well-cut and combed. So far so like so many other veterans I've interviewed. It was what was on the inside of his flat that was interesting – or rather what wasn't – Andreas is the head of the local old comrades' society, and was evidently proud of his service, and yet there wasn't a single book, photo, plaque, flag or memento of the war, the Waffen-SS, or his time in it – not a thing. Andreas's wife had passed away some time before but she had clearly left her mark on both him and their home – it was still her place really and didn't belong to the Totenkopf.

He brought in the fresh coffee and some more confectionaries – mini-chocolates and sweet biscuits, and a bottle of something he described with a smile as a 'traditional liqueur'. He poured me, my translator (although Peter wasn't really needed in that capacity as Andreas's English was very good), and himself a glass, and then started again:

AF: You know Herr Trigg, since the war I have been asked many times about the fighting in the forests – you know in 1944 – but

I can't do it, I won't describe it. Why not? Because they wouldn't understand it. Maybe you would understand it because you've been a soldier, but most people – no, so I don't talk about it – it was terrible, terrible I tell you.

His face darkened and he seemed lost in thought for a time, and then as if a switch had been flicked he looked up, smiled and made a toast to us all. I took a slug of the liqueur – a drink called *Gammeldank* – and thought I'd swallowed paint-stripper – trust me, don't drink it if you don't have to.

Needless to say, Andreas laughed as I sat there gasping, and he poured me another, sat back in his armchair and carried on.

AF: After I'd recovered from my Stuka-arm, I went back to my unit, and in the meantime while I had been away we had gotten a new recruit, his name was Werner, he was from Berlin and I knew him from before the war. So, I told my platoon leader – he was from Aalborg, you know, up in the north of Denmark – that he would come to my squad, and he said no, he was going to another, and I said 'NO! He's coming to me.' That was that, he came to my squad! We didn't get many replacements at that point in the war, in fact we got fewer and fewer replacements as time went on, and the ones we did get weren't as well trained as we were, in fact most of them were barely trained at all, so my Gruppe was meant to have 12 men, but we usually had just eight and there was no way I was going to let a lad I knew go somewhere else when we needed the men and I could look after him if he was with me.

I remember – it was about that same time in 1944 – we got 200 ex-Luftwaffe men to help fill the ranks – some who were ex-pilots, but most were ground crew – and they had no infantry training these guys, they were useless. I was told I had four days to train them – that was it, just four days, they didn't have a chance and didn't last long; they were all killed soon enough.

One such 'willing volunteer' was the Dane Hans von Vultejus from Ry. The son of a German father and Danish mother, he initially volunteered for the Luftwaffe, but as the manpower shortage for the front bit hard, just like Andreas's 'new comrades' in the Totenkopf, he found himself ordered to report to the Waffen-SS.

Hans von Vultejus: I was given a Waffen-SS uniform and was then told to get in line to have my blood group tattooed on me. However, I refused to get the tattoo on my left arm as was common practice in the SS, so, while waiting in line, I quietly moved over to the file of guys who'd already had it done. I didn't make a fuss or say anything, I just did it, so I was never tattooed.

The combing through of the Luftwaffe, the Kriegsmarine and the Army's own rear area units was only ever going to be a sticking plaster to try to cover the yawning gaps in the line, especially as the Red Army continued to grow in power and effectiveness.

AF: We had to put up with these replacements that were no help at all – but it wasn't like that for the Russians I can tell you, they had excellent units, called Guards,[6] they had different uniforms from their normal infantry, we could tell when we were up against the Guards because they had proper belts – leather belts – while the rest – we called them 'second-line units' – they just had rope holding up their trousers. They weren't as well-trained or as well-armed as the Guards, not all of them even had weapons. They were told before they went into an attack, 'take the weapons from the dead', they were still soldiers though. Mind you, they weren't happy when they heard they were facing the Totenkopf, when they heard we were there, they tried to move away, they were afraid of us! Anyway, the Russians had so many men that from October 1944 onwards they were sending frontline soldiers back home, and their place was taken by new men with little training and no experience.

Another thing the Russians had lots of was sharpshooters – snipers – they were very good. They could stay still for hours, not move for hours and then shoot. I remember I spoke to some Americans – after the war – who had fought at Iwo Jima, you know where they raised the flag in that photo [Author: famous shot of the Stars and Stripes being raised on Mount Surabachi], and I asked them why they did that when there were still snipers about? They could have been shot. They said the snipers were usually out at night and stayed hidden during the day. They told me they used flamethrowers to burn them out. We used flamethrowers too, I saw one burn a T34 tank up once.

Anyway, I used to warn my men 'don't stand up, don't put your head up', but one of my men stood up anyway and I said to him: 'Are you trying to get killed?'

I had to teach this lad a lesson, to try and keep him alive. I had a special rifle at the time, one with a telescopic sight, and I put my helmet on a stick and told one of my men to put it up in the air, and at the same time I was looking at the Russian lines through the telescope on my rifle. A Russian sniper fired, and hit my helmet, but I didn't see him for a little while. Then he made a mistake, he moved, and I shot him. I'd got him. We had no more firing from him. More coffee?

At the same time as Andreas was dealing with the Russian sniper, Karin Matre had returned to Oslo from the Warthegau.

KM: I was very close to my younger brother who joined the Waffen-SS, and I also had a very good girlfriend who was engaged to a Norwegian front fighter. With those connections I thought I needed to do something for the war too, so I enlisted in the Deutsches Rote Kreuz [Author: DRK the German Red Cross] as a nurse in the autumn of 1944. We were trained here in Oslo, near the castle. Our leader was an experienced front nurse called Grethe Knutsen, and when my training was finished, I was sent to work in the diphtheria department of the Aker Hospital for German soldiers. We looked after the patients; bandaging them, giving them medication, feeding and washing them. There were Germans and Norwegians there, all from the Eastern Front. I felt sorry for them. I met my future husband there – he was a German – but I had nothing to do with him during the war because he was a German. But he came back to see me after the war and we got together – six years after the war it was.

I hadn't been there long when the British tried to bomb the Gestapo headquarters here in Oslo – we were sent lots of wounded men then – some of their injuries were horrible.

The bombing raid Karin described in the interview was one of a number carried out by the RAF's Mosquito squadrons during the war, targeting Gestapo headquarters across the Continent involved in trying to destroy the Resistance. The most famous was the Amiens attack – Operation Jericho – with Oslo first being hit in 1942 to coincide with one of Quisling's NS rallies, and then followed up at the end of October 1944 with the destruction of the Gestapo's Aarhus HQ. On that occasion the Aarhus University building used by the Nazis was hit, killing an estimated 200 members of the Gestapo and associated organisations. Unfortunately, about 30 imprisoned Danish resistance fighters also died. Canadian Bob

Boyden was one of those flying with 627 Squadron who later remembered the RAF's return raid to Oslo on 31 December:

> *Our first information about the trip to Oslo was that we were to fly to Peterhead in the northern part of Scotland, which would be our advance base ... Briefing told us that Oslo was the target – not the target for tonight – as this would be a daylight raid, which we did not do very often. In fact, I believe I flew only three trips in daylight. It's quite different as you feel like you stand out like a sore thumb ... Wing Commander Curry was our new squadron commander and would lead the group, which was made up of two flights of six Mosquitoes each. Flight Lieutenant Mallender would lead the second wave. The North Sea is a long trip and we had been told that the water was so cold, we'd last only two minutes. I don't remember worrying too much about it – it was such a beautiful day ... We cleared the Norwegian coast, with the Oslo Fjord to our right. The target was ahead of us but not in sight, lost in the haze. Suddenly bursts of flak came up, seemingly one for each aircraft and right on altitude. This was the first time that I had seen, heard and smelled it all at the same time as we flew through the cloud ... Everything happened so quickly. We had, of course, fooled the flak defences by our diving attack and at last – the target. Bomb doors open, wait for the right moment, push the button, hold 1,000 feet. I felt concussions that closely followed one another. There was no smoke, no dust. I then pushed lower over the city and I remember seeing an open-air skating rink with people skating around, unaware of the chaos and explosions behind them ... All aircraft returned to base and all had some flak marks. Mine also had a cracked landing light cover, which they said had been caused by the concussion. Only one crew member was injured by shrapnel.*

Bob Boyden was awarded the Distinguished Flying Cross (DFC) for his part in the raid. Only the first six of the 12 aircraft on the raid dropped their bombs, the smoke obscuring the target for the second wave. The RAF at first believed the raid had been successful but it later transpired that the Victoria Terrasse building that housed the Gestapo was undamaged. Instead other civilian buildings had been hit and one bomb had bounced off the ground and hit a crowded tram, killing 44 civilians. In total 78 Norwegians and 27 Germans were killed. It was the worst single action loss of life in Oslo during the war.

Owen Carlstrand is the son of an eyewitness to the attack, and spoke about it in December 2016:

My father lived at 60 Ruselokkveien during the war, in fact until he married my mother in 1952. He used to tell us about the night of the Gestapo raid as he was there that night. Ruselokkveien was, and still is, just around the corner from Victoria Terrasse and one of the bombs went right through the flat and out the other side, exploding the other side of the courtyard. He also told us that the daughter of the founder of Broderene Dahl was a casualty on the tram which was hit. By coincidence dad was their UK managing director in the 80s.

His favourite story though was at a New Year's Eve party in Epsom – where they lived – in the 80s, he was talking to a bloke who, when he found out that dad was Norwegian told him that he had been hanging about Oslo on New Year's Eve 1944. Dad's response was thanks a lot, you bombed us out that night. The man responded with 'Happy New Year, I'm very glad you could make it here tonight.' Unfortunately, I don't remember his name, if indeed dad ever mentioned it.

Over in the east, Army Group North could no longer hold the Narva position it had defended for so many months, and the last retreat beckoned for Bjørn and his comrades.

BL: The Russians broke through near Riga, and we were the furthest troops east at that point and on 18 September 1944 we retreated.

Estonia is very flat and we could see soldiers and vehicles everywhere, lots of horses too, and lots and lots of civilians. As we drove down the road, the horses and civilian cars would get out of the way – and then when we got close to Riga, we attacked the Russians. We held the Russians until all the refugees had gotten away. We then packed everything away, the cannons were taken off as well, and all the time the infantry were coming past us saying they were the last ones and there were only Russians behind them. Then a wagon came back to get us and took us to a farm. I was with my two Volksdeutsche friends and they were joined by another one, and when they were talking I heard them say 'Bubi' and that was my nickname so I knew they were talking about me. They were saying that Bubi has to join them for something but I didn't know what. Theft was strictly forbidden you know, but it turned out to be stealing a chicken from a coop. We went and one of the Volksdeutsche 'hypnotised' one of these chickens and off we went with it. We ate well that night for a change.

Then we were surrounded – cut off – in Courland.[7]

During the battles in Courland some 400,000 Russians were killed you know, and about 50,000 on the German and Latvian side.[8]

So, we were cut off in Courland, and General Steiner wanted us all to evacuate the place, to escape, but Hitler said no, we had to stay. All those lives were lost for nothing. I knew then that we had lost the war, in fact I never thought we were going to win, not ever, not since before I volunteered.

It's never been good to be on the losing team in a war! Most of my comrades didn't agree, they believed in Hitler's 'secret weapons' and were always talking about them. Some also thought that when the Russians advanced into Germany itself, then the Allies would join the Germans in fighting the communists – they thought the Western Allies and the communists was an unnatural alliance that would fall apart pretty soon – but I never really believed that.

We arrived in the dark at Preekuln [Author: modern-day Priekule in southwest Latvia] and started to dig trenches. I dug a hole on my own and one for my commander – Abels – and I could hear my neighbour digging too, he was from the infantry and had the same job as me except it was for a mortar crew – he was Norwegian too – so we could speak to each other in Norwegian. The two of us discussed what would happen when we lost the war, even though we didn't really think we would survive that long, but we both wanted to see what would happen at the end. That's why we carried on fighting, to try and survive.

We were fired at then, and I jumped down into my hole and fell asleep, and woke up when someone was shouting at me that we were retreating and we had to go – it was my Norwegian friend from the next-door hole. I grabbed my stuff and began to run, and after a few yards I saw that my Norwegian friend had been shot in the head and was dead. I took his ID disc – it was difficult to break off – and his Soldbuch[9] *so at least his family would know what happened to him.*

I remember always being tired – we never got enough sleep – and, of course, there was never enough food either, but it was the lack of sleep that was the worst thing. I was eight months at the front without any leave, and some of my comrades then carried on for another six months right up to the end in Berlin – if you ended up at the front at that time you were stuck there.

We didn't have set positions in Courland, we were always moving around and digging our holes. We hoped that the troops behind us would dig trenches for us, but they never did.

My commander, Abels, he was killed on 28 October 1944, and I had to take over, and then I was wounded on 1st November 1944. I was near my hole and a Volksdeutsche was in the hole next to me, and I was walking to the telephone when I heard Stalinorgeln being fired at us. It was a very imprecise weapon and usually when they tried to hit us in the frontline with them they hit their own men too, so they normally used it to fire at our rear areas. But I'd forgotten we were slightly further back than normal and so we were in the firing zone for the rockets. One landed near me and the explosion knocked me back into my hole. I was covered in blood – I'd been hit by shrapnel at the top of my right leg – but I didn't pass out. I got up and was shaking from shock. My comrades put me on a sledge and dragged me out to a field dressing station, and then I was taken further back through an area under fire from Russian artillery, so we had to go really quickly through there, and that was a very painful journey. I was so thirsty and kept on calling to another soldier to give me water. I was on my back, lying in my own blood – it was a Heimatschuss [Author: a 'Homeland wound', this was the type of wound that was so serious it meant you were sent home and could be out of the war] – but I didn't think it was possible to be evacuated as we were surrounded, but we were sorted into categories depending on how badly we were wounded. I arrived at the hospital for surgery and there was a big line waiting to be operated on – there were Russians waiting to be treated too, but they weren't prioritised.

The surgeons were working on two tables each and their aprons were covered in blood. There wasn't any anaesthetic, someone put a cigarette into the surgeon's mouth and then he turned to me to start the operation. An orderly was holding me down and the surgeon took out the shrapnel in my leg – the wound it left was six centimetres by two centimetres – and he also took out bits of shrapnel in my right shoulder and lower down in my right leg. He left some smaller bits in me and over time they moved around and just disintegrated, it looked like I had 'rust'!

I was evacuated out of Courland on a fishing boat to Stettin [Author: modern-day Szczecin in Poland] and I ended up in Ingolstadt in Bavaria. I was there for six weeks, but the wound hadn't healed, and then more wounded arrived from the Ardennes. I was meant to be sent home, but they wouldn't transport me to Norway, so I was sent to the home of one of the nurses' mothers – in Ulm, in Swabia. I was on my way there when it was bombed. The church was the only thing that survived the bombing. The mother was living in a pile of ash. She had some family elsewhere in Herrlingen and we started walking there, I was limping and we went about 10 kilometres and arrived at the nurse's grandparents, and I ended up living with the nurse's aunt – it was near where Rommel was buried.

I've been there since the war too, you know. The English had put small crosses on Rommel's grave, and they had written on them; 'To the Desert Fox from the Desert Rats.'[10] *I myself was going to put flowers on the grave of the woman I stayed with, but she had donated her body to medical science. So there was no grave.*

When I was finally healed I was given two weeks leave and was then sent to Breslau, which was near the front then. I was posted to the NCO School there but had to wait until the course started, and in the meantime I was sent home to Norway via Berlin as I hadn't been sent there on my sick leave. I had to watch the execution of a deserter before I left Breslau – a Dutchman – I didn't know him. I was made to watch it to teach me a lesson so I wouldn't desert myself.

Bjørn was extremely lucky to be wounded as he was and evacuated from Courland – although when I said this to him he laughed and said he hadn't felt lucky at the time! However, the fact remains that the men who were left in the Pocket had to endure months more of vicious fighting with Soviet forces that far outnumbered and outgunned them, and at the end the only thing they had won was a surrender that saw the survivors marched off en masse to the horrors of Soviet POW camps.

The end of the war was definitely in sight now. As 1944 drew to a close the Anglo-Americans stood on the Rhine, a liberated France and Belgium behind them. In the east the mass grave that was Poland was also free, although the term was relative given Stalin's determination to hold the country in a vice-like grip from then on.

In Europe's south-east, the Bulgarians and Romanians had switched horses to try to avoid calamity – it would be a forlorn hope – and the Germans and their Croat fellow-travellers were desperately marching north-west out of Greece and Yugoslavia to the Austrian border before the noose tightened around their necks.

Food was becoming increasingly scarce in what was left of the Nazi empire, with even frontline soldiers on short rations: 11 ounces of bread and just a single ounce of fats (whatever that was…) per day.

The great oilfields of Ploesti had been lost to the Wehrmacht when Romania turned on them, further degrading the Nazi capacity to wage war – *blitzkrieg* was swiftly becoming *Pferdkrieg* as horses took the place of vehicles. Hungary was the Reich's last source of oil, although the production from its main fields around Nagykanizsa[11] was a drop in the bucket against what was needed. Nevertheless, Hitler fixated on Hungary, even as Soviet tanks aimed at Berlin began to mass on the Vistula. The Nazi dictator – now more than ever lost in his own fantasy world – believed he could win a resounding victory on the Magyar plain that would turn the tide of the war.

Andreas Fleischer and Ivar Corneliussen would bear witness to his folly.

AF: I was in the line from October '44 and we were fighting hard, and then, just before New Year 1994/45, we were loaded up onto trains and sent down towards Budapest, in Hungary. We were sent with an Army division. We arrived and I found my brother there. He had escaped from Budapest – he was with an Army unit, a special unit, but I can't remember what it was called – it wasn't the Brandenburgers[12] I don't think... No, it wasn't them. Anyway, he told me that they had had to split up into small groups and escape that way – it had been their only chance.

It was very good to see him, but we didn't get much chance to talk – that was the way things were at the front, and before you ask, Herr Trigg, is it necessary to answer questions about my brother? No, it isn't.

So, my division – the Totenkopf – the very first day we attacked towards Budapest we cost the Russians 250 tanks! We had Tigers, Panthers and some old PzKfw IVs, and we attacked some of their Guards units, you know, the ones I told you about – they were good – not as good as us but good anyway.[13] But before we attacked we were moved from one place to another, we had to change our insignia – hide our SS insignia – you understand, all to confuse the Russians so they didn't know where we were or what we were doing. We carried quite a lot of rations too at that point – usually when we knew we'd be going into a fight we'd carry enough food and so on for two to three days, but we had more then. Maybe they thought we'd have problems getting resupplied, I don't know.

It didn't matter to me as it turned out because I was wounded then, on 4 January 1945, in Hungary. It was the second time I'd been wounded.

What happened was that we attacked the first town we came to and there was a minefield there, the mines were in wooden boxes so they were difficult to find, you know with mine detectors. Our panzers could then only use the roads, to stay away from the mines, you see, but it meant that the Russians could hit the panzers from the flank, from the side, you see, that's the best way to kill a panzer, from the side, the armour is thinner there. Anyway, a Tiger was hit, the commander managed to get out and we grabbed him and brought him back. There was so much machine-gun fire, it was like snow in the air. One round hit the panzer next to me like that 'dummmm', that's the noise it made, it was so close. A shell landed just behind me then and shrapnel hit me here, in my right shoulder. The bone wasn't broken though, just scraped. I got a lift back to a small dressing station with a guy who had a little moustache – you know like Hitler – that was popular back then!

Another laugh from Andreas.

The doctor I saw said it was lucky the shrapnel hadn't gone into my lung. I lay there in the dressing station – like I said, a small place with just two beds, me and another guy next to me. This guy next to me said: 'Hey, do you recognise me, do you know who I am?' and at first I didn't, he was all burnt up and bandaged, and then I realised who he was, he was the Tiger commander we'd grabbed. He was very worried, though, that they were going to take his legs off, as they were in a mess. He kept on saying, 'please don't take my legs, please don't take my legs' – again and again he kept on saying it.

The next day they told us they were going to send us back to a bigger hospital on a train. They loaded us up and he was there again, the Tiger commander, in the same wagon as me. We were waiting there on the railway track and I fell asleep. Then I woke up, and something was wrong. I opened the door and the Tiger guy said what's going on, and I said: 'Shut up! Can you hear that? It's Russian fire!' He said, 'Are you crazy, how do you know?' and I said, 'Trust me, I've heard it a lot of times before! That's Russian fire!' So, I then said that if another train doesn't come and take us away in 20 minutes, then I'm off. Another train didn't come so I got out and left. I found out later what had happened; a Hungarian general had surrendered to the Russians and taken his whole division across with him, so there was a big hole in the line and the Russians had come through it, that's why they were so close to the train. Luckily, the train managed to get away anyway.

I was given some leave and then went back to Prague, and a doctor there told me my shoulder wasn't healed and I couldn't go back to the division yet. After a while I was OK and I went back to the division and that was when I was wounded for the third time, a bullet hit me on the left side of my face and my left ear, well I think it was a bullet – it hurt like hell I can tell you, and there was blood everywhere, I couldn't see much out of my eye.

Incredibly, Andreas wasn't a rarity in being wounded multiple times; six per cent of front fighters received three or more injuries, and well over half had at least one.

IC: Between Christmas 1944 and New Year 1945, we were ordered to pack up our gear and move to Hungary where the Russians were close to Budapest. We were supposed to try and push the Russians back, and we did some very heavy fighting around a brick-works factory on the Pest side of the Danube, and then had to withdraw to the Buda side of the river. At this point in time I was withdrawn from the frontline and transferred to a supply unit. During the withdrawal from Hungary we went over Stuhlweissenberg {Author: modern-day Hungarian Szekesfehervar] and on to Varpalotta, where for quite a while I managed a depot of food supplies and spare parts. I lived with a local family in their house in Malom Utska, and had a good friend called Rossi Feher.[14]

The biggest problem we had was the lack of gasoline and diesel oil. We only had enough fuel to fill up one panzer at a time, and that panzer then had to pull a whole string of other vehicles along behind it. One day a message came that said the Russians were just outside of town, of Malom Utska that is, and I opened my depot and told the villagers to take whatever they wanted – everything went very fast I can tell you!

It was all very close. When I drove out of town the Russians were arriving at the other end of town at the same time. After this we went back to the north of Lake Balaton [Author: in German the Plattensee], along Fürstenfeld, and here we got a whole lot of cigarettes from some cigarette factory, then past Graz, then Leoben and Judenburg until we ended up in Kleinarl.

For the Scandinavian Waffen-SS volunteers, and for the Third Reich itself, the war was coming to an end. Ivar's Wiking and Andreas's Totenkopf – once immensely powerful panzer divisions – were shadows of their former selves, and the remnants were withdrawing into Austria with half an eye on surrendering to the Anglo-Americans rather than the Soviets.

As for Bjørn Lindstad, he was doubly lucky; firstly in escaping the Courland Pocket on account of his leg wound, and secondly by avoiding the fate of his Nordland Division comrades who then found themselves in the eye of the storm in Berlin, where they became one of the lynchpins of the city's defence, and suffered enormous casualties as a result.

There was one last chapter to be written by some of the veterans – pretty much exclusively by Norwegians – before a blessed peace broke out across Europe, and it was one that involved Bjørn, Jostein Berge and my last interviewee in Norway, Stål Munkeberg.

> *SM: When I finished my training I was sent north to Finland, to the SS-Skijägers, but I was only there for 14 days before the Finns made peace.*[15] *I hadn't heard a shot fired in combat, and then we were told we had to go home. It was a 1,100-kilometre walk back – 1,100 kilometres, can you imagine that!*
>
> *It was very, very hard indeed. We had hardly any food, no change of clothes or anything, it was awful. My feet were always in pain, I was always hungry – dreadful, absolutely dreadful. I finally got back to Bergen on 24 April 1945 – and I was just happy to be alive, I can tell you!*

Following Gust Jonassen's death in combat and the withdrawal from the frontline of the SS-Ski Company, a new battalion was formed in the spring of 1943 on the same lines and christened the SS-Schijäger-Bataillon 'Norge', with three companies and a staff company. The battalion was then attached to the 6th SS-Gebirgs-Division Nord based in Finland. Staying on the defensive, the Norwegians suffered heavy losses during the great Russian offensive in the summer of 1944, when the Red Army assaulted and captured the positions they were holding on Kaprolat and Hasselmann Hills on 25 and 26 June 1944. The SS-Nord Division was then sent back to Germany in December 1944, and the remainder of the Ski battalion went to Norway. Amalgamated with some German police troops, the unit was re-christened the 'SS-Polizei-Schijäger-Bataillon 506 (mot.)'. The new unit never saw frontline service against the Soviets or the Anglo-Americans, but did some small-scale fighting with the Norwegian Resistance as the war drew to a close in May 1945. Some of its members were also assigned to Skallum farm in Bærum to keep watch over some of the most prominent Norwegian Nazis including Henrik Rogstad, Jonas Lie and Sverre Riisnæs.

JB: From December 1944 I was in training for the S-Skijägers, first at Vikersund, and then at Mysen. My instructors were all Norwegians, but there were Germans there too. As the war was obviously coming to an end I expected to be set free from the Waffen-SS at any time, but instead we received orders to go to Haglebu where we ended up fighting a battle there. That was on 26 April 1945, and was just 12 days before the end of the war. We had a high-ranking Norwegian SS officer there – Reidar Egil Hoel[16] *– and he stopped a German officer who wanted to burn down the whole village, so only a summer farm was burnt down in the end.*

While I was there, me and a comrade saw three Resistance men passing by and we could have easily shot them but we didn't, they were Norwegians and our fight wasn't with them, and in any case the war was as good as over. But the Resistance didn't do the same for us. They took a Norwegian Waffen-SS man prisoner and shot him – I knew the man, not well, but I'd spoken to him a few times, he was just 21 years old and they murdered him.

We'd been there before, to the Egdal region, to go skiing and we'd seen some weapons stored there by the Resistance, but we didn't do anything about it. We always tried not to hurt Norwegians or take Norwegian lives. One day we went to check a hut in the mountains – no one was in the hut – but we found a British Enfield rifle behind the door and we hid it from the Germans who were with us so they didn't burn the hut down. In another hut we found a radio and it was forbidden to have a radio, of course – this was all in April 1945 – and again we didn't tell the Germans. We found out afterwards that the hut was supposedly owned by an NS member who was the uncle of one of us in the battalion so he was allowed to have a radio as an NS member, but we didn't know that at the time. The German soldiers weren't bad guys, though, they were just foreigners in a strange country, you know. We weren't all angels either, of course, but I was an angel!

My company was then sent to help guard Quisling. We joined some of his own bodyguard – one of whom was Bjørn Østring, whom you knew of course, Herr Trigg – and all the talk then was of what would happen to Quisling and all the rest of us when the war ended. I think some people were telling Quisling he had to escape but he didn't want to run away – he had decided to stay and face the music – isn't that what you English say? I then went home on compassionate leave for my grandfather's funeral – we buried him on 5 May 1945, just a few days before the war ended.

BL: The SS-Skijäger battalion had come back from Finland, and was now in Norway and I wanted to apply to join them – that was during my leave in the middle of February 1945. I had to go to Germany to apply for some strange reason – military thinking, eh! I was told I had go all the way to the SS-Hauptamt[17] *in Potsdam in Berlin. I told them I was Norwegian, so I spoke Norwegian of course, so it made more sense for me to be in that battalion – I didn't know that my regiment, the Norge, was outside Berlin at that point, I thought it was still in Courland and I couldn't get there. If I had stayed with the Nordland I would have stayed around Berlin until the end.*

Anyway, I got my transfer papers. By coincidence I met my old Norwegian liaison officer on a tram in the city and he told me that the Norge was close by, but when I said I should join them he said no, the war was as good as over, he told me to go home. I joined the SS-Skijäger Battalion in Oslo – they were infantry, without cannons or anything like that – so I had to re-learn a lot. We had motorbikes, and there were three of us to a motorbike with a sidecar, and we had to learn how to jump on and off the bikes. One of our commanders was an Austrian, and we would go with him to a house on the outskirts of Oslo where he had a lady friend. He would go in and 'entertain' her and we would wait outside and look after the bike. He would then come out with a big smile and talk to us about his wife – we couldn't believe it!

One day the whole company was called to the Gestapo HQ in Oslo, our officer went in and then came out with a Gestapo man and a prisoner, a Norwegian from the Milorg.[18] *They got into a car and went east and we escorted them. The prisoner was meant to tell the Gestapo where there were other Milorg men, but he didn't know. They stopped after a while – outside the city – and were talking to him about it when a woman on a bike came by and it looked as if she and the Milorg man knew each other. The woman carried on her way and after that the Gestapo men started to beat the Milorg man up pretty badly, but he didn't say anything and they just kept on beating him. He still didn't say anything so then they stopped hitting him and we all left and went back to our barracks.*

A little later I was sent back to school again – to the NCO School at Elverum. I met someone there from my old company in the Norge, the 8th, who had been wounded like me in Courland. There was a rumour that the next day we would be sent to hunt down Partisans, to hunt locals – fellow Norwegians. I told my old comrade what I had seen with the Gestapo; you know, the Norwegian man being beaten up, and the two of us decided to desert because we didn't want anything to do with something like that. In the end it turned out that it was just a rumour, and we weren't sent out to hunt Partisans, it was actually the Germanske SS who were supposed to go out and hunt them down. But enough was enough, and so I deserted on 1 May 1945.

Notes to Chapter Six

1. Atkinson, Rick, *The Guns at Last Light; The War in Western Europe 1944–1945*, Abacus.
2. Ibid.
3. Butar, Prit, *Between Giants: The Battle for the Baltics in World War II*, Osprey. The 214th Infantry Division, with its two regiments; the 355th and the 367th, was sent to Estonia in early 1944 and was attacked by the Soviet 59th Army's 43rd and 109th Rifle Corps in March. After three days of fighting it was driven back and virtually destroyed.
4. HKL – in German the *HauptKampfLinie* – Main Battle Line i.e., the main defensive trench line.

5. Kudowa-Zdrój is one of the oldest spa towns in Europe, traditionally where heart and circulatory system diseases were cured, Winston Churchill was a famous visitor.
6. Guards status was awarded to units and formations that distinguished themselves during the Second World War by the order of People's Commissar for Defence of USSR No.303, instituted on the 18th of September 1941, with accredited units considered to have élite status.
7. The Courland Pocket (in German: *Kurland-Kessel*) refers to the Red Army's isolation of Axis forces on the Courland Peninsula from July 1944 to May 1945. The Pocket was created during the Red Army's Baltic Strategic Offensive Operation, when forces of the 1st Baltic Front reached the Baltic Sea near Memel. The Soviet commander was General Ivan Bagramyan (later Marshal). This action isolated German Army Group North (in German: *Heeresgruppe Nord*) from the rest of the German forces between Tukums and Libau in Latvia. Renamed Army Group Courland (in German: *Heeresgruppe Kurland*) on 25 January 1945, the Army Group remained isolated until its surrender at the end of the war.
8. As ever it is difficult to be accurate as to Soviet losses but Krivosheyev, Grigoriy F., ed. (2001), in his *Russia and the USSR in the Wars of the Twentieth Century: Losses of the Armed Forces, A Statistical Study*, OLMA-Press, calculates that from 16 February to 8 May 1945 the Soviets lost 160,948 men, killed or wounded, attacking the Pocket, so during the whole six battles for the Pocket a figure of 400,000 dead Soviets could well be accurate. As for Axis casualties, Grier, Howard D. (2007), *Hitler, Dönitz, and the Baltic Sea: The Third Reich's Last Hope, 1944–1945*, Annapolis: Naval Institute Press (p81–88) claims the figure for killed and wounded throughout the Pocket's life was just in excess of 150,000 killed and wounded. Some 180,000 men survived to surrender to the Soviets at the end of the war.

9. The German Soldbuch was an A6-sized document containing 24 numbered internal pages, bound within a tan-coloured leather-grain style card cover. Although often referred to as a soldiers' pay book, it was actually a very detailed booklet containing identification details, a record of equipment issued to the holder and it also kept track of the individual soldier's service history. The booklet held very little information regarding pay, but did give authority for the holder to draw pay. It first began to be issued to serving soldiers in mid-1939, during the general mobilisation, and from then on was issued to new recruits soon after their induction to the army. This practice continued until the end of the war. At the end of hostilities, many soldiers retained their Soldbuch as it would often be the only form of identification they would have.
10. Field Marshal Erwin Rommel was respectfully nicknamed the Desert Fox by the British and Commonwealth troops he faced in North Africa when he commanded the Afrika Korps. One of the units Rommel fought in the desert was the British 7th Armoured Division, which adopted the nickname the Desert Rats while fighting there.
11. After successful exploration by the American corporation Eurogasco, the Hungarian-American Oil Inc. was formed. Nagykanizsa became the centre of the Hungarian oil industry. During the Anglo-American Oil Bombing Campaign from 1943 onwards, Nagykanizsa was bombed and so were the Hungarian refineries at Almásfüzitö, Budapest and Szöny.
12. The Brandenburgers were a German Special Forces unit during World War II. Originally the unit was formed by, and operated as, an extension of the military's intelligence organisation, the Abwehr. Members of this unit took part in seizing operationally important targets by way of sabotage and infiltration, and were often either fluent foreign language speakers, expatriates or Volksdeutsche.

13. The Totenkopf's opponents were the Red Army's 4th Guards Army and the 6th Guards Tank Army – the German offensive met strong resistance from the outset and achieved little progress.
14. The name *Rossi Feher* means 'white rose', and at the time it was often used either as a nickname or a pseudonym, usually for a prostitute.
15. On 4 September 1944 a ceasefire between Moscow and Helsinki was agreed, and the armistice was signed on 19 September. Under the conditions of the peace treaty, the Finns were obliged to expel all German troops from their territory by force if necessary. The German response was to withdraw all their personnel to Norway in an epic march.
16. Also called the Battle of Egdal, Haglebu cost the lives of 14 men, seven from the SS and seven from the Resistance. The 2nd SS-Police Company was the first to be formed, and was led by the ex-Norwegian Army engineer captain, SS-Hauptsturmführer Reidar-Egil Hoel. Its 160 men were sent to Finland to serve alongside the Reconnaissance Battalion of the SS-Nord. Hoel was awarded the Iron Cross 1st Class, imprisoned after the war and passed away in 1971. Trigg, Jonathan, *Hitler's Vikings*, The History Press, p161.
17. Commanded by Gottlob Berger, the SS Main Office – *SS-Hauptamt* – was the central command office of the SS until 1940. Thereafter it lost much of its pre-war power but still carried out multiple administrative functions throughout the sprawling SS empire.
18. The Milorg – an abbreviation of the Norwegian *militær organisasjon* – military organisation – was the main Norwegian resistance movement of the war.

7

RETRIBUTION

By the beginning of May 1945, the Third Reich was fast collapsing. Adolf Hitler had committed suicide and Berlin was burning. The Ruhr and most of western Germany was in Anglo-American hands, and in the east, hundreds of thousands of soldiers and civilians were on the roads fleeing to try to escape the anticipated Soviet wave of vengeance.

Outside Berlin there was still sporadic fighting going on, but it was little more than the dying embers of the mighty conflagration that had consumed Europe for almost six long years.

Naively, the Americans believed that Stalin was not only a trustworthy ally, but that he would stand by the letter and spirit of all the agreements he had made with the Anglo-Americans during the war, and that this would lead to the establishment of peaceful democracies across Europe once the Nazis were destroyed – the British were more worldly-wise. London realised that for Stalin, possession was nine-tenths of the law, and the key to the post-war settlement was to end the fighting sitting on top of as much land as you could grab. For the British armed forces under Montgomery, this meant driving forward and meeting the approaching Soviets as far to the east as possible. However, Monty was never a general to be rushed, and the upshot was that for the Danes it was a close-run thing; British paras only reached Wismar on the Baltic – to block entry to Jutland – just two hours before the Red Army arrived from the other direction.[1] Somewhat disgruntled at being beaten to the prize, the Soviets settled for occupying the Danish island of Bornholm, and proceeded to stay there for almost an entire year.

Bottled up in Denmark were tens of thousands of Axis soldiers; not only Germans, but Hungarians and Romanians who had carried on fighting alongside their previous allies after their countries switched sides, while in Norway there were a staggering 400,000 German troops[2] – all now wondering what to do. While the Germans scratched their heads, the Danes – most of them – began to celebrate liberation. People came out onto the streets to wave the *Dannebrog* – the Danish flag – and everywhere households burnt their blackout curtains and put lit candles in their windows as a sign the war was over.

There was still uncertainty though, and nowhere more so than in Odder, and who else could sort it but our old friend Assistant Police Commissioner Lemvigh-Müller.

On the 1st of May 1945 I was serving as adjutant to Martensen-Larsen, the then chief of the police's illegal opposition forces for Jutland-Funen. In consultation with the local resistance movement representatives, we had to prepare for what might occur at the point the Germans capitulated.

I was informed the Resistance had 150 men and about 15 policemen, but only enough weapons for about 120. That armament consisted of two machine-guns, some rifles and pistols. The stock of ammunition was sufficient. On the first night, at a meeting, the local representatives of the liberation movement and

I discussed our three main tasks. 1) The detention and disarming of any remaining German forces in Odder, as well as 2) the establishment of military roadblocks at the city's four main roads, and 3) ***the internment of Danish nationals who had behaved improperly during the occupation years. [Author's emphasis in bold]*** *The details for the solution of these three tasks were discussed at meetings in the following days. On the fourth evening, after the announcement over the radio from England of the German surrender in Denmark, the local Resistance leaders along with parish council chairman Aage Knudsen and me, gathered in the home of the grocer, P.W. Christensen, in Rosensgade. After some negotiation, it was agreed that Knudsen would contact the German commander in the city to arrange the surrender, and he asked me to join him in negotiating with the German commander.*

At midnight we were received by the commander, Major Erdmann, at the Phoenix. The garrison at that time consisted of the following units: 1 Battalion 'Weisbach' of the Grossdeutschland, a smaller unit of the Luftwaffe (about 100 men) and 200 wounded German soldiers. Major Erdmann told us that he had received no orders and that the radio announcement was probably an English lie. He added that his battalion belonged to one of Adolf Hitler's premier units and that they would never surrender. He said in a sharp tone that if there was even the smallest demonstration in the city, he would crack down with an iron fist. He said that if any house in town flew any flags, it would be blown up, and if just one shot was fired at his men, he would immediately take 25 hostages, including Knudsen and me, and we could be executed.

On the question about whether he would resist Allied troops, he declared that if the British or the Americans approached, he would march out of town and possibly go into position to the south, but if the Russians came, the city would be levelled. He promised to inform me if he received any orders from his superiors.

The next morning we met again. The situation in the city was becoming more and more difficult, partly because the people had to take their flags down, while we heard on the radio how the rest of the country were celebrating the day … it was decided that I should contact the German High command in Silkeborg.

At this point, with tensions high, Lemvigh-Müller decided to play his old trick of relying on the Germans innate respect for uniforms, authority and military pomp.

I returned to the commandant's office wearing full uniform with peaked cap, and after some discussion, he declared that the police could take over responsibility for law and order, apart from the German military areas in the city, but that it was only the police who were allowed to maintain order. I made him aware that when the Germans took over from the police back in September 1944, they had taken their uniforms so he agreed that we would be identified by an armband. He promised to keep the German troops in their quarters, and only officers and orderlies – the latter equipped with passes issued by him – would be allowed to walk in the streets.

Roadblocks were set up and by the evening, the internment of Danish collaborators had begun. We interned about 125 people, all listed on the local Freedom Council's arrest lists. These were people who had directly worked for the Germans or who had been informants, but it was also in the interest of peace and order to arrest an additional number of people who had had intercourse with Germans or who had expressed German sympathies. As soon as was possible, examinations were held on all the easier cases, and the vast majority of detainees were released within a few days. About 50 people of those arrested were convicted and later sentenced.

The rest of the day was peaceful with no incidents of any kind. There were many people on the streets, but the Germans remained, as promised, in their own areas.

On the 6th of May we extended the agreement with the German commandant for a further 24 hours. On the 7th of May the commandant came to see me and informed me that his men would depart the next morning for a position five kilometres south of the city. Handguns with five shots per man were left with them, all other equipment was taken over by the Resistance. The main task of the Resistance had been accomplished without human lives being lost or Danish property having been destroyed.

What was left was the surrender of the remaining German troops, including the Luftwaffe unit who were accommodated at Odder University under the command of Lieutenant-Colonel Jessnitzer and who were ordered by the Royal Air Force to remain in Odder, as well as about 1,000 German refugees who had hitherto been billeted in holiday cottages in Hou and Saxild. From there they were transferred to Malling agricultural college, Testrup University, Rathlousdal and Holsatia in Hou. From these camps over the course of 1946, they were sent to other camps outside the area.

Visible traces of the German troops' stay in the district during the War hardly exists, but the years of occupation with all their moving events for those who experienced them will nevertheless always be remembered as a national disaster, which it is hoped the country will never see a repeat of.[3]

One of those 150 Resistance members Lemvigh-Müller was referring to was the local accountant, Poul Louring-Andersen, who wrote of the time:

> *On May 4, 1945 we heard the London liberation message. It was a moment I will never forget. We looked at each other and it was some time before it really dawned on us that the Germans in Denmark had capitulated.*
>
> *I went to see Thorvald and said I was ready if he needed me. There were lots of people in the streets, lots of joy and also relief that 'the five cursed years' were now over. But the very next day, May 5, when the capitulation was due to take effect at 0800 hours, everything took a turn for the worse. There were reports that the German commander in Odder would not surrender unless he received orders from the commander in Denmark, General Lindemann, who had his headquarters in Silkeborg.*
>
> *Conditions were pretty chaotic and it was impossible for him to contact Lindemann, and the commander in Odder threatened that his men would shoot freedom fighters if they appeared in the streets.*
>
> *It all quietened down and soon the Resistance took over. Some might argue that the M groups didn't make much effort, but I think, however, that the M groups were very important in helping us avoid a 'night of the long knives'.*

For Louring-Andersen it was indeed a time of blessed relief and celebration, but the same could not be said for the surviving Danish Waffen-SS veterans. They were most definitely on the 'Freedom Council's' arrest lists, and their future looked bleak as Denmark was convulsed by quasi-judicial revenge and acts of petty violence.

Magnus Møller had been home and out of the Waffen-SS for almost two years when the new authorities came calling.

MM: When the war ended nothing really happened straight away. My name wasn't on the lists of people they were arresting, but they did arrest my father as an NSDAP member, that was on 11 May 1945. He had been the local contact for anyone who had wanted to volunteer for the Waffen-SS and they charged him with 'agitation for German Army service'. I was working on a nearby farm at the time and was told of my father's arrest. I was pretty angry I can tell you.

Then on around the 10th or 11th of June 1945, I can't remember exactly which, I found out that the Danish police had discovered I had been in the Frikorps and so were going to come and arrest me. So, someone rang me and told me it would be better for me if I handed myself in first, which I did. I went to the police station and told them who I was, and that yes, I had been in the Frikorps, but now I was working on a farm and I said that if I was arrested who would look after the animals, but they just said, 'Fuck you, we're going to arrest you anyway.' Then they said that my father would be released if I went quietly and didn't make a fuss, and I would then take his place in prison, so that's what I did. I was sent to Faarhus Lajren Camp[4] *at first, and just sat there and waited to be told what was going to happen.*

They then told me that I had to go to prison for one and a half years! I didn't understand at all! I had done nothing wrong – I still think about it now, all these years later, and it still makes me so angry. I did nothing wrong and was still punished and sent to prison. Denmark is the only country in the world to have made a retrospective law that made it illegal to do something – that was to join the Frikorps – something that at the time was perfectly legal![5]

As it was, I went to prison and served about a year before being released, that was normal, to do about two-thirds or so of your sentence.

Magnus's astonishment at being arrested and charged may seem unutterably naïve to us, but it was a widespread belief amongst volunteers at the time, of whom a full third just didn't expect to be treated that way. Considering the legal position of the volunteers – particularly the original *Frikorps* men, which was questionable to say the least in terms of any guilt – Denmark turned on its own with real vehemence. Was this thirst for vengeance justifiable given how long the country had been occupied, or was this more about trying to whitewash a sense of national shame at the official policy of co-operation and the relative lack of resistance? It's impossible to tell, but there is more than a whiff of the latter.

The reality though was that Magnus was just one of the 15,274 Danes arrested and charged with collaboration. Of that veritable football crowd, 1,229 were acquitted, while the rest were convicted and handed prison sentences of anywhere between a year and life – although only 62 got the latter. For the majority it was one to two years, like Magnus, although 3,641 were penalised with four years or more. Alongside their prison terms, most lost their civil rights; the right to vote, to hold public office, to join the armed forces, etc. – 9,737 lost them temporarily and 2,936 lost them permanently.

Even more controversial was the special law of 1 June 1945 that brought back the death penalty in Denmark – something that had been abolished before the war. One hundred and twelve Danes were given this ultimate sentence by the courts, but in the end just 46 executions were actually carried out – Kobe

Martinsen being one of course – but Frits Clausen wasn't another as drink finally got the better of him and he died of a heart attack awaiting trial.[6]

Most veterans, who found themselves scattered across Europe as the war ended, now began an odyssey to return home.

IC: We were in Austria when the war ended, in a small village called Kleinarl. There was a farm-house by a lake and that's where we were staying at the time, and an officer came and told us that the war was over. We collected all our weapons into a big heap and our officers told us that from this point on we were relieved of our oath to the Waffen-SS and we would have to fend for ourselves, as we saw fit. Nobody told us what was to happen and that we were surrendering to the Americans, and I was naive enough to think that the Russians would soon show up and we would be handed over to them, and none of us wanted to be handed to the Russians, so that's why I decided to escape so I would not end up in Siberia.

The Americans put us all into a POW camp, not that it was a proper camp, it was a big field with some barbed wire, and there was very little supervision, not many guards at all and they were very relaxed. After a few days I decided the best thing to do was to get out of there and get home to Denmark. I was friendly with one of my Danish fellow soldiers – Jens Pørksen – he was from southern Jutland and he was promoted to Unterscharführer while we were in the POW camp, I asked him to escape with me but he didn't want to, so I promised to tell his parents that he was alright when I got home.

I got out past the wire – it was easy – and then headed off west. To avoid potential bloodhounds tracking me I walked for a long time in a stream on my way out of Kleinarl. I then put my Soldbuch in a small tin box and hid the box in a stone wall.

Trying to blend in with the local civilians I 'organised' some civilian clothing that was hanging from a clothesline and left my uniform behind.

My journey back to Denmark took me a couple of months, lasting from about the 15th May and ending in mid-July 1945. I mostly travelled on foot, but also got rides in cars and even became a stowaway on a train. Many times I hitched a ride on military vehicles – American or British. All of Germany was in chaos at this point with so many people travelling back and forth trying to get back home. The population was very helpful too and supplied food and shelter and also information about Military Police check-points so I could avoid them.

At some point in June I was close to Hamburg and thus the British occupation zone. When I asked around I learned that the River Elbe was heavily guarded and on all crossings there were check-points. After talking to a railway worker I learned that there was a train loaded with coal going north to a power plant somewhere. I told the railway worker I was trying to get home to Denmark and he showed me the waggons and I crawled into the coal and dug myself in so only my nose and mouth were above the surface, my face was all black anyways. After some waiting time the train finally started up and I crossed a railway bridge heavily guarded with spotlights and soldiers looking down from higher up. They didn't see me and I managed to get across. On the far side of the bridge the waggons were pushed onto a side-track to await their next leg of their journey. This was where I jumped off the waggon, and landed just besides another railway man who said 'you look a mess' and then he said 'follow me, I'll show you where you can get cleaned up and I'll also find you some new clothes' and he gave me some green soap too. It was a good feeling to have a real bath and have new – well, second-hand – clothes, and I looked somewhat civilized once again. I thanked the railway worker many times and jumped on the next north-bound waggon. This train was bound for Lübeck so I jumped off and continued on 'the thumb', a skill I had become quite good at.

As I had passed Schleswig and was close to the border I went into a house to ask directions. I was lucky because the man that lived there was a former customs officer and the border was literally just in his backyard. He said 'sit down and get something to eat and tell my why you are so interested in the border.' I told him I was heading home to Denmark but had no papers so had to cross without the authorities knowing. He understood, and said, 'Stay in the garden and wait for the border patrol to pass, the border here is nothing but a ditch anyway and you can cross even without getting your feet wet. After crossing the ditch, go into a plantation and through it, and then after a few kilometres you will come to a road, and that leads to Aabenraa (Åbenrå), and that's where you want to go.'

And that's exactly what I did – I waited until the border patrol had gone and headed over the ditch and into Denmark. Early next morning I came to Stolling, which is close to Aabenraa and it's where Jens Pørksen's family lived, so I went to their address and told them their son was still alive and was in Austria and would come home later on. They gave me a meal and some clothes and bought me a train ticket to Odense, my hometown. When I arrived in Odense I went straight away to see my mum and step-dad. It was my mum who opened the door and she just said, 'So there you are, about time you got home,' but I could tell she was happy to see me. A short time after there was a knock on the door and I hid behind the front-door – that opened inwards – and outside were two guys from the Resistance. One said: 'Mrs Nielsen, have you seen your son?' and she replied: 'No I have not, have you?' The

Resistance guy went on: 'We have been told he was sighted on the Fredericia railway station' and my mum answered: 'That's great, so he's alive after all.' After this the Resistance guy finished by saying: 'If you see him please tell him we wish to speak with him at the Domhus [Author: courthouse] on Albanigade [Author: Albani street]' and after this they said a polite farewell and left. Who and how anybody recognized me at the Fredericia train station is a riddle to this day.

After the Resistance had left, I got a cup of coffee and a piece of bread and said to my mum: 'I better go to the Domhus and find out what they want.' When I arrived at the Domhus I went to the front desk and said to the person behind the counter: 'My name is Ivar Corneliussen, you want to talk with me?' This created an uproar right away and I had a machine-gun barrel shoved in my back and was ordered to put my hands up. I said: 'No way, if you want to shoot me, do it! The Russians never got me, so you try your luck!' They didn't like that and I got a beating and was thrown into a cell.

There were three other guys in the cell, they were: Peder Borg, 55 years old; a farmer and member of the Danish Nazi party, Martin (I can't remember his last name), 25 years old; and a former member of the Westland's 3rd Company. Martin later bought a gravel pit and did very well, he wanted me in on the business but I didn't have the money, and possibly I wasn't motivated either. The last one was Uffe (I can't remember his last name either), he was 20 years old and had been working for the Wehrmacht. So, we were four men in the cell; Peder slept on the bed because of his age, the rest of us on mattresses on the floor. After some time, I think it was about September or October 1945, the staff guarding us were changed to normal prison staff, and then on the 16th of October 1945 I was presented to a court in the Domhus in Albanigade in Odense. I was to face a jury of lay assessors. The court comprised one judge, E. Lunøe, and three lay assessors whose names I can't remember.

The charges were read out to me; I had participated in the war on the German side as a Waffen-SS volunteer and as such I was charged with treason! I declared 'not guilty' as I had volunteered on behalf on an official Danish government call for arms to join the Waffen-SS. Then the judge said 'you should have understood that was pure performance' and then went on 'why didn't you desert when you were on leave in August 1943' – and I answered back, 'Your honour, have you ever been a soldier?' He answered no and I said, 'Then you have no ability to understand me. You do not turn your back on the oath you have given as a soldier.' Then the judge handed down my sentence, one year and three months, and a five-year loss of all civil liberties.

It is very clear in my memory that this was a light sentence as I knew the penalty for treason was a minimum of four years.

After my verdict I was moved to the 'Tvagen' [Author: no translation possible, it's a nickname] in Klaregade in Odense and was sent to a cell up under the roof. Here I met the painter Claus Clausen with whom I later worked out an electrostatic pulver coating system, he had the idea and I the know-how. This system was later sold to the Cabinplant factory, you know.

About a month later I was moved to Bogense prison, this was a nice place to be. The cell doors were open during the daytime, we had free passage inside the jail, and the prison warden's wife cooked a great meal. Here I was up till Christmas time, and I was getting sick and tired of braiding straw for door mats and shoes, so I applied to be transferred to an outdoor prison camp, and was sent to Nyborg prison. It was an old barracks built by the Germans and we worked most of the time on nearby farms so we were all outside most of the time.

Everything was fine there, and then one day I was called to the prison warden's office – now it gets hard to remember – but I'm pretty sure I had done eleven or twelve months by then and was only a few months short of the end of my sentence when I was called in, and the warden told me, 'Sign this, saying you regret everything you have done and you will be released right now.' My answer was, 'I sign no papers and I do my time in full.'

Two days later I was once again called to the warden's office and he said: 'We don't want you anymore, you're free to go.' I got my civilian clothes back and about 45 Danish krone that I had earned for my work while in prison, and that was that, they let me go home.

I got a job then, as a sailor; it was what I'd always wanted to be. I joined a Norwegian merchant marine company and worked my way up until I became the 3rd Engineer on a tanker.

By far the luckiest of all the Danish volunteers I interviewed – in terms of the way their own war ended – was Andreas Fleischer. His unit, the Totenkopf, had a reputation both as a fearsome fighting force, and as a perpetrator of some infamous war crimes such as the Le Paradis massacre of British troops in 1940. The Red Army certainly had no love for it – or for any Waffen-SS formation to be fair – and so as the war fizzled out, the division disengaged from fighting the Soviets in Austria and attempted to surrender itself en bloc to George Patton's Third Army on 9 May 1945. The Totenkopf's commander – Hellmuth Becker – reached an agreement with the Americans whereby they would accept the surrender on condition that his men disarmed the remaining SS guards at the nearby Mauthausen concentration camp. Job done,

Becker and his men handed themselves over to the Americans, only to be immediately gifted to the Soviets over the next two days. The gulags then swallowed them up. Within six months many senior Totenkopf officers simply disappeared – presumably executed or dead from maltreatment, starvation or disease – along with large numbers of their men. Becker himself was tried in Poltava for war crimes in November 1947 and sentenced to 25 years' forced labour. He was tried for additional crimes some time later, convicted and executed in February 1953[7] in Camp No. 337 near Sverdlovsk.

AF: I knew I was very lucky. Some of the men from the Totenkopf got home, but most of the division was handed over by the Americans to the Russians and sent to the gulags. I had a friend who was with them and survived, a driver, Danish like me, and I asked him what happened when I saw him again years later, and he said a lot of them died. He said he once saw a Russian tank shoot down 500 Totenkopf men because they couldn't work anymore, that was the rule, if you couldn't work you were shot. The Totenkopf men then said – those who survived – that if they'd known they were going to be handed over to the Russians they wouldn't have surrendered but would have gone further west and carried on fighting. But so many were handed over to the Russians – the Vlasov Army for example, they were all shot, all of them.[8] *The Americans handed over so many, and the British too.*

So, getting wounded and being sent to the rear may well have saved his life.

AF: I was sent to a hospital in a small town in the Bavarian Alps – a hospital town – and we were told we couldn't have any weapons there – no weapons were allowed in the whole town – so, all the weapons were thrown away, most of them were dumped in a nearby lake – that was May 1945.

The war finished then, it was over, so we were now Prisoners of War. We just sat there and an American officer came, Major Salman, and he wanted a German officer to talk to, to represent us, and a Leibstandarte[9] *Hauptsturmführer came forward and he was called Salman – could you believe it, they were half-brothers! Their mother had left Germany years before and gone to America and remarried an American, and they had had a son – the American Army Major Salman.*

The Americans knew we were Waffen-SS of course, we had our blood group tattoos – on our left arms here – I still have mine, it's an 'O'. They took us all to a big camp near Regensburg, and we were searched by Americans who tried to take everything off us ... they were always after souvenirs the Americans, anyway, both Salmans, American Major and German Hauptsturmführer, told them to leave us our pocket knives and so on. I hid my cuff title for the Theodor Eicke Regiment in the lining of my trousers, I sewed it in, but later on we were given new trousers and I forgot it was there and handed my old trousers in and they were burned, and so my cuff title went up in smoke.

We were put in tents behind some barbed wire, and American soldiers would come up and stare at us through the wire like we were animals in a zoo.

One day an American officer with a loudspeaker appeared and called out to us all, 'All Wehrmacht men go over there to the left, and all Waffen-SS men on the other side to the right'. We all went where we were told, and it turned out there were more than 200 of us Waffen-SS – that shocked them, the Americans, especially as the camp had a rule that the guard had to be doubled if there was even just one Waffen-SS man in it, and now they had over 200!

We were from all sorts of Waffen-SS units as well; Totenkopf, Leibstandarte, Reich,[10] *and lots of volunteers; Dutchmen, Danes, Norwegians. Then, one night in February 1946, we were taken to a new camp and there was nothing there, just a bit of wire, no tents, no nothing. An officer of ours, a Leibstandarte Hauptsturmführer who was from here, from the Denmark borderlands just like me, he went up to the Americans and said he wanted to see an officer. A sergeant appeared and asked what he wanted and he said he would only speak to an officer, so an officer then appeared, a lieutenant, and the Hauptsturmführer said he wanted wood for fires, and tents for us to sleep in, and the American said: 'Who do you think you are?', and the Hauptsturmführer asked him if he knew who he had in the camp, he said 'We're Waffen-SS, and if you don't get us these things then we're going to come over this wire and take them from you!' Anyway, we got what we asked for! Those Americans were new, they hadn't fought in the war and they were scared of us – very scared I can tell you. Even though we were unarmed and the war was over they knew better than to mess with us!*

I got to know one of the American drivers you know, a guy from Boston, and he was a nice guy but he didn't like black people, and he was very rude to his own Negro soldiers. I remember once he was asked by a Negro soldier for a match for his cigarette and he said, 'No, I don't have any,' when I knew he did, so I asked him why he did this, and he said, 'I don't give anything to blacks.' He wouldn't even allow black soldiers on his truck.

In the end I was kept prisoner by the Americans until July '46, and then I was sent back to Denmark. I was sent home with a group of other volunteers, and we went via Hamburg, and when we arrived there we were staying just outside the city, and the Americans told us they were going into town and we had to stay where we were. It was a real shame, we'd have loved to have gone into the city and enjoy ourselves a bit.

One of our guards on the journey home was Danish, he was from Greenland of all places, but had gone to America years before and was now an American citizen.

When we finally reached the border we were held by the Danish police for 14 days. I was interviewed by the police and I said: 'It was allowed, the Danish government said I could join the Waffen-SS', and the policeman told me: 'You shouldn't believe everything you're told!', and I thought that was that, but a few days later they let me go, and so I went home. I saw my father then. He was being held in a prison camp and I saw him through the wire, and I went up to him and the guard told me to stay away from him, but I said: 'Shut up, it's my father, I haven't seen him for two years and I'm going to talk to him now and you can't stop me.' He had been imprisoned for being a civilian worker for the Germans, but he was released soon after that.

As for me, I got a job working on an airfield.

Having spent his time behind barbed wire in Germany, Andreas avoided the judicial trawl that captured the likes of Magnus and Ivar in its net. The result is that all these decades later Andreas is relatively sanguine about the Danish State, while Magnus and Ivar simmer with resentment about the way they were treated.

MM: Thousands of young men, all volunteers, so many died, and those that survived were then punished – not the politicians, oh no, they weren't punished, just us, just the ones who fought. It was humiliating, and even now it's seen as a bad thing to say that you were in the Frikorps, but I don't care, I say I was in anyway! I was sent to prison and I can't forgive them for that, not ever, they made me a criminal when I'm not.

The anger felt by some of the Danish veterans was as nothing though compared to what I found among most of the Norwegian ex-front fighters and their families and friends. In fact, I would describe it as visceral – it was like a festering wound with them – always there, just covered with a scab, and if I scratched it, even just a little, it would bleed anew, releasing an outpouring of indignation.

Elizabeth Kvaal (EK): I was a governess on a farm during the war. After the war, because I was ex-NS, I lost my civil rights for 10 years, and a 10,000-krone bequest left to me by my aunt was confiscated. I suppose I was lucky though because so many others were sent to prison and I wasn't. But the worst thing was that everyone who hadn't been NS looked down on me as well, as if I was a lower form of life, as if I wasn't quite human. It made me so angry!

Anyway, I had to find work, to get a job, and it was very difficult because of my background, and then by accident I bumped into an ex-pupil of mine in the autumn of 1947 who offered me a job picking apples during the harvest, and that was where I met Ørnulf, he was picking apples too.

We talked a lot as we worked and he told me about how he had volunteered, and that after enlisting he stayed in Norway for a while because his parents were elderly and he needed to look after them, and then off he went to Germany. He ended up in Berlin and was there at the end of the war. He changed into civilian clothes to try and escape the city, but was taken prisoner by the Russians.

He managed to escape and was given shelter by two women, but was then recaptured by the Russians.

They sent him to a camp northeast of Moscow at first, and then onwards to another one – he spent eight months in those two camps. The second camp was far better than the first, but even so there was very little food. The second camp was for captured officers and those the Russians considered 'specialists'. He was treated as a spy because of a mix-up with his surname as they thought he was another man called 'Kvaal'. He was then sent west in coal wagons to Vienna along with other prisoners. That was 21 December 1945 – I remember that because it was his birthday. He then was sent on to Holland and then finally Belgium on New Year's Eve. He was worried at the time because lots of other prisoners were being arrested in their home countries, then tried, convicted and sentenced to death. He was put on a boat at Antwerp and shipped to Gothenburg in Sweden in either January or February 1946 – I can't remember exactly which – and from there he came back to Norway by train.

When he got back he thought he would be arrested, but he wasn't, but when he went home his parents told him to go away. He ended up staying with some friends, and called himself 'Christian' to try and hide his identity, but after a few months the police knocked on the door and took him away. They only kept him for a couple of months because by then it was 1947, all the trouble had died down, he was still ill from the war you know, but even so he was convicted and they fined him 10,000 krone – that was about ten years' wages back then – and sentenced him to three years in jail, but he didn't serve any of it – so he was lucky! He also had to report to the local police twice a week until 1955. I remember in 1949 we went on our honeymoon to Copenhagen and had to get the permission of the police to do it, and one of the police had to act as the guarantor that we would return – I brought him back a lovely cheese from Copenhagen to say thank you. Having children helped too – we had four children in five years and they were reluctant to take him away from his pregnant wife and young children.

Eventually Ørnulf got his dental licence back, but it cost us 10,000 krone to secure it – my father helped by giving us some money for it – he was ex-NS too, of course, and knew how hard it was for us.

KM: When the war finished, some members of the Home Front[11] *came to the hospital in the middle of the night and took away those injured and sick Norwegians who had served or worked with the Germans – that included a 16-year-old lad whose leg was in a cast – but the Home Front men didn't care, they just carried him out and threw him in the back of a truck.*

My family were all punished because we were NS. First, the police came and arrested my father. My sister was at home at the time and as he was being led out of our building a large crowd had gathered – many of them were our neighbours whom we had known for years and had always been friendly with. My father was very upset, and ashamed at being arrested in front of his daughter and all these people that he knew, so his shoulders were slumped and his head was down, but my sister called out to him so everyone could hear; 'Stand up straight, father, you haven't done anything wrong and have nothing to be ashamed of.' – Well, that was it, the crowd went mad and started to shout at my father and sister, and then they began to push them and shove them, and the next thing you know they're attacking them, punching, kicking and spitting – my father and sister said it was very scary, they thought they were going to be killed, and if the police who were there hadn't intervened and protected them then I think they would both have been killed.

JB: I was arrested on May 9 1945, and the only weapon I had on me at the time was a shotgun. I told the men who arrested me that I wasn't dangerous, I even knew some of them; they were from my district. There were about four or five of them and they had a lorry with some other prisoners in it. They also arrested my 17-year-old younger brother who hadn't joined the Waffen-SS but had signed up for some sort of 'behind the lines'[12] *stuff for after the war that the Nazis were planning – Quisling had stopped all that nonsense thank goodness, but my brother still spent two to three months in prison despite having never done anything.*

They also arrested a 15-year-old lad in Hamar! Unbelievable, a 15-year-old! Tell me, what could he have done?

After I was arrested my comrades told me not to say I was trained at Vikersund as it would make my punishment worse – one guy who had been trained there got seven years' hard labour! I was never convicted in a court of any crime but was instead made subject to an administrative order – the forelegg[13] *– and was in prison from May to 23 December 1945. I lost my civil rights and my right to join the armed forces, but I was called up anyway – but I refused to go – I told them they had sent me to prison and taken away my civil rights so why should I be a soldier and protect them?*

After I got out of prison it was Christmas of course, and it was that Christmas that I met Ingeborg – for the third time, I have to say – at a party, and I realised there and then that she was the one for me, and that was that. I was 19 and she was 18.

I had to find a job and start earning some money, and that wasn't a problem for me because I could work on my father's farm, so work wasn't a problem for me like it was for a lot of others.

They just couldn't get a job, and were scratching around for money to live.

It was good that work wasn't a problem, but the attitude of some people towards me was terrible. Several people refused to even say hello to me. I remember I was working on my parents' farm and a neighbour used to cycle by every day and wouldn't say hello, even though he could see me and had known me for years. Then after a while he started to say hello and he told me he'd forgiven me for what I'd done.

I was so angry I can tell you – I didn't want forgiveness – forgiveness for what? I hadn't done anything, and who was he to say he 'forgave me'? I have always been tall and I was a big, strong lad then, so, I went right up to him and just stared at him, my face was inches away from his, and he blinked and backed off, got back on his bike and cycled off pretty fast. And you know what, he never cycled past our farm again, not once, but went a longer way around.

Jostein's fellow ski troopers – Asbjørn Narmo and Stål Munkeberg – were more matter-of-fact about their punishments.

SM: I was arrested a few days after the war ended. As I said, I hadn't heard a shot fired in anger, not one, but that didn't matter to the authorities; I was still tried, convicted and sentenced to three years in jail. I ended up serving two years, two months and 14 days in the end. I'm sure those last 14 days were for the 14 days I spent at the front!

AN: I was arrested in May 1945 on my elder brother's farm, by a well-known local man who came with about five or six other men in an open-backed lorry – they were all armed – I don't know why, were they expecting trouble? So, they all had guns, but they hadn't practised with their weapons – you could tell – and it was a miracle there weren't any accidents, they were so sloppy with them. I was sent before the preliminary court at the end of 1945 – when that should have happened in 24 hours after my arrest – and I was sentenced to three years and three months in prison. I also lost my civil rights for 10 years.

Bjørn Lindstad being Bjørn Lindstad, things were somewhat different for him – not least because he had deserted. It can't be overstated how big a deal that was. Desertion is a crime that all militaries take extremely seriously and have traditionally punished in the harshest possible manner, and for entirely understandable reasons – if soldiers can just leave when they wish then there is very little chance of maintaining any sort of discipline under the stress of combat. The Wehrmacht was no exception, and during the war it issued death sentences to no fewer than 50,000 of its own men – with more than half of them carried out.[14] As it was, Bjørn ended up being arrested and punished like everyone else, but unsurprisingly the veteran with the never-ending smile looked back on it all a bit differently from many of his former comrades.

BL: I have no regrets about my service, and I am not bitter about what the State did to me, not bitter at all. They just did what they thought was right – I don't think it was the right thing, but that's that.

My war ended when we deserted, of course. We went home to my father's house and he rowed us – there were two of us, me and my friend Gustav Svalland from the Norge – over to a cabin on a little island. We were outlaws then. My brother came with a girl in a lorry and rowed over a week later to tell us the war was over. We were so pleased I can tell you!

We left the island and went to Hamar to celebrate but the town was just full of rubbish as everyone had been celebrating and we'd missed the party. We went back to the cabin and my father came across again with food and drink for us and so on.

We just stayed there for a while and played games – like outlaws! A few days later I went home, the police had been there, and I went to the prison to hand myself in, but the guard said I couldn't go in as it was a prison, so I told him who I was and that I was a front fighter and all of a sudden, he pointed his gun at me and started to wave it around – he was so scared – he thought I was going to pull a gun or something and shoot him down!

They marched me inside and the next thing I knew they put me with a lot of other arrested men – mostly ex-NS members. We were sorted into groups and screened so we weren't with friends, and five of us were put in cells meant for one person. In my cell there were two farmers and a goldsmith among the five of us – what danger were they?

Conditions weren't great; there was a bucket in the corner for our toilet, which was filthy and stank. It was a good thing we weren't fed much so we didn't have to use it a lot!

I considered myself innocent, I wasn't NS, and I thought they would soon sort it out so I wasn't worried. My cellmates were nice guys, they weren't criminals either.

I was in that prison for six months, and my total sentence was one year and nine months hard labour. They moved me to an old Arbeidstjensten camp[15] *and we turned it into a prison by converting it ourselves with materials supplied to us.*

After that we were put to work during the days to go and work on local farms, and that was good as we got more food, and on release after 15 months there I was given a tiny bit of money from the State for my work. I then went home.

In truth I think I was lucky to be locked up at that time as it meant I was away from all the trouble that went on when some Norwegians took revenge. I didn't like that, as I knew there hadn't been much resistance during the war and I thought people were just putting it on now that the Germans had lost. There was a Norwegian historian who said that five percent of the population was active on the German side, five percent on the Allied side and the other ninety percent were in the middle and just sat watching and doing nothing. In the end, though, everyone wanted to be part of the Resistance, and the less they had actually done the more they made out they had done. That's on their conscience, though, not mine.

Prison was also good for me in one other way – inside there were lots of highly educated prisoners, so I took courses run by them to learn lots of things. It put me on a different path in life. When I got out, I even took exams in business studies – I did a three-year course in one year and passed it.

The prosecutor at my trial helped me get a job after I got out of prison. I found out later – when they opened the archives – that this same man applied for me to get my civil rights back early so I could vote. He was very kind and I was grateful for what he did for me.

Notes to Chapter Seven

1. Atkinson, Rick, *The Guns at Last Light; The war in Western Europe 1944-1945*, p617, Abacus.
2. Ibid, p634.
3. As with all Lemvigh-Müller and Louring-Andersen's testimony, these accounts are held in the Odder local archives.

4. *Faarhus Lajren* – commonly called the Frøslev Detention Centre, was built in the municipality of Frøslevlejren in 1944, just next to the German-Danish border, and used by the Nazis to imprison political prisoners, resistance members, etc. Its official German designation was *Polizeigefangenenlager Fröslee*. With the end of the war it became a major destination for those arrested for suspected collaboration, and soon held more than 5,500 prisoners. Conditions were very bad and treatment could be severe, and there were deaths in the camp. The last inmates were released in October 1949. A part of the camp is now a museum and belongs to the Danish National Museum, but only the time pre-1945 is mentioned.
5. There is some dispute about the Danish government's role in the creation of the original *Frikorps Danmark*, with some opinions stating that whilst the government did sanction its establishment, it didn't actually form it, and therefore when it retrospectively made enlistment illegal it was acting appropriately. This can be seen as legal semantics, the fact being that as far as the volunteers themselves were concerned enlistment was perfectly legal and they were being victimised after the fact by a nation trying to cover up its own record of co-operation with the Germans.
6. Littlejohn, David, *The Patriotic Traitors*, p82, Heinemann.
7. Parrish, Michael, *The Lesser Terror: Soviet State Security, 1939–1953*. Praeger Press.
8. The Russian Liberation Army, also known as the Vlasov Army, was a group of primarily Russian forces that fought under German command during the Second World War. The army was led by Andrey Vlasov, an ex-Red Army general who had defected after being captured by the Germans in the 1942 Volkhov battles.
9. The 1st SS-Panzer Division Leibstandarte SS Adolf Hitler – Hitler's Bodyguard division.
10. The 2nd SS-Panzer Division Das Reich.

11. The Home Front was another name for the main Norwegian resistance movement during the war. During the occupation some 1,433 of its members were killed, of whom 255 were women. Dahl, Hans Fredrik, ed. *Norsk krigsleksikon 1940-45*, p414–415, Cappelen.
12. I assume this 'behind the lines stuff' refers to the Nazi Werewolf programme. This last-ditch diehard resistance movement never really got off the ground, although there were attacks on Anglo-American and Soviet personnel by Werewolf members (mainly teenagers) for months after the war in Germany itself.
13. The post-war Norwegian legal purge that allowed the government to act against ex-NS members, front fighters and so on, was the *Rettsoppgjøret*, enacted on 8 May 1945 – it followed an immediate law enacted on 5 May 1945 that – just as in Denmark – brought back the death sentence. It criminalised all Norwegians who had joined the Waffen-SS or any German military organisation, anyone who had volunteered for the German Red Cross and all members of the NS.
14. Atkinson, Rick, *The Guns at Last Light: The War in Western Europe, 1944-45*, p528, Abacus.
15. This was the Norwegian equivalent of the German Reich Labour Service. The *Arbeids-tjensten* was compulsory and was instituted in September 1940 to replace the previous conscripted military service. Due to a range of issues – not least the unwillingness of large numbers of those called up – the service was not a great success.

8

LEGACY

It is now more than 70 years since the guns at last fell silent at the end of the Second World War – a lifetime almost exactly, and yet in modern, three- or four-storey apartment blocks scattered across Denmark and Norway sit men and women for whom those war years were the defining times in their lives. Since then they have got married, had children, had careers, had grandchildren, retired, and had great-grandchildren, and yet the memories of that time are still there, still remarkably fresh – and for some, still painful.

Those flats they now almost all live in are light and airy, comfortable and clean, and filled with the mementoes and keepsakes we all seem to accumulate almost absent-mindedly as we wander through our lives. If you know what to look for, you can see clues to their past in some of those self-same mementoes; Magnus's biography of the controversial Danish Waffen-SS Knight's Cross winner Søren Kam on a bookshelf next to *The Da Vinci Code*, Karin's collection of Jonas Lie books, Asbjørn's front fighter award signed by Quisling on top of a shoebox in a closet – but even Sherlock Holmes would be hard put to find any evidence in some of the homes; Andreas, Elizabeth, Ivar and Bjørn's log cabin in the woods spring to mind.

But you would be wrong if you thought that a lack of chattels or photos on the mantelpiece indicates regret.

AN: After the war it was very hard to get a job if you were ex-NS like me, so I ended up setting up my own business – a concrete business – Narmo Concrete – 24 years it took me to build that company, and it did very well, I'm glad to say. It was hard work, though, and I used to give jobs to other ex-front fighters as no one else would hire them.

As for my service in the Waffen-SS I don't regret it at all, I volunteered for Norway and to stop the communists.

I stayed in touch with a lot of my old comrades after the war, but they're all gone now. We were all the best of friends. Was I scared at the front? Yes, I was, several times, like when Gust Jonassen was killed just a few metres away from me, I thought it could have been me, but I tried not to think about it if I could.

MM: After I was released from prison I met a lovely German girl and I didn't have to say anything to her about the war, she understood, she was from Pomerania, in eastern Germany, it's part of Poland now, so we got married and had three children. They knew I had been in the Frikorps and didn't like it, they thought I had been foolish.

I don't regret being in the Frikorps, not at all, and not ever, in fact I'm very proud of it, to have served and to have fought the communists. A German general, Gørtz[1] I think his name was, said he was very proud to have soldiers like us Frikorps boys to fight alongside them. I can't change anything from the past but I have no regrets.

I stayed in contact with other Frikorps veterans after the war, lots of them actually. My own group of veterans was called 'Memory Love of 1967' [Author: an ironic reference to the summer of love!]. We all lived in the southern part of Denmark, so we had good local contacts – trust me, there were lots of us. Mind you, the whole veterans thing wasn't special for me, what I really liked about it was seeing old friends, having some good coffee, talking about old times, you know how these things are – it wasn't about anything Nazi, or anything national socialist at all.

I don't know of any other surviving Frikorps veterans now, they're all gone, all except me and Helmuth Rasmussen in Copenhagen. Even now it's seen as a bad thing to say to people here in Denmark that you were a member of the Frikorps, and that you fought the communists.

IC: I am happy to talk to you about my service in the Waffen-SS. I have no regrets. I was never a hero! Not at all. *I was just a soldier. While on leave in Denmark in 1943 I met a girl, her name was Karen Margrethe Rigmor Jensen and I had written back and forth with her while I was in Russia. She was 11 years older than me. Karen was the only one to visit me while I was in jail. She'd rented a summerhouse and we spent a few days there after I got out. After the war I was really restless and had a hard time settling and I was suspicious of anything and everybody.*

SM: I learned English and German in prison and then went to work for Scandinavian Airlines. In the '50s – I can't remember exactly when – me and some other ex-Waffen-SS comrades went to Austria to a meeting, a reunion, with other ex-soldiers from America and Britain, we were just old soldiers then, you know. I am not interested in politics and all the comrades I served with are dead now.

I was so young back then – I was only just 17 at the time – I don't deny anything, but I don't brag about it either, that's not my style. I don't ask for forgiveness for what I did, but I have always wanted to move on. I don't owe anything to anyone else at all. I told my son about what I did when he was 13 or 14, I told him because I don't lie – I never lie. I have a good relationship with my son, but not with my brother or sister and their families because they haven't told their own children what really happened in the war.

I'm not afraid of dying, and I don't want to live to be 100. I'm not religious either, when you're gone it's just lights out! My wife died 12 years ago and I live alone now, and I am quite happy looking after myself.

JB: I have no regrets about my service – none. When you're a soldier, you're a soldier, nothing more, nothing less. For example, my father-in-law's uncle was the NS man who sank the Blücher in Oslo fjord in 1940, and that was the biggest success the Allies had during the whole invasion.[2]

It hurts though that people still talk about the NS and its members as if they were all bad and no one else was. We didn't do anything wrong, so we don't have anything to regret or ask forgiveness for, and that's what people on the other side don't, or won't, understand, and that's why there's been no reconciliation.

Let me tell you a story; my wife and I had a couple we were friends with, he was one of three brothers and all three had been front fighters – his wife had been a DRK nurse – anyway, to avoid trouble they hadn't told their children about what they'd done in the war, they kept it a secret, but their kids found out – one was a policeman and the other was in the health service. When they knew, they told their parents that they were 'Nazis' and that they shouldn't have had children – can you imagine that? Can you imagine your own children telling you that they shouldn't have been born because of what you did – and when what you did, you didn't feel any shame or regret for?

I don't think the opposing sides from the war can talk to each other – even now – that's what it's like here in Norway. It's such a shame, and for both sides it's the same.

Bergljot Østring: Bjørn never regretted his service in the war, he never hid his past and was very open about it – but he did have his blood group tattoo removed after the war because of the stigma attached to Waffen-SS service – most front fighters tried to hide their service, but weren't ashamed of it, if that makes sense.

Bjørn was far from being the only veteran who made an effort to disguise his past. Tales abound of German doctors removing the tell-tale tattoos to leave bullet-wound-resembling scars, and if no doctor was available then many men resorted to a razor blade and a slug of schnapps to perform a home-made operation.

This theme of 'no regrets' was familiar to me from my interviews with Flemish Waffen-SS veterans the previous year, but in Scandinavia one of the things that struck me most was that it wasn't just the veterans themselves, it was their families and more or less everyone connected in the wider sense, and it most definitely crossed the gender barrier.

KM: After the war it wasn't easy finding work as people didn't want to give jobs to ex-NS members like me. But eventually I managed to get a job in the tax department here in Oslo. It was a good job but it wasn't what I really wanted to do – I wanted to be a clothes designer – and so after a while I left and went to Stockholm to learn tailoring and cloth cutting, and I learnt sewing too.

I have no regrets about being in the NS or doing what I did in the war, but I told my children 'please don't go into politics!'

EK: Ørnulf died in 1992 aged 78. He used to tell people about his service, if asked, but he didn't talk about it too much as he didn't want to bore people with it all. He used to have nightmares, about being behind bars and having me and the children on the other side of them. He never told me what it was like at the front during the war, he just wanted to forget it. He didn't have any regrets though, we agreed on that, I did what I thought was right, and not to get any advantages or benefits. I've tried to explain that to my grandchildren, as they all think it was just black and white – the NS was bad, everyone else was good, and so on – and that isn't right. I joined the NS because I felt it was the right thing to do, and I have no regrets about it at all – none!

I had two cousins who served in the Waffen-SS during the war, and I thought that was fine, I didn't have a problem with it. I know the Waffen-SS were looked on as devils, but they looked at us all like we were devils anyway!

Both my cousins survived the war, but they're dead now. One died when he was 80 and the other when he was 94 years old. One of them even became the Mayor of his town, a small place of 800 voters near the Swedish border – Axel Stang[3] *was a neighbour of his. They both kept diaries during the war – just for the family – in them they wrote about what it was like at the front.*

After the war so many of us had nothing – nothing at all – so we used to help each other out all the time, for instance my husband had several ex-NS patients who couldn't pay him, but he treated them anyway.

I don't think I'll live to see it, but I hope that in the future there is a bit more objectivity about the NS, the war, and what really went on. I really enjoyed being in the same group of friends as the Østrings and all the others, they were my friends and the NS was a common bond between us – a special bond.

An interesting postscript to the post-war treatment and legacy of the Scandinavian volunteers was what happened to the black sheep of Iceland's first family, the Björnssons.

Having served in the Caucasus with the Kurt Eggers in 1942, the 34-year-old Björn Sveinn found himself in Copenhagen in 1943, taking on the role of Director for the national radio broadcaster after the previous incumbent was sacked for tacitly supporting the wave of strikes and demonstrations that swept the country. However, it was obvious that Björn did not feel that he was receiving the sort of support and recognition – either financial or in terms of rank – that he felt he deserved, as denoted by a number of letters he wrote to his superiors and which are now held by the US National Archives NARA (National Archives and Records Administration).

On 6 June 1944 – even as British, American, Canadian and Free French forces were storming the shores of Normandy – he wrote to his superior enquiring rather resentfully about his expected promotion, and asking for money to pay for his new uniform.

Unfortunately, I must discuss with you the issue of my promotion. Since I last contacted you a number of batches of candidates have graduated and received their promotions whilst I have not. It seems almost as if something stands in the way of my progress, and my promotion has been forgotten about. I would be very grateful to you if you could discuss this issue with your colleagues and send me a message on the matter as soon as possible.

I also received a message from my tailor – Chr. Schwarz & Sohn in Munich – which states that the jacket that I ordered last year is ready and will be sent to me. I would be very grateful to you if the 'Kurt Eggers' could transfer on my behalf 110 RM and 35 Pfennig to them as I have no bank account in Germany.

Heil Hitler!

Björnsson's correspondence must have had an effect, as there is also a letter in the Archive from a senior officer based in Berlin recommending the Icelander for promotion and detailing his 'good SS character'.

Justification:

Björnsson has an impeccable personality and sound ideals. He has a disciplined temperament and good mental ability. A hardworking and energetic soldier, he is disciplined and has a refined and exemplary bearing. As head of the Copenhagen League regimental structure, Björnsson has done an excellent job in recruitment efforts for the Waffen-SS and has increased our presence in the Danish media. He also proved successful in battle as a soldier in the invasion of the Soviet Union. He is the son of the current President of Iceland, which should be especially considered in the evaluation of his performance and his work.

The letter recommends a promotion date of 20 April which, as Hitler's birthday, was a date traditionally used by the Nazis to hand out awards and promotions.

At the end of the war Björnsson was caught up in the Danish judicial dragnet, arrested, and sent to prison, where he spent more than a year behind bars as a cause célèbre between Denmark and its former Icelandic possession – the Danes feeling pretty aggrieved that the islanders left them in the lurch – as they saw it – whilst they were under German occupation. Then in the winter of 1946, Björn's formidable mother and political *grande dame*, Georgia Hoff-Hansen, travelled to Denmark on a 'holiday' and privately lobbied the royal family and government for her wayward son's release.

It worked.

Despite howls of protest from the public, he was set free and quickly got himself to Sweden and out of harm's way, before being smuggled back home on a fishing boat.

I can only imagine how uncomfortable his homecoming was as he was reunited with his father and the rest of his family after so many years away in Waffen-SS and then prison uniform.

Iceland's President made his son promise to stay out of the limelight and try to bury his past, and Björnsson responded by strongly denying he had ever applied to join the Waffen-SS, insisting instead he had volunteered for the German military but had been assigned to the armed SS against his wishes. He further distanced himself from his past by taking himself and his family to Argentina to start a manufacturing business – making washing lines of all things. But the venture failed and he ended up back in Iceland. He then did all sorts; selling the British *Encyclopaedia Britannica* and acting as a tour guide for German tourists amongst other things. He wrote a memoir about his experiences too, and said of his service:

I never thought of myself as an accomplice in the Nazis crimes, although I was impressed with their policies and issues. I was deceived like millions of others.

This statement sat uncomfortably with the discovery a few years later of his original Waffen-SS application, where he stated: 'I certify that I am of pure Aryan stock. Heil Hitler!'[4] Perhaps he would also have recognised the US reporter Martha Gellhorn's sarcastic commentary on the Germans she met following the advancing Anglo-American armies into Germany in 1945:

> *No one is a Nazi. No one ever was, it would sound better if it were set to music, then the Germans could sing it as a refrain.*

Only one of the veterans ever carried a gun again after the war – Andreas Fleischer. He had been wounded three times while serving in the Totenkopf, but still hadn't gotten soldiering out of his system – in truth, having met him, I never thought he would. Andreas was no 'gentleman soldier', no civilian in uniform, he'd taken to the life and clearly found a vocation there.

> *AF: After the war I didn't think I should be a soldier anymore, then in 1946, or was it 1947, I got orders to report to the Danish Army. I didn't want to go but I did, and so I was sent to Haderslev for training. I turned up and all the corporals and lieutenants didn't know about my past, but the captain did, he knew. He said to me, 'You will see things here that are rubbish, things that aren't right, but you must remember that most of the men here have only learnt about being a soldier from books.' The rules at the time meant that if you had been in the Resistance during the war you got promoted, you were a corporal or a sergeant or even an officer – not because you knew anything or were a good solider, but because you had been on the 'right' side in the war. I remember talking to some of the men who were ex-Resistance and they were very proud of what they had done, and I said to them: 'Do you know you acted against*

the Geneva Convention?' They weren't happy I said that, but it was OK. They all soon found out about my time in the Waffen-SS and gave me a hard time about it, and then we got a new captain who had been in the Resistance, and everyone said that I was going to be in real trouble with him, but that was total rubbish! The captain and I became best friends!

I found soldiering in the Danish Army to be very easy. Most of our weapons at the time we had bought from Sweden, like our rifles, they were K98s – which were German, the same ones we had in the war. I knew how to handle all our weapons and use them to the best effect. I remember being called to see the company commander in his office one day and he told me that because of my service in the war I knew more than all the other platoon leaders about machine-guns, mortars, and even anti-tank guns – the guns we had were 37mm ones, again the same as the Germans had in the war – but he told me I just had to let them get on with it.

I spent ten years in the Danish Army in the end. Oh, one thing you might like, Herr Trigg – when I was in the Danish Army we trained with the British Army in Germany – on the Lüneburger Heide [Author: Lüneburg Heath – a famous German Army training area] and they could shoot those British boys, they were good.

Andreas made that last comment with a wink and a smile, proving that he wasn't past trying to butter up an author if he had the chance, but despite his amiability and hospitality, I couldn't leave without asking him about the elephant in the room whenever you interview a Waffen-SS veteran – war crimes. It's unnecessary to outline here the complex story of the Waffen-SS and wartime atrocities – other works do it far better and in far more detail than I could – suffice to say that alongside the battlefield exploits of the armed SS there are numerous well-documented instances of massacre and cold-blooded killing, which encompassed captured POWs, unarmed civilians of various nationalities, and Jewish people in particular. Some members of the Waffen-SS were even involved in the concentration camp system as guards and functionaries, both at work camps and extermination camps.

It is always an extremely difficult subject to ask the veterans about, but to not do so would be to purposefully leave out an extremely important part of history, and would be akin to refusing to see the dark side of what are ostensibly military narratives.

I also asked Ivar, Bjørn, Stål, Asbjørn and Magnus:

> *IC: We were just soldiers, we didn't have anything to do with the concentration camps, which were utterly horrible, by the way. I saw atrocities done by the Russians – I told you about that – but not by us.*

> *MM: I never committed any war crimes myself, and I never heard of any atrocities or war crimes being committed, and I definitely didn't see any; not in Demyansk, or Velikiye Luki, or anywhere. The Frikorps was just for volunteers and we had nothing at all to do with war crimes or concentration camps or anything like that.*

This was standard – the brick-wall of denial. That isn't to say at all that the veterans weren't telling the truth, but to deny even hearing or seeing something – anything at all – seems to be stretching credulity a bit far. After all, atrocities were (and still are) part and parcel of war.

Rick Atkinson – in his masterful book about the fighting in north-west Europe, *The Guns at Last Light* – details a whole string of American 'incidents'; on 22 December 1944 George Patton told his staff that no SS prisoners were to be taken until further notice, and then followed that up, when he and one of his staff were shot at by a sniper in Germany, by ordering all the local houses to be torched in retaliation. Then Eisenhower himself had to admit that 104 German POWs had suffocated to death while being transported across France in locked freight cars – the investigators found 'evidence of teeth marks and clawing' in the carriages once they were opened. Eisenhower was again called in after the Dachau concentration camp was liberated by horrified GIs from the 42nd and 45th Infantry Divisions, who shot several dozen of the SS guards who were standing amidst the mounds of murdered souls. At first the Allied Supreme Commander said that 'America's moral position will be undermined if these crimes went unpunished'[5] – can anyone think that a senior Nazi would have said the same had the positions been reversed? In the end the investigation and subsequent charges were quietly dropped, and I for one have no moral qualms about that decision.

Terrible as many of these crimes were, the fact remains that the incidents listed above were errors or simply old blood'n'guts excess, and not State policy, which was exactly what the Nazis' extermination of the Jews and vast swathes of the Soviet Union's peoples was.

Speaking of which – during my interview with Magnus, he went quiet for some time as he did throughout the interview, his blue eyes looking down as the shadows lengthened in the room, and then blurted out:

MM: When we were in Demyansk we were fighting together with troops from the SS Totenkopf Division and I'm pretty sure – but not 100% – that they committed some crimes, but I never saw anything personally, so I can't say whether they did or they didn't.

Before I could react to that statement, he spoke out again:

> *MM: Hitler had Jewish genes himself, did you know that? He was probably at least one quarter Jewish himself. As for Bobruisk it's a lie! There wasn't a camp there, nothing at all, it's all just been made up!*

He fell silent once more, his fingernails scratching away on the edge of his food tray.

Bobruisk was the topic that had almost killed off my trip to Denmark before it began – it was, after all, the main cause of the Wiesenthal Institute investigation that had silenced Helmuth Rasmussen and almost silenced every other living veteran. An article by the historian Dr Lea Prais on the Bobruisk camp is included as an appendix.

Clearly Magnus is mistaken in his assertion there was no camp at Bobruisk – there was, and it was a labour camp where Jewish inmates were imprisoned. The case against Helmuth Rasmussen is that for a short period of time, whilst he was in transit to his unit at the front, he was detailed as a guard on the camp's outer perimeter. There is no evidence (or suggestion) that he was involved in any killing or abuse of the prisoners, but it would seem next to impossible that he would be unaware of the terrible treatment inflicted upon them. I am no legal expert in what constitutes a criminal offence in such matters, but as the case was dropped by the Danish prosecutors then it would seem that the weight of judicial opinion is that his behaviour did not equate to a war crime.

As for Jewish Danes and Norwegians – Magnus brought the topic up himself, after all – the war was a tale of two very different outcomes.

Denmark's 'politics of co-operation' had shielded its Jewish citizens for the first years of the occupation, and then when the order finally came at the end of September 1943 to round them up and ship them off to their deaths, a middle-ranking German official – Georg Ferdinand Duckwitz – tipped off the Danish authorities and in the space of a fortnight the vast majority of the country's 8,000-strong Jewish community were shipped over to neutral Sweden and safety by fishing boat, ferry and trawler.

Norway's Jewish citizens were not so fortunate.

The treatment meted out to the Feinberg family from Oslo was typical; called to their local police station in the winter of 1942, they arrived to have their ID cards compulsorily stamped with the letter 'J' for 'Jude' in red. Monitored from then on, six months later the whole family was sent to Auschwitz and gassed.[6] Of the 2,000-plus Norwegian Jews, more than 700 were murdered in total.

Why does all this matter in regards to Scandinavian Waffen-SS volunteers? It matters for exactly the same reasons as for any veteran of the Waffen-SS, and there is evidence that atrocities were known about by some Scandinavian volunteers – and some even participated in them – albeit a very small minority.

Three Danish historians published a study on Danes in the Waffen-SS[7] based on diaries, letters etc., and interviews with 13 veterans. In their study they cite a number of cases including one in the Demyansk Pocket in 1942 where a Danish *Frikorps* volunteer wrote in his diary that he shot dead a POW who stole three packets of cigarettes from him; and that a company from the Regiment Danmark burnt down a Croatian village in the autumn of 1943 after it was fired at from that village.

While these incidents have been published, there wasn't a single instance where a Norwegian veteran had admitted to any involvement in atrocities – until 2013 when it so happened

I was in Oslo on a promotional visit for my books *Hitler's Vikings* and *Hitler's Jihadis*, which were being published there. I did a number of interviews for radio, television and the print media, and was looking forward to my TV appearance on the national NRK network being broadcast in particular, when at that precise moment a Norwegian ex-front fighter decided to speak up.

His name was Olav Tuff, he was 91 years old and the TV presenter who interviewed me – Mari Allgot Lie (a very nice woman indeed) – rang me to apologise that my piece was being put on hold so she and her fellow journalist Ola Flyum could devote the programme to Tuff's revelations.

Tuff, as it turned out, was born into grinding poverty on a farm in Sparbu, and after the war came he volunteered for the Wiking Division. While in the Ukraine in 1941 he took part in a massacre of local people:

> *In one instance in Ukraine during the autumn of 1941, civilians were herded like cattle into a church. Shortly afterwards soldiers from my unit started to pour gasoline onto the church and somewhere between 200 and 300 people were burned alive inside. I was assigned as a guard on the outside – no one came out ... There was a lot of yelling and screaming, and we barely believed what we became a part of, but there was little we could do, we had to do what we were ordered to ... The episode at the church was terrible, but it was only one of many episodes. I did not feel bad because we could not do anything to stop it. I am just telling you how I experienced it.*

This assertion, that he couldn't do anything about it, was not the case in a later instance when Tuff said he was ordered by a

German officer to shoot 16 unarmed Soviet prisoners. Thinking on his feet, Tuff told the officer that as a Norwegian citizen he could not – under Norwegian law – carry out the execution. The officer accepted this bold assertion and ordered some other soldiers – presumably non-Norwegians – to murder the POWs.

Strangely, Tuff went on to state that in his view he had not done anything he regretted but understood that other people would see it differently – and clearly his actions did affect him in some way as he later wrote to his younger brother Hermod, warning him not to enlist, citing the terribly harsh conditions in Russia, and also the extreme brutality he would be subjected to.

As it turned out the letter was too late – Hermod had signed up already – and ended up fighting on the Eastern Front. He survived the war along with his brother and both were tried and convicted of collaboration, with Olav sentenced to three years and eight months in prison.

There are no excuses for committing war crimes – but there is context – and it is that context that can help us understand how hitherto 'normal' human beings can be caught up in horrible events. The context for the Scandinavian front fighters fits that description, being as the war was one of the most brutal conflicts in Europe since the religious wars of the Reformation. This horror was further compounded by the sheer scale of the fighting, which was so vast as to be almost incomprehensible to the human mind – for example; in less than three weeks after the launch of Barbarossa, the German's Army Group Centre advanced 360 miles and inflicted 417,790 casualties on the Soviets, plus it destroyed 4,799 Red Army tanks, 9,427 guns and mortars and 1,777 aircraft.[8] The following year the Red Army amassed an armada of in excess of 32,000 tanks, and the Ostheer obliterated 15,100 of them[9] – the average Soviet T34 tank survived just six months after production – and it wasn't just machines either, it was men – 310,000 Soviet tankers were killed in action during the war, that's 78 percent of all trained Red Army tank crew.[10] The average Soviet infantryman at the time lasted just three weeks at the front before he was killed or seriously wounded.[11] Little wonder that studies at the time carried out by the US Army found that a man's combat skills began to decline after only a single month of fighting, and that many frontline soldiers appeared 'close to a vegetative state' at the 45-day mark – after about 200 days a man was judged to be permanently worn out – if he lived that long.[12] The trauma of modern battle also tended to be concentrated in a relatively small number of men – those the German Army referred to as the 'bayonet strength' of a unit; for example, a typical infantry division might be 14,000 men, with the same number or more supporting it in ancillary units, but there would only be around 5–6,000 frontline riflemen in there, and so it wouldn't take too long before a formation became relatively combat ineffective, or at the very least 'damaged'.

The brutality of it all must have been mind-numbing for both sides.

The historian Robert Forczyk said of the Russo-German war:

> *...there were brave and extraordinary soldiers on both sides, but it is a sad truth of military history that some of the most remarkable warriors have fought for some very shabby causes.*

The ex-front fighters themselves were more than aware of that particular truism.

> *IC: Stalin didn't care about his soldiers' lives, not at all. I even saw with my own eyes a Cossack attack, with all of them on horseback*

and waving their sabres. They charged towards us, it was madness, I couldn't believe what I was seeing. It wasn't just a handful either, there was lots of them, all those men and horses – what were they thinking? They must have been ordered to attack us. We had just been issued MG42s, and we mowed them down, dozens and dozens of them – men, horses, everything, it was just slaughter, the machine-guns shredded them. We had a Dutch commander at the time and he loved horses, so, after it was all over he sent us out into the steppe to shoot the injured horses and put them out of their misery – they were making a terrible noise – it was awful.

MM: What did I think of the Russians? The Russian soldiers weren't good or bad, they were just the enemy you know, killing them was just a job, that was all it was, a job. You killed them or they killed you – simple.

It wasn't just horses and the Soviets who suffered, it was their own SS comrades too, and reading between the lines I sometimes got hints of what might have happened in the heat of battle to enemy prisoners.

AF: I remember we found a Dutch Waffen-SS volunteer once who had been nailed to a gate, crucified, and he had been used for bayonet and bullet practice. That's what happened with the Russians. I heard our officers tell our soldiers when we had prisoners; 'No, you can't do that, stop it,' but officers can't be everywhere at once, so sometimes things could have happened, but war is like that, it's the worst thing you can do.

As a generation, those who became front fighters are fading now, and there is undoubtedly a sense that their own countries would like to erase their actions through neglect. Understandably, what Norway and Denmark want to remember from the war is their united struggle against occupation, the battle against tyranny, and not any inconvenient reminders that might conflict with that view. But to not remember, to not document, that there was a flip side to that coin, is both historically untrue and does a disservice to everyone who lived through those times – resistance and collaboration co-existed, anti-communism was strong, as was anti-Nazism – history is laced with nuance and the veterans provide us with a context we need in order to try and make sense of what happened.

In today's world, extreme political ideologies of the left and right are not the threats they were when the Scandinavian veterans I interviewed for this book were young and made the choice to volunteer. Turn on the television and you may see the occasional be-flagged march by a few hundred masked white supremacists, or another semi-farcical parody of communism in North Korea (and don't even mention China where communism has long been nothing more than a cover story for the dictatorship of the country by a self-serving oligarchy) – but in the 1940s and beyond Soviet communism was a genuine danger, seemingly hell-bent on fomenting revolution on a global scale – that's why we had the Cold War after all – and Nazism plunged us into the Second World War of course.

The Norwegian SS-Germania volunteer, Ørnulf Bjørnstad, said in his post-war interviews with the British Imperial War Museum that anti-communism was a big driver for his own enlistment:

I was never into politics – my brother-in-law was in the NS but I wasn't – but he knew a lot and he said to me that the best chance

> *of Norway being free was if we fought with the Germans. So, at the start of the war when I joined I made it clear to everyone that I was fighting with the Germans because they offered the best hope of beating communism. I had a lot of encouragement from my family and friends and I was glad to fight communism I can tell you, especially with everything I saw over in Russia ... It was only when the war started going against the Germans that peoples attitude changed to hostility against me and the whole German cause. This change of attitude dated from the defeat at Stalingrad in 1943 and the subsequent retreat.*[13]

People in the West were afraid, and that meant Scandinavians too – not least the Swedes. When quizzed about their reasons for smuggling themselves over the border and enlisting, Swedish veterans usually said they volunteered to fight ***against*** Stalin and communism and not ***for*** Hitler and Nazism.

Having said that, the list of Waffen-SS volunteers from the land of Volvos, Saabs and Abba might have only run into a few hundred at most, but there was alarm at an official level at the possibility of a Soviet invasion through neighbouring Finland, or even the northern tip of Norway.

Part of Stockholm's answer was to create an underground network of volunteers supported by secret arms and supply depots across the country, just in case the Red Army came barrelling in – it was called 'Sveaborg' – a name shared with the association of Swedish national socialists who fought in Finland during the Continuation War (some 20 percent of Finland's population were actually ethnic Swedes at the time).

The Reuters journalist, L. Foyen, wrote of it in December 1990:

> *The Sveaborg network, supported by the US CIA and Britain's MI6, was created by the Swedish government in 1958, and existed until at least 1978. It included 150 standby resistance leaders and special arms depots across Sweden. Its existence was known only to the Prime Minister, a few selected cabinet ministers, military leaders and leading industrialists ... It was led by the Swedish businessman, Alvar Lindencrona, whose work for the International Chamber of Commerce made it possible for him to travel inconspicuously to the US and Britain for briefings with the CIA and MI6 ... It is unclear what happened to the organisation after 1978 when Lindencrona retired. He died three years later.*

What makes this relevant to the story of the Scandinavian Waffen-SS was that according to a report in the British newspaper, *The Guardian*, at around the same time in 1990, the Swedish Army's Chief of Staff, General Bengt Gustafsson, not only confirmed Sveaborg existed but that it had strong links to Swedes who had fought in the Finnish-Soviet war and went on to join the Waffen-SS:

> *Right wing extremists in Sweden were part of the stay behind set-up and I cannot understand why the Swedish authorities never took a closer look at it.*

The anti-fascist publication and website, *Searchlight*, insists that Sveaborg still exists and that adherents – including several who were members of the Waffen-SS – come together on the 14th of April every year in Stockholm's northern burial site to honour the memory of Gösta Hallberg-Cuula, a Swedish-Finnish member of Lindholm's pre-war movement who was later killed in action on the Finnish front.

But in reality the gathering of a handful of right-wing extremists at a graveside means very little, and has no linkage to the story of the Scandinavian front fighters.

I will let the veterans and their widows have the last word – this is their story after all – and it is their voices that this book means to capture.

EK: I'm old now – very old – and who cares, no one, I think, not really, we just get on with life. Do you know that my daughter-in-law is a well-known member of the Norwegian Labour Party? We get on well, her and I. It can be quite difficult sometimes but we both try hard for the sake of my son – next Sunday I'm going to her 70th birthday celebration – that'll be her THIRD 70th birthday by the way!

BL: My conscience is clear, the biggest crime I committed when I was in the Waffen-SS was that I stole a chicken! I told that story to a Norwegian-American who was in the American Army, and he told me that when he and his friends were fighting across Germany they didn't 'steal' any chickens, they 'freed' them! He told me they also 'freed' paintings and anything else they could lay their hands on.

In the '60s I had a lump in my leg and I went to the doctors and had it removed, and it was sent away and it turned out to be a piece of shrapnel. Once I was X-rayed to see if I had tuberculosis and I asked them to check if I still had any shrapnel left in me.

Do you know one of the things I remember the most from the war? It was the swamps at Narva – they were full of mosquitoes and this attracted lots of birds, one of which was a cuckoo that got closer and closer until it was sitting in the same tree as me. Then

> *it flew over to the Russians. It happened again the next day – the same thing. There's a saying in Norwegian fairy tales that if you sit under a tree with a cuckoo in it and it sings then you get three wishes and they all come true as long as you're not too greedy – if you are then you will be punished. I thought it was just superstition but then I thought why not, no one will see or hear me or think I'm stupid, so I spent a couple of days deciding what to wish for. One of the things I decided to wish for was marriage, as my commander was married and he used to get letters from his wife back home and he used to read us bits of them and it sounded wonderful. My second wish was that I survived, and the last one was to have a good life. I climbed up to the cuckoo bird and made the wishes and then climbed down, and then I did the same thing the next day. And, you know, all my wishes came true!*

As for Magnus and Ivar, the last time I saw Magnus he pointed to the glass-fronted cabinet in his flat, where there was a framed pencil drawing of him as a young man:

> *MM: That was done by my best friend Max. He was in the Frikorps with me and survived the war, just like I did. He drew that picture in 1946, it's a good one isn't it? I can't remember his surname now, I can see his face in my mind, but can't remember his surname, that's age for you!*

For Ivar it is all gone – less than two months after I interviewed him I received word he had passed away in his sleep.

I remember interviewing him in his neat, over-heated bungalow, family photos vying for wall space with cheap oil paintings of generic mountain and nature scenes, the floor covered with rugs, all neatly laid out and not a hint anywhere of his wartime service.

Physically he'd been quite frail, the eyelid drooping over his left false eye, the short-sleeved shirt revealing old merchant navy tattoos, but his mind was still clear, his arms waving around as he sought to emphasise this point or that – now gone, his last words captured by my dictaphone.

An American rifleman in the 26th Infantry Division wrote a letter home from Europe in late 1944 and included the following line: 'No war is really over until the last veteran is dead.'[14]

While it is a great line, I would suggest that a better one might be 'No war is ever really over – ever.'

Notes to Chapter Eight

1. This is most likely to be Heinrich Götz (1 January 1896 – 31 of January 1960), a German general who commanded the 21st Infantry Division during the war.
2. When the Germans invaded Norway and sailed up the Oslo fjord, the overall commander of the Oscarsborg Fortress guarding the fjord was the 65-year-old Colonel Birger Kristian Eriksen, and the main gun battery's deputy commander was Lieutenant August Bonsak – the latter was an NS member. Even though the guns were obsolete and war hadn't been declared, Eriksen didn't hesitate and ordered the battery to open fire, sinking the German flagship, the 16,000-ton heavy cruiser, *Blücher*. Eriksen's words apparently were: 'Either I will be decorated, or I will be court-martialled. Fire!' Lofoten Krigsminnemuseum.
3. Axel Stang was Quisling's Minister of Sport and Chief of Staff of the NS Rikshird paramilitary wing.
4. All details on Björnsson reproduced by kind permission of Jökull Gislason.
5. Atkinson, Rick, *The Guns at Last Light: The War in Western Europe, 1944–1945*, p466, p568, p525, p613, Abacus.

6. S-1708 Sosialdepartementet, Våre falne, Ec 21 A. Riksarkivet/ National Archives of Norway.
7. Christensen, Claus Bundgård, Poulsen, Niels Bo, Smith, Peter Scharff, *Danskere i Waffen SS 1940–1945 – Danes in Waffen-SS 1940–1945*.
8. Glantz, David M., *Before Stalingrad – Barbarossa and Hitler's Invasion of Russia 1941*, p35, Tempus.
9. McNab, Chris ed., *Hitler's Armies: A History of the German War Machine 1939–45*, p224, Osprey.
10. Merridale, Catherine, *Ivan's War – The Red Army 1939–45*, p187, Faber and Faber.
11. Clark, Lloyd, *Kursk: The Greatest Battle, Eastern Front 1943*, p98, Headline.
12. Atkinson, Rick, *The Guns at Last Light: The War in Western Europe 1944–1945*, p341, Abacus.
13. Imperial War Museum, Oral History, catalogue number 17649.
14. Atkinson, Rick, *The Guns at Last Light: The War in Western Europe 1944–1945*, p641, Abacus.

APPENDICES

APPENDIX A – Waffen-SS and Comparable British Army Ranks

SS-Schütze	Private (this was the basic private rank, any speciality would be reflected in the title, e.g. Panzerschütze – tank trooper)
SS-Oberschütze	Senior Private (attained after six months' service)
SS-Sturmmann	Lance corporal
SS-Rottenführer	Corporal
SS-Unterscharführer	Lance Sergeant (this rank above full Corporal but below Sergeant is only used in the British Army in the Brigade of Guards)
SS-Junker	Officer candidate (acting rank only, substantive rank of SS-Unterscharführer)
SS-Scharführer	Sergeant

SS-Standartenjunker	Officer candidate (acting rank only, substantive rank of SS-Scharführer)
SS-Oberscharführer	Colour/staff Sergeant
SS-Hauptscharführer	Warrant Officer Class 2
SS-Standartenoberjunker	Officer candidate (acting rank only, substantive rank of SS-Hauptscharführer)
SS-Sturmscharführer	Warrant Officer Class 1 (after fifteen years' service)
SS-Untersturmführer	Second Lieutenant
SS-Obersturmführer	Lieutenant
SS-Hauptsturmführer	Captain
SS-Sturmbannführer	Major
SS-Obersturmbannführer	Lieutenant-Colonel
SS-Standartenführer	Colonel
SS-Oberführer	Brigadier equivalent
SS-Brigadeführer	Major-General
SS-Gruppenführer	Lieutenant-General
SS-Obergruppenführer	General
SS-Oberst-Gruppenführer	Colonel-General (only Sepp Dietrich ever attained this rank)

APPENDIX B – DNSAP 1933 Electoral Programme & Interview with the DNSAP leader, Frits Clausen, on the death of the ex-Prime Minister, Thorvald Stauning

In 1933 the Danish Nazi party (DNSAP), the National Socialist Workers' Party of Denmark, adopted a new programme that replaced the party's first manifesto of 1930. This package of policies was developed by the Party's then-new leader, Dr Frits Clausen. Clausen had acceded to his post by leading an internal coup that toppled the previous leader, Cay Lembcke, at a meeting of district leaders on 23 July 1933. The programme was somewhat hastily put together and struggled to reconcile the Party's earlier thinking with the 'imported' German Nazi idea of the infallibility of the leader. Because of this the programme was only first printed in the pamphlet 'What we want!' in September 1933, and then on 8 October it was reprinted in the Party organ the 'National-Socialist' as part of an article entitled 'Denmark must be awakened'.

The 1930 programme had no fewer than 25 policy planks, but the new one only had eight, and all were fairly broad and designed to be non-controversial, thus allowing the Party to come together after the bruising strife that removed Lembcke. The points were as follows:

Programme for National Socialist Workers' Party of Denmark, September 1933

The National Socialist Workers' Party of Denmark will unite the Danish people to the point where there is neither Right or Left, Socialists and Radicals, only Danish.

1) *We want a recovery of the Danish people, economic and moral, based on our Nordic Culture and Race.*
2) *We demand the right to work be guaranteed. We will fight exploitation, and those who labour will be rewarded for their efforts.*
3) *We demand far-reaching social services for all our old, sick and invalids through an inclusive Peoples Retirement.*
4) *We demand that Danish businesses aim to cover the needs of Danish society, instead of as now serving exclusively capitalism*

and the pursuit of profit. From this we demand the abolition of the gold monopoly, and as the basis for issuing money a national currency based on land and work as a Co-operative 'Land, labour and capital'.

5) *We require ownership of land and homes to be secured by legislation that stops all speculation.*
6) *We are fighting the Marxist class view of our people, and we regard the people as a national, organic whole. From this we fight against the parliamentary form of government that we want replaced with the co-operative statism, based on businesses.*
7) *We are fighting the liberal and materialistic forces and we require protection for the idealistic and socialist forces in our nation during this struggle.*
8) *Based on this requirement, we support the Church in its struggle for a Christian Danish People.*

We require the Conservation of Denmark's National Independence and under the symbol of the swastika are looking for fraternal co-operation with the Nordic-Germanic people, to whom we are linked with the tie of blood.'

Born in 1973, Thorvald Stauning was the first Social Democratic Party Prime Minister of Denmark from 1924–26, and again from 1929 until his death on 3 May 1942. He is the longest-serving prime minister in the history of Denmark. Especially for the working class who he championed, his life was a symbol of the social, cultural and democratic development that he and the Social Democrats had aspired to lead in Denmark since the turn of the century.

On his death most of the country's newspapers wrote obituaries of the deceased PM, in which his life and political career were summarised and assessed. The DNSAP leader, Frits Clausen, gave the interview below on Stauning and his legacy to his party newspaper – *Fædrelandet* ('*The Fatherland*').

> *With Prime Minister Stauning's death an era goes to the grave. In his time the parliamentary system evolved from the old Right of the landowners and the Left of the peasant to that of the worker. Stauning ... voluntarily gave his power to an Assembly Government, this strange conglomerate of various special interests. I do not doubt that there are many workers who mourn Stauning's death because they have not yet understood that he long ago forsook their interests. Many workers have, of course, in reality been more Stauning-followers than they have been Marxists. Personally, I have no reason to lower my sword for the late Prime Minister as he is the man who first of all has used the word 'traitor' about me and my companions. However, I would say that, at his death, we have not done the same in return. None of us National-Socialists have ever denied that Stauning was a personality. If he had not been Marxist, he would probably also have done his people great service...*

When asked by the reporter what Stauning's death might mean for the DNSAP in electoral terms, Clausen responded dismissively:

> *I do not want to be connected at all with the democratic system, and therefore we National-Socialists will be spectators until the time comes when our ideas can be implemented without parliamentary haggling with one lot or another. Of course, we will*

closely follow events with the greatest interest, but without interfering actively in them.

APPENDIX C – Article by Dr Lea Prais (historian at the International Institute for Holocaust Research at Yad Vashem) on the Bobruisk Camp

At the beginning of the 1970s, in order to collect testimony about crimes committed in a forest camp (*Wald lager*), the prosecutor from the city of Hamburg appealed for help to the Israeli police unit responsible for the investigation of Nazi crimes. The Nazis had established this camp near the city of Bobruisk in Belarus. This appeal by the prosecutor was related to an investigation that was underway in regard to *SS* Obersturmbannführer Rudolf Pannier, who had been commandant of the Wald lager from June 1943. The investigation had already revealed that a *Jude lager*, a camp for Jews, had been set up in this location, which served as the main supply base for the *Russland-Mitte* front. In the process of the investigation, the Israeli police drew the attention of staff members of the Yad Vashem Archives Division to the fact that a number of Jewish youths had been transported from the Warsaw ghetto to the camp at Bobruisk.

Until the investigation, the staff at Yad Vashem's Archives had not encountered a single survivor of the camp at Bobruisk, nor did the archives hold any single testimony about the camp. Moreover, there was no reference to the camp in the International Tracing Service (ITS) files in Bad Arolsen, Germany in 1949, or in Yad Vashem's catalogue of concentration and labour camps in Nazi-occupied territories.

The German Army needed to establish a central supply base for the Waffen-SS in central and southern Russia. For this purpose, they set up a central supply base in the forest camp close to the village (in Russian the *sovkhoz*, or state farm) of Kissyelevichi, 8 kilometres southeast of the city of Bobruisk, in an area under military administration, in early 1942. Established as it was, the camp came under the auspices of the SS Leadership Main Office (*Führungshauptamt*), headed by Hans Jüttner, and not the more-usual administration of the concentration camps of the SS Economic and Administrative Department (SS-*Wirtschaftsverwaltungshauptamt* – WVHA), headed by Oswald Pohl and Theodor Eicke. This meant at war's end the camp almost disappeared from the records.

The first commander of the camp, in charge of its construction and operation, was SS Standartenführer Georg Martin. Martin required manpower for the construction of the camp and for its continuing operation. This necessary manpower was, however, not available to him from the German military forces serving in this location. Therefore, he decided to use Jewish labourers under the authority of the Main Office of Security of the Reich (RSHA). Before the Jewish labourers arrived, a unit of 60 SS men who had been tried by SS courts and punished for various infractions were sent from the SS camp at Debica in Poland to the forest camp in Bobruisk to prepare the camp for the arrival of Jews and to guard them afterwards.

The Jews arrived at the camp in two separate transports. The first group was made up of approximately 1,000 Jewish males from the Warsaw ghetto, including about 150 youths between the ages of 13 and 16, transported on 28/29 May 1942 to the camp in Bobruisk. This, in fact, was the first mass deportation from the Warsaw ghetto.

The second transport of around 1,400 Jews left the Warsaw ghetto at the end of July 1942, during the first week of the 'great transport' of the Jews of this ghetto to the death camp of

Treblinka. Thus, two transports of approximately 2,400 Jews were sent to Bobruisk from the Warsaw ghetto.

The Jewish camp was surrounded by a fence that enclosed an area of 150 square metres with four stables and a number of barracks, including ones for prisoners who were forced to clean, build, dig, load wood and coal, work as assistants in the supply depot, tend to pigs, tailor, make shoes, cook and assist other Jews with special skills. Their numbers declined daily. The vast majority of them were killed in two murder pits that had been dug in the neighbouring forest.

In mid-September 1943 the Jewish camp was liquidated, although the military camp continued to function, mainly as a base for actions against the local Partisan fighters. At that time, about 90 Jewish prisoners remained alive. They were transferred first to Minsk and then, about a week later, to the Lublin District, where they were dispersed among several concentration camps.

It should be stressed that information about the Jewish camp in Bobruisk derives only from survivor testimonies. There are no other sources. Plus, the number of testimonies is very small, and is mainly from the low-ranking SS men who guarded the camp.

By its very nature, testimony was not uniform among those who gave accounts. Three of the testimonies deserve particular attention: those of a gravedigger, a cook, and a youth or rather a boy, because Avraham Fabishevich was only 13 when he was deported to Bobruisk.

Shraga Zisholtz was 18 years old when he was deported in the second transport to Bobruisk. The SS forced him and another prisoner, who did not survive, to dig graves in the forest. They were kept extremely busy at that task. Zisholtz provided testimony twice, in 1972 and in 1994.

APPENDIX D – Lists of Scandinavian Waffen-SS officers: Finns, Danes, Norwegians, Swedes

The following appendix is my attempt to compile a list of Finnish, Norwegian and Swedish Waffen-SS officers. Most – but by no means all – attended the Waffen-SS officer academy at Bad Tölz, graduated, and then achieved their officer rank.

In terms of the Finns, some 104 achieved officer rank in the Waffen-SS, but only a minority of 21 graduated from Bad Tölz, however, even though Finnish volunteers in the Waffen-SS in general are not covered by this book as I stated at its beginning, it would be remiss of me not to at least mention them in some way, and therefore I have all of them below as an exemplar of their service.

I must stress though that any such list is open to error and correction. Individuals may have attended, got sick, left, re-joined, failed etc., and a lack of complete records hampers exact detail – so I would crave readers' indulgence for all the mistakes I have made.

The key to the list is: Surname, Christian name, rank achieved in the Waffen-SS; date of birth and date of death, if known – and Killed in Action (KIA), again if known., except for the Danes where the list is simply a surname followed by the Christian name.

I have also included some notes, such as which course they attended at Bad Tölz – if they attended at all and if known. On that point *KJL* stands for 'Kriegs-Junker-Lehrgang'.

Finns

Aaltonen,Antti,Nikolai–SS-Obersturmbannführer.Born22June1933. Died 26 September 1996. 8th KJL (8 June 1942–5 December 1942).

Aarnio, Aarne, Olavi – SS-Untersturmführer. Born 16 November 1913. Wounded in Action 27 September 1941 at Mog.Ostroja. Died on 7 December 1941 in Liegnitz Military Hospital.

Aejmelaeus, Nils, Gustaf – SS-Hauptsturmführer. Born 31 May 1915. Wounded in Action, summer 1941 – remained in Germany until return to Finland in 1947. Died 11 June 1966.

Alhonen, Tuure, Allan – SS-Untersturmführer. Born 15 October 1916. Killed in Action on 23 April 1942 at Shemenski while in the Finnish Army.

Anttila, Ensio, Johannes – SS-Untersturmführer. Born 31 May 1919. Died 7 September 1993.

Autio, Matti, Antero – SS-Untersturmführer. Born 3 November 1920. Died 8 February 1999.

Backberk, Seppo, Aatto, Ilari – SS-Untersturmführer. Born 24 March 1921. Died 16 May 1984.

Duncker, Kaj, Henrik – SS-Obersturmführer. Born 21 November 1917. Wounded in Action autumn 1943. Died 28 November 1992.

Fagerholm, Lars, Henry, Matts – SS-Untersturmführer. Born 7 April 1919. Killed in Action 26 September 1943 at West Syväri while in the Finnish Army. 8th KJL (8 June 1942–5 December 1942).

Hakkarainen, Ilkka, Uljas – SS-Untersturmführer. Born 10 December 1920. Killed in Action 12 October 1942 at Malgobek.

Hallavo, Veikko, Sakari – SS-Untersturmführer. Born 7 January 1917. Died 7 August 1993.

Halonen, Uuno, Antero – SS-Untersturmführer. Born 4 December 1914. Killed in Action 30 September 1943 at Vansjärvi while in the Finnish Army.

Hannus, Erich, Oskar – SS-Obersturmführer. Born 18 March 1917. Killed in Action 26 September 1942 in Malgobek.

Hatara, Teuvo, Olli – SS-Obersturmführer. Born 23 April 1915. Killed in Action 17 October 1944 in Rovaniemi while in the Finnish Army.

Heiskanen, Erkki, Veli – SS-Obersturmführer. Born 16 September 1919. Died 20 August 1994.

Helske, Jaakko, Juha – SS-Untersturmführer. Born 4 May 1922. Died 9 September 1994. 9th KJL (October 1942–August 1943). The Danish ethnic German Nordschleswiger, Georg Erichsen, graduated from this intake at the top of the class.

Hortling, Kai, William – SS-Obersturmführer. Born 14 April 1916. Killed in Action 4 December 1942 at Tschikola.

Hukkanen, Juhani – SS-Untersturmführer. Born 6 September 1916. Died 18 July 1966.

Ingerö, Kauko, Alpo– SS-Obersturmführer. Born 22 June 1919. Killed in Action 23 June 1944 at Alanoskua while in the Finnish Army.

Inkinen, Eino, Iivari – SS-Untersturmführer. Born 14 June 1918. Killed in Action 15 June 1944 at Kivennapa while in the Finnish Army.

Jaakkola, Heikki, Matti, Tapio – SS-Untersturmführer. Born 19 April 1923. Killed in Action 25 June 1944 while in the Finnish Army. 9th KJL (October 1942–August 1943).

Järvinen, Sakari, Kustaa – SS-Untersturmführer. Born 25 February 1922. Died 28 September 1994. 9th KJL (October 1942–August 1943).

Kaila, Yrjö, Paavo, Ilmari – SS-Hauptsturmführer. Born 30 July 1912.

Mikkola (Kalli), Sakari, Viljo, Volevi – SS-Untersturmführer. Born 21 December 1920. Died 2 January 1995. 9th KJL (October 1942–August 1943).

Karila, Erkki, Otto, Pentti – SS-Untersturmführer. Born 1 October 1914. Died 5 April 1995.

Karinen, Antti, Kalervo – SS-Hauptsturmführer. Born 26 September 1916. Wounded in Action 18 July 1941 at Stukolanskaja. Died 9 July 1954.

Karjalainen, Kauko, Ensio – SS-Obersturmführer. Born 21 May 1910. Died 18 March 1985.

Karvinen, Gösta, Antti – SS-Untersturmführer. Born 7 June 1918. Died 7 January 1953.

Kihlström, Lennart, Väinö, Valdemar – SS-Untersturmführer. Born 14 September 1920. Died 1 December 1991.

Kilpinen, Oiva, Veikko, Urho – SS-Untersturmführer. Born 8 November 1916. Wounded in Action 29 September 1942. Died the next day from his wounds in Terekskoye Field Hospital.

Koiranen, Veikko, Rafael, Aleksanteri – SS-Obersturmführer. Born 9 January 1915. Died 23 June 1944 at Turku.

Koivula, Martti, Oskari, Bengt – SS-Untersturmführer. Born 22 June 1920. Killed in Action 15 April 1942 at Vorbenitsa while in the Finnish Army.

Koivuvaara, Paavo, Kaarlo – SS-Untersturmführer. Born 10 February 1918.

Kokkola, Armas, Kaukovalta – SS-Untersturmführer. Born 2 November 1915. Died 1 February 1997.

Korhonen, Erkki, Oskari – SS-Untersturmführer. Born 27 August 1917. Died 19 January 1987.

Kosonen, Herkko, Ilmo, Olavi – SS-Untersturmführer. Born 30 May 1920. Killed in Action 13 July 1944 at Vuosalmi while in the Finnish Army. 8th KJL (8 June 1942–5 December 1942).

Kotkanen, Pentti, Ilmari – SS-Untersturmführer. Born 20 June 1919.

Kurkiala, Kalervo, Lauri – SS-Obersturmführer. Born 16 November 1894. Died 26 February 1966 in Sweden. Liaison Officer and priest for the Finnish volunteers.

Kulovaara, Aslak – SS-Untersturmführer. Born 18 August 1919. Killed in Action 18 August 1941 at Balanow.

Kuutti, Kaarlo, Börje – SS-Obersturmführer. Born 5 November 1918. Killed in Action 2 February 1943 at Kagalnitskaja.

Käppi, Erkki, Olavi – SS-Untersturmführer. Born 2 June 1916. Died 27 December 1980.

Laakso, Yrjö, Ilmari – SS-Untersturmführer. Born 21 February 1922. Died 28 April 1987.

Ladau, Karl-Erik, Gustaf – SS-Hauptsturmführer. Born 3 June 1916. Wounded in Action 26 March 1942 and again on 18 February 1943.

Lange, Erich – SS-Obersturmführer. Born 1 January 1920. Killed in Action 21 July 1944 in Suojärvi while in the Finnish Army.

Laurell, Kaj, Vilhelm – SS-Intersturmführer. Born 25 November 1920. Died 23 April 1967. 9th KJL (October 1942–August 1943).

Lautia, Erik, Rafael – SS-Obersturmführer. Born 29 August 1914. Killed in Action 1 October 1942 at Malgobek.

Lehmus, Uuno, Mikael – SS-Intersturmführer. Born 24 January 1915. Died 19 January 1976.

Leino, Mauno, Josef – SS-Untersturmführer. Born 12 December 1916. Died 26 April 1969.

Liljavirta, Lauri, Veikko – SS-Obersturmführer. Born 2 December 1910. Died 19 November 1941 in the field hospital at Golodajewka from wounds sustained the previous day.

Lindberg, Kim, Konrad – SS-Hauptsturmführer. Born 1 September 1916 in Stuttgart, Germany.

Manni, Tauno, Mikael – SS-Untersturmführer. Born 29 September 1921. 9th KJL (October 1942–August 1943).

Mansala, Heikki, Karl, Theodor – SS-Obersturmführer. Born 3 April 1914.

Mansala, Matti, Theodor – SS-Obersturmführer. Born 18 March 1911. Died 26 December 1992.

Massinen, Pekka, Veli – SS-Untersturmführer. Born 4 November 1921. Died 4 December 1997.

Nieminen (Mattelmäki), Auvo, Birker – SS-Untersturmführer. Born 21 October 1916. Died 18 December 1976.

Miettinen, Arno, Ilmari – SS-Obersturmführer. Born 13 November 1918. Killed in Action 19 June 1944 while in the Finnish Army.

Myllykangas, Maunu, Johannes – SS-Untersturmführer. Born 8 October 1917. Died 9 February 1962.

Myllymäki, Paavo, Aarne, Henrik – SS-Untersturmführer. Born 12 January 1919. Killed in Action 11 September 1941 at Kamenka.

Nevalinna, Eino, Edward – SS-Untersturmführer. Born 2 February 1923. 9th KJL (October 1942–August 1943).

Noisniemi, Torkel, Richard – SS-Untersturmführer. Born 28 August 1916. Died 23 August 1963.

Norrmen, Lars, Herman – SS-Untersturmführer. Born 25 April 1920. 9th KJL (October 1942–August 1943).

Norvio, Viljo, Kaarlo – SS-Obersturmführer. Born 27 December 1911. Died of wounds sustained on the 18 and 19 November 1941 at Darjewka.

Nummi, Pekka, Sakari – SS-Untersturmführer. Born 13 February 1919. Wounded in Action date unknown.

Oinonen, Matti, Olavi – SS-Untersturmführer. Born 2 March 1922. Died 9 September 1977.

Ojanen, Reino, Johannes – SS-Untersturmführer. Born 15 March 1922. 9th KJL (October 1942–August 1943).

Olin, Ulf-Ola – SS-Obersturmführer. Born 18 July 1917. Died 11 January 1995 in Germany. Stayed in the SS-Wiking until the end of the war.

Olki, Antti, Olavi – SS-Untersturmführer. Born 11 September 1917. Died in the 1980s.

Paikkala, Antti, Veikko, Antero – SS-Untersturmführer. Born 9 October 1909. Died 11 April 1963.

Pajunen, Tauno, Olavi – SS-Obersturmführer. Born 11 August 1912.

Palmgren, Brynolf – SS-Untersturmführer. Born 20 October 1920. 9th KJL (October 1942–August 1943).

Parvilahti (Boman), Unto, Ilmari – SS-Untersturmführer. Born 28 September 1907. Wounded in Action, date unknown. Died 27 October 1970 in Malaga, Spain.

Paukkala, Kosti, Juha, Julius – SS-Untersturmführer. Born 12 September 1911. Died 20 July 1989.

Pihkala, Ensio, Samuli – SS-Untersturmführer. Born 26 May 1915. Killed in Action 6 August 1941. Liaison officer and priest.

Pitkänen, Erkki – SS-Untersturmführer. Born 12 April 1915.

Pohjanlehto, Tauno, Poju, Verner – SS-Obersturmführer. Born 30 August 1920. Died 23 July 1995.

Polon, Tauno, Eino, Edvard – SS-Untersturmführer. Born 5 September 1921 in Paris, France. Killed in Action 10 July 1944 at Pitkäranta while in the Finnish Army. 9th KJL (October 1942–August 1943).

Purio, Claes, Bror – SS-Untersturmführer. Born 10 January 1918. Died 27 March 1996. 9th KJL (October 1942–August 1943).

Puuperä, Erkki, Yrjö, Jalmari – SS-Obersturmführer. Born 16 January 1915.

Rantasila, Pekka, Ilmari – SS-Untersturmführer. Born 8 April 1921. Died 30 May 1989. 9th KJL (October 1942–August 1943).

Rautala, Simo, Esko, Johannes – SS-Untersturmführer. Born 27 October 1920. Died 29 November 1991. 9th KJL (October 1942–August 1943).

Rautala, Jouko, Verner – SS-Untersturmführer. Born 17 February 1920. Died 22 August 1989.

Riekki, Tero – SS-Untersturmführer. Born 26 November 1919. Died 14 May 1967.

Roiha, Erkki, Kalevi – SS-Obersturmführer. Born 18 March 1917. Died 31 January 1994.

Saarnilahti, Sakari, Sami – SS-Untersturmführer. Born 13 January 1913. Died 18 December 1964.

Sahlberg, Tom, Olof – SS-Untersturmführer. Born 17 June 1910. Died 18 September 1976.

Sarasalo, Juhani, Kaarlo – SS-Untersturmführer. Born 28 February 1923.

Sartio, Mauri, Holger – SS-Obersturmführer. Born 19 August 1916. Died 5 March 1986.

Seppälä, Osmo, Verner – SS-Untersturmführer. Born 10 July 1917.

Sirviö, Samuli, Johannes – SS-Untersturmführer. Born 3 May 1918. Died 28 April 1985.

Somersalo, Olli, Artturi – SS-Obersturmführer. Born 20 January 1915. Died 4 August 1963. Finnish Battalion doctor.

Sorko, Osmo, Ylermi, Kullervo – SS-Untersturmführer. Born 18 June 1921.

Suonio, Reino, Olavi – SS-Obersturmführer. Born 2 August 1913. Died 1992.

Suorttanen, Sulo, Elias – SS-Untersturmführer. Born 13 February 1921. 9 KJL (October 1942 – August 1943). Served as Finland's Minister of Defence from 27 May 1966 to 14 May 1970.

Tenomaa, Yrjö – SS-Hauptsturmführer. Born 27 June 1916. Died 1986.

Toivonen, Elja, Kalle, Sulevi – SS-Untersturmführer. Born 5 November 1922. Died 18 January 1996 in Spain. 8th KJL (8 June 1942–5 December 1942).

Törni, Lauri, Allan – SS-Untersturmführer. Born 28 May 1919. Killed in Action 18 October 1965 in Vietnam while serving with the Special Forces of the US Army where he was known as 'Larry Thorne'.

Vaaramo, Toivo, Perttuli – SS-Obersturmführer. Born 30 September 1920. Died on 12 November 1944 from wounds sustained earlier while in the Finnish Army.

Vainio, Valle, Voitto – SS-Untersturmführer. Born 22 May 1918. Died 1974 in South America. 8th KJL (8 June 1942–5 December 1942).

Viikama, Veikko, Kalevi – SS-Untersturmführer. Born 16 December 1919.

Virtaniemi, Kyösti, Vilho – SS-Untersturmführer. Born 1 October 1923. Died 1 July 1978 in Norway. 8th KJL (8 June 1942–5 December 1942).

Vuori, Olli, Yrjö – SS-Untersturmführer. Born 3 January 1921.

Wallen, Lennart, Simeon – SS-Obersturmführer. Born 25 April 1913. Killed in Action 9 October 1942 at Malgobek.

Ylinen, Olavi – SS-Obersturmführer. Born 14 October 1920. Killed in Action 6 September 1941 at Aunus while in the Finnish Army.

Danes

This list of Danes was kindly supplied by Lars Larsen, and drawn from John Moore's superb *Führerliste*. I apologise for the lack of biographical information.

Abraham, Kaare
Ahelfeldt-Laurvig, Hans

Andersen, Hans
Andersen, Leo
Arentoft, Holger
Binnerup, Björn
Birkedahl-Hansen, Svend
Bonde, Christian
Bonnek, Dirck-Ingvard
Broberg, Poul
Brörup, Erik
Christensen, Holger Winding
Christensen, Holger Toft
Christensen, Jürgen
Dall, Christen
Dircksen, Hans
Dumas, Holger
Efsen, Wilhelm
Eggers, Christian-Ulrich
Ellehoj, Jens
Ellekilde, Helge
Erichsen, Georg
Erikson, Erik
Feilberg, Kaj
Fenger, Erik
Frederiksen, Johannes
Fuchs, Hermann
Gordon, Ib
Grammens, Claes
Gregersen, Mogens
Gyldenkrone, Emil
Gylstorff, Arthur
Halles, Erling

Hansen, Robert
Harebye, Hans
Hellmers, Johannes
Herlov-Nielsen, Erik
Höjmark, Bornemann
Höjmark-Christensen, Bent
Holm, Peter
Holmgaard-Jensen, Johannes
Hyllestad, Börge
Jacobsen, Carsten
Jacobsen, Erik
Jensen, Hans-Peter
Jensen, Paul-Englehardt
Jensen, Poul-Jörgen
Joachimsen, August
Johannsen, Olaf
Johannsen, Peter
Johnsen, Karl-Johann
Kaergaard, Tage
Kall-Bertelsen, Mogens
Kam, Paul
Kam, Sören
Karschies, Georg
Kierulff, Aage
Kjersgaard, Kell
Knudsen, Aksel
Koopmann, Paul
Korsgaard, Henning
Krabbe, Oluf von
Kryssing, Christian Peder

Kryssing, Niels
Kuba, Günther
Kuhnert, Jörgen
Kure, Ole Peter
Laerum, Erik
Langermann, Armand
Larsen, Erik
Larsen, Hartwig
Larsen, Poul
Lorenzen, Lorenz
Lund, Ove-Iwan
Lund-Nielsen, Aref
Madsen, Leo
Marcussen, Tage
Marquardt, Otto
Martinsen, Knud
Mortensen, Jörgen
Müller, Hans-Olsen
Munch-Christensen, Kaj
Neergaard-Jacobsen, Paul
Nielsen, Erik
Nielsen, Fredrik
Nielsen, Jens-Bent
Nielsen, Vagn-Viggo
Norreen, Octavius
Nybo, Karl
Olsen, Richard
Park, Arne
Pedersen, Carl
Pedersen, Olaf

Petersen, Jens
Petersen, Johannes
Petersen, Tage
Petersen, Walter
Poulsen, Egill
Rasmussen, Ellef Henry
Rathje, Kurt
Salskov, Jörgen
Schalburg, Christian von
Schok, Knud
Schröder, John-William
Schütt, Gerhard
Schwartz, Mogens
Skov-Nielsen, Arne
Sörensen, Bendix
Sörensen, Per
Steenholdt-Schütt, Christian
Steen-Jensen, Erik
Teisen, Christian
Thomsen, Kaj-Holm
Thorgils, Knud
Thorius, Johan
Thorkilsen, Paul
Thornberg, Ove
Tingleff-Hansen, Johannes
Velde, Johann
Viffert, Ernst
Vögg, Ejvind
Weidlich, Jörgen
Weidlich, Paul
Worsoe-Larsen, Bent

The following is a list of Norwegian officer candidates who attended Bad Tölz, graduated and achieved the rank of SS-Untersturmführer. It has been complied with the aid of the internet and then cross-referenced with the excellent *Norske Offiserer I Waffen-SS*, but I make little claim as to its completeness.

Aakervlk, Torstein – Born 1 August 1907.

Aanonsen, Knut Agnar – Born 12 January 1919. Killed in Action 5 February 1944 at Narva.

Aarbu, Rolf – Born 10 February 1922. Killed in Action 26 June 1944 at Hasselmann Hill.

Amundsen, Willy Thorwald – Born 9 July 1913. Died 3 November 1982.

Arntzen, Tor Dischenthun – Born 3 July 1919. Died 30 July 1989.

Bae, Per Henry – Born 26 November 1910. Died 1992.

Bakke, Halvor – Born 1 October 1922. Died 17 September 1989.

Bakke, Olaf-Andreas – Born 13 October 1920. Died in Sao Paolo, Brazil, 15 September 2010.

Bakken, Knut Trygve – Born 29 June 1924.

Balstad, Peter Johan – Born 25 September 1924. Died 18 June 1985.

Bang, Oscar – Born 9 April 1916. Died 30 March 2003.

Barrum, Eivind – Born 27 September 1921. Died 16 June 2004.

Bay, Hermann Henrik – Born 18 November 1921. Died 24 November 2003.

Bech, Eystein – Born 17 September 1918. Killed in Action 7 March 1944.

Berg, Aage Henrik – Born11 August 1914. Died 21 November 2003.

Berg, Anton Jenssen – Born 16 August 1916. Killed in Action 27 October 1944 in Courland.

Berg, Magne – Born 4 August 1918. Killed in Action 28 July 1944 at Narva.

Bjørkelid, Njaal – Born 3 March 1924. Killed in Action 19 March 1945 at Stettin.

Blegen, Per – Born 29 November 1924. Died 21 October 1990.

Bøe-Simonsen, Ferdinand – Born 8 April 1919. Killed in Action 27 July 1944 on Grenadier Hill at Narva.

Borch-Flatebø, Gustav – Born 11 June 1923. Died 8 March 1996.

Boresen, Richard Ole Nils – Born 1 January 1922.

Børstring, Kåre – Born 17 April 1923. Killed in Action 27 June 1944 at Hasselmann Hill.

Braseth, John – Born 2 December 1914.

Brekke, Bernhard – Born 1 September 1914.

Bruland, Gunnar Rossland – Born 21 March 1916. Killed in Action 1 February 1944 at Dubrovka.

Brunaes, Ole Kristian – Born 24 September 1918. Died 20 May 1987.

Bruun, Henrik Bjarne – Born 25 July 1989. Died 6 December 1971.

Bruun-Evers, Emil – Born 1 September 1921. Killed in Action 7 May 1944 at Iyeesare.

Brynestad, Kåre – Born 18 June 1924. Died 27 September 2001.

Brynjulfsson, Bjørn Dic – Born 21 January 1921. Taken prisoner by American soldiers on 29 April 1945, he was executed by them the same day, near Neustadt.

Cappelen, Johannes Jan – Born 14 August 1922.

Christensen, Finn Bratlie – Born 11 November 1919. Died 5 August 2009.

Christensen, Lauritz Ruud – Born 12 April 1924. Died 16 June 2011.

Dahl, Kristoffer Stovner – Born 7 March 1919. Died 27 December 2001.

Ekeland, Siegfried – Born 18 October 1908.

Ellsroth, Reinhard – Born 19 November 1915. Died 26 March 1989.

Erichsen, Knut – Born 21 August 1917. Killed in Action 27 October 1944 in Courland.

Kalkum, Magne – Born 6 September 1916.

Fermann, Olaf – Born 17 February 1892.

Fogstad, Jacob – Born 3 May 1914. Died 13 February 1996.

Furusteh, Ola Olsen – Born 31 May 1908. Died 3 October 1983.

Gauslaa, Alf – Born 20 July 1917. Died 23 July 2001.

Glestad, Einar – Born 26 December 1915. Killed in Action 28 January 1944, at Narva.

Gramnes, Einar Julius Martin – Born 3 February 1923. Died in 1970 in Sweden.

Grønnerød, Ivar Marentius – Born 1 August 1918. Died 29 May 2003.

Gulliksen, Gullik Odd – Born 26 March 1917. Died 22 June 1998.

Gurholt, Thomas Hersleb – Born 3 January 1922. Killed in Action 23 September 1944, in Latvia.

Gustavsson, Johan Ragnar – Born 4 March 1924. Killed in Action 5 March 1945.

Hagtun, Sverre – Born 13 July 1914. Died 23 September 2000.

Halle, Frode – Born 15 March 1906. Died 10 January 1995.

Halse, Per Weien – Born 1 January 1922. Died 18 January 1987.

Hansen, Ralph Born 5 May 1925. Died 12 December 1989.

Hanssen, Arne Einar Olav – Born 18 August 1917. Killed in Action 10 February 1944, at Hungerburg.

Hegnar, Håkon – Born 3 May 1910. Killed in Action 18 December1943, at Kestenga, Russia.

Heiberg, Anton Wilhelm – Born 17 June 1915.

Hembre, Aksel Magnus – Born 18 May 1920. Died 3 July 1992.

Herigstad, Leiv.

Herseth, Kristian – Born 22 January 1920.

Hildebrand-Myhrvold, Gøsta Ragnar – Born 9 September 1919. Killed during a Soviet bombing raid on the hospital he was in in Tallinn, Estonia, on 9 March 1944.

Himberg, Ran Lykke – Born 29 September 1921. Killed in Action 25 June 1944 at Hasselmann Hill.

Hoff, Hans Petter – Born 10 June 1917. Died in 1952.

Holmen, Thorbjørn – Born 19 April 1919. Died 27 August 1977.

Hørvik, Harald – Born 22 May 1917.

Høve, Einar – Born 21 October 1912. Killed in Action 14 February 1943.

Høve, Jørgen – Born 14 November 1916.

Hvistendal, Thomas – Born 28 December 1918. Died 21 August 1992.

Jacobsen, Knut August Toftegaar – Born 5 July 1921. Died 5 October 2002.

Jadar, Arild Berner – Born 19 February 1921. Died 9 December 2010.

Jansen, Rolf Harry – Born 1 November 1917. Died 9 May 1945, from wounds received in action.

Jensen, Fredrik – Born 25 March 1921. Died 31 July 2011.

Johannesen, Johan Arnt – Born 25 November 1919. Died 21 December 1985.

Johansen, Per Ragnvald – Born 29 December 1920. Died 6 May 1999.

Johnsen, Gunnar – Born 18 November 1923. Died 3 August 2006.

Jonassen, Johan August 'Gust' – Born 19 May 1911. Killed in Action 26 May 1943 in Karelia.

Jonsson, Birger Ernst – Born 9 October 1923. Killed in Action 26 June 1944 at Kaprolat Hill.

Jøntvedt, Olav Wendelboe – Born 27 March 1921. Died 4 July 1980.

Kahrs, Sophus Magdalon Buck – Born 28 March 1918. Died 18 November 1993 in Buenos Aires, Argentina.

Kjelstrup, Johan Bernt Sverre – Born 20 May 1920. Died 27 October 1993.

Kjølner, Per – Born 14 August 1921.

Knudsen, Hans-Christian – Born 25 July 1917 in Salzburg, Austria. Died 25 February 1943 in Krasnoje Selo hospital from wounds sustained inn fighting earlier that month.

Knudsen, Leif- Born 30 September 1911. Died in 1975.

Kracht, Kjell – Born 20 November 1919.

Kvammen, Birger Magne – Born 5 May 1919.

Larsen, Borger Dahl 'Bobbo' – Born 30 March 1922. Killed in Action 2 February 1944, at Dubrowka.

Larsson, Lars Ove – Born 6 February 1922.

Linde, Sverre – Born 12 December 1918. Died 1 February 1976.

Lindvig, Olaf Trygve – Born 9 September 1917. Died 2 February 2007.

Lislegaard, Othar Øvind – Born 28 July 1899. Died 19 November 1976.

Lofthus, Torgeir – Born 13 February 1921. Died 6 February 1981.

Lund, Jens-Bernhard – Born 20 May 1918. Killed in Action 22 November 1943, in a Partisan ambush in Yugoslavia.

Lundbye, Trygve – Born 17 September 1920. Died 16 May 1973.

Marthinsen, Kjell Andreas – Born 24 September 1924. Wounded in Action in August 1944, he was invalided home but died when his plane crashed in Norway on 16 October 1944.

Moe, Johannes – Born 14 August 1918. Died 1 March 1967.

Mytting, Eirik Hans – Born 19 March 1916. Died 29 March 1997.

Nakken, Hans Thomas – Born 15 February 1924. Killed in Action 10 February 1945, at Landeck.

Nielsen, Paul – Born 29 May 1910. Died 14 April 1991.

Nybøle, Kaare – Born 5 April 1921.

Nygaard, John Willy – Born 22 April 1918. Killed in Action 4 March 1945.

Olsen, Bjarne Arnt – Born 22 September 1920. Died 24 April 1975, in Sweden.

Østerdahl, Sverre Andersen – Born 4 November 1911. Killed in Action 26 June 1944, at Hasselmann Hill.

Østring, Bjørn – Born 23 September 1917. Died 27 November 2012.

Østvig, Karl Aagaard – Born 24 October 1924. Killed in Action 25 December 1944, at Modlin in Poland.

Øverland, Julius – Born 30 November 1913. Died 30 November 1988.

Pedersen, Henrik Skaar – Born 23 April 1917. Killed in Action 30 January 1944, at Jamburg.

Plünnecke, Per Schwalenberg Biesterfeld – Born 7 December 1922. Died 10 January 1987.

Prytz, Kristian Peder – Born 16 August 1910. Killed in Action 13 February 1944, in Estonia.

Prytz, Trond – Born 23 July 1921.

Reppen, Asbjørn – Born 31 December 1915. Died 16 September 1998.

Riise, Reidar – Born 20 February 1920. Died 2 January 1968.

Røer, Harald – Born 7 March 1923.

Røkenes, Bjørn Kjell – Born 12 February 1923. Died 26 June 1992.

Rønningen, Olai – Born 14 August 1921. Killed in Action 4 August 1944, at Grenadier Hill, Narva.

Rosnaess, Frithjof – Born 5 April 1921. Killed in Action 27 January 1945 at Pettend in Hungary.

Rossnaes. Knut Andreas – Born 2 September 1918. Died 1983 in Germany.

Rustad, Finn – Born 30 April 1914. Died in Spain, date unknown.

Ruud, Sverre Tiedemann – Born 27 July 1911. Died 18 June 1988.

Sandborg, Peter Thomas – Born 1 September 1907. Killed in Action 23 September 1944 at Baldone, Latvia.

Sandnes, Finn Bjarne – Born 1 November 1918. Died 1 May 1966.

Sandstad, John – Born 5 February 1925.

Sandved, Gunnar Bloch – Born 28 June 1921.

Sanner, Olaf – Born 8 February 1924. Died 29 January 2001.

Schneider, Jan – Born 27 December 1919. Died 22 March 2004.

Seeberg, Alf – Born 10 November 1895. Died 4 March 1973.

Schrøder, Eyvind Andreas – Born 6 January 1922. Died 9 April 1995.

Seljelid, Odd – Born 23 February 1921. Died 3 May 1968.

Selnes, Ole Bernhard – Born 16 November 1917. Died 27 November 1982, in Berlin.

Sesseng-Fjeseth, Ola – Born 19 March 1918. Killed in Action 1 February 1944, at Jamburg.

Skjefstad, Kjell – Born 14 February 1922. Died in 1948 (probably).

Skjefstad, Martin – Born 23 September 1918. Died 7 May 1992.

Skui, Odd – Born 13 August 1923. Died 8 December 2010.

Smith, Arne Gunnar – Born 23 April 1922. Killed in Action 15 August 1944, at Jasienica in Poland.

Sødahl, Harald Normann – Born 5 October 1915. Died 3 October 1987.

Solberg, Knut Johan – Born 9 August 1923. Died 31 July 2009.

Sommerhaug, Ole Andreas – Born 14 August 1923.

Sønstebye, Torfinn – Bprn 24 October 1918. Died 17 January 1970.

Staff, Helge – Born 12 September 1918. Died 22 June 1968.

Steen, Axel – Born 16 November 1915. Killed in Action 25 June 1944, at Kaprolat Hill.

Steen, Walter – Born 15 July 1917.

Stensvaag, Sigurd Ivar – Born 3 August 1920. Killed in Action 26 June 1944 at Hasselmann Hill.

Storm, Thor – Born 10 May 1917. Killed in Action 27 January 1945.

Stridskler, Arne – Born 24 September 1916.

Strømsnes, Hans – Born 19 May 1920. Died 10 September 1999.

Strømsnes, Oskar Anton Erik – Born 15 July 1920. Killed in Action 19 March 1945 at Inota in Hungary.

Sundberg, Håkon – Born 5 February 1923. Killed in Action 9 August 1944, at Talsen in Latvia.

Sundlo, Christian Nikolai Lassen – Born 6 January 1919. Died 24 October 2001.

Sveen, Bjarne – Born 16 February 1921. Killed in Action 1 March 1945, at Arnswalde.

Svelle, Hallvard – Born 14 April 1918. Died 30 September 2006.

Svendsen, Jochen Per Greiner – Born 5 October 1915. Died 7 February 1997.

Svenke, Harald – Born 24 September 1914.

Svenneby, Tor – Born 6 March 1917. Killed in Action 7 March 1945, at Krepcewo in Pomerania.

Sylten, Stein Sture – Born 27 September 1921. Died 28 November 2001 in Sweden.

Theodorsen, Gunnar Magnus – Born 25 March 1919. Died 26 December 1999.

Theting Johannessen, Roald – Born 29 June 1921.

Thoresen, Felix Patrick – Born 30 January 1923. Died 22 February 1991.

Thorkildsen, Egil Horst – Born 21 July 1916.

Thunold, Oskar Lauritz – Born 23 December 1918. Killed in Action 8 November 1943. at Bos Nowi in Croatia.

Tordarson, Odd – Born 24 February 1924. Killed in Action 30 August 1944, in Estonia.

Torjussen, Tor – Born 4 June 1924. Killed in Action 24 June 1944, at Hasselmann Hill.

Tryti, Oddvar – Born 19 September 1913. Died 11 June 1993.

Ugelstad, Rolf Ivar Kruse – Born 8 May 1916. Died 9 September 1990.

Vik, Arnfinn Tor Holmesland – Born 20 June 1920. Died 6 January 1995.

Vinje, Jan Henry – Born 28 July 1921.

Wahlmann, Olaf – Born 11 October 1918. Died 10 June 1981.

Wahlstrøm, Rolf – Born 11 October 1917. Reported as Killed in Action 26 June 1944, at Hasselmann Hill; he was supposedly seen by three other Norwegian POWs in the Soviet camp at Tambov, however the Soviet authorities denied they had him and there were no further sightings.

Waksvik, Erling Loktu – Born 8 May 1909. Died 20 March 1999.

Westad, Knut – Born 23 January 1916.

Wiik, Asbjørn Jäger – Born 20 June 1920.

Windingstad, Inge Håkon – Born 24 May 1924.

Swedes

This list was kindly compiled and supplied by Lars T. Larsson.

Ahlgren, Rune – SS-Untersturmführer. Killed in Action 29 October 1944 in Second Battle of Courland. 3rd KJL.

Baecklund, Per-Sigurd – SS-Untersturmführer. 11th KJL.

Bergqvist, Gunnar – SS-Hauptsturmführer. Served in the Imperial German Army in First World War, and the Allgemeine-SS in Second World War.

Blom, Lars – SS-Untersturmführer. Dual German-Swedish nationality. Died in Germany in 1978.

Borg, Gösta – SS-Untersturmführer. 3rd KJL.

Eklöf, Gunnar – SS-Untersturmführer. 9th KJL. Charged and imprisoned for the murder of Sven Rydén in Berlin in February 1945.

Eldh-Albiez, Wolfgang – SS-Untersturmführer. Graduated 11th KJL as top of his class. Badly wounded in action in August 1944.

Gustavsson, Johan-Ragnar – SS-Untersturmführer. Born in Norway in 1924. Killed in Action 5/6 March 1945 near Massow. 14th KJL.

Hassler, Bengt – SS-Obersturmführer. Committed suicide after the war. 2nd KJL.

Hellenborg, Yngve – SS-Untersturmführer. 8th KJL (probably). Compulsive liar who served at the Grini concentration camp in Norway, probably as an informant.

Holst, Axel – SS-Untersturmführer. Honorary cavalry officer, 1930s. Died in a riding accident in 1935.

Jürgenssen, Dr. Olaf – SS-Untersturmführer. Received his rank as a medical doctor in the Waffen-SS.

Krueger, Hans-Caspar – SS-Untersturmführer. Died in a car accident in 1977 in Buenos Aires.

Laggberg, Are – SS-Untersturmführer. Ex-Swedish Army officer, he left the Waffen-SS in October 1941. Bad Tölz 1941.

Meyer, Heino – SS-Untersturmführer. Wounded in Action three times in March 1944 and reported killed, but survived. 3rd KJL.

Norberg, Kurt Birger – SS-Obersturmführer. Thought not to have attended Bad Tölz. Deserted in March 1943.

Nordborg, Yngve – SS-Obersturmführer. Received his rank due to having a Swedish officer's rank in the Home Guard.

Pehrsson, Hans-Gösta – SS-Hauptsturmführer. 9th KJL. Most decorated Swedish Waffen-SS officer. Died of cancer in 1974.

Raab, Harry – SS-Untersturmführer. Probably received his rank due to having held an officers rank with the Red Cross. Killed in Action with the Swedish Volunteer Company on the Finnish front.

Rydén, Sven – SS-Obersturmführer. Bad Tölz 1941. Murdered in Berlin on 19 February 1945 – fellow volunteer Gunnar Eklöf was charged and imprisoned for his killing.

Svensson, Carl – SS-Obersturmführer. 8th KJL. Died in 2000.

Tillman, Torkel – SS-Untersturmführer. 11th KJL. Killed in Action on 26 June 1944, at Cheux St Manvieu, France.

Wrang, Carl-Olof – SS-Obersturmführer. Received his rank due to his previous service as an officer in the Swedish Army. Commanded a Swedish UN battalion in the Congo in the 1960s and retired a lieutenant-colonel.

In addition, Hans Lindström, Frank Gustavsson, Kurt Allan Lundin and Nils-Erik Eriksson all went to Bad Tölz, but never became Waffen-SS officers; Lindström and Gustavsson due to the end of the war, Lundin deserted and Eriksson flunked out.

BIBLIOGRAPHY

Bauer, Eddy, *Lt. Col, World War II,* Orbis, 1972

Beevor, Antony, *Berlin the Downfall 1945*, Penguin, 2003

Bellamy, Chris, *Absolute War – Soviet Russia in the Second World War*, Macmillan, 2007

Bishop, Chris, *The Military Atlas of World War II*, Amber, 2005

Bjerregaard, Jens Pank & Larsen, Lars, *Danish Volunteers of the Waffen-SS: Freikorps Danmark 1941–43*, Helion, 2017

Brenden, Geir & Natedal, Tommy, *Norwegian Volunteers of the Waffen-SS*, Helion, 2016

Brenden, Geir, Natedal, Tommy & Thoresen, Knut Flovik, *Norske Offiserer I Waffen-SS*, Forlaget Historie & Kultur, 2012

Butler, Rupert, *SS-Wiking*, Spellmount, 2002

Buttar, Prit, *Between Giants: The Battle for the Baltics in World War II*, Osprey, 2013

Calvocoressi, Peter, & Wint, Guy, *Total War*, Penguin, 1974

Carell, Paul, *Hitler's War on Russia Volume One*, (translated by Ewald Osers), George G. Harrap, 1964

Carell, Paul, *Hitler's War on Russia Volume Two: Scorched Earth*, (translated by Ewald Osers), George G. Harrap, 1970

Christensen, Claus Bundgård, Poulsen, Niels Bo & Smith, Peter Scharff, *Danskere i Waffen SS 1940–1945 (Danes in the Waffen-SS 1940–1945)*, Aschehoug, 1998

Clark, Lloyd, *Kursk: The Greatest Battle, Eastern Front 1943*, Headline Review, 2011

Dahl, Hans Fredrik, ed. *Norsk krigsleksikon 1940–45* (Norwegian War Encyclopedia 1940–45), J. W. Cappelen, 1995

Davies, Norman, *Europe at War 1939–1945*, Macmillan, 2006

Dorrill, Stephen, *Blackshirt*, Penguin Viking, 2006

Edwards, Robert, *White Death: Russia's War on Finland 1939–40*, Weidenfeld & Nicolson, 2006

Estes, Kenneth. W., *A European Anabasis – Western European Volunteers in the German Army and SS, 1940–1945*, Columbia University Press, 2003

Evans, Richard J., *The Third Reich at War*, Allen Lane, 2008

Foot, M. R. D., *Resistance – European Resistance to Nazism 1940–45*, Eyre Methuen, 1976

Forczyk, Robert, *Where the Iron Crosses Grow – The Crimea 1941–44*, Osprey, 2014

Glantz, David M., *Before Stalingrad – Barbarossa and Hitler's Invasion of Russia 1941*, Tempus, 2003

Glantz, David M., *The Battle for Leningrad 1941–1944*, BCA, 2004

Graber, G. S., *History of the SS*, Diamond, 1994

Hausser, Paul, *Wenn Alle Brüder Schweigen (When all our brothers are silent)*, Nation Europa, 1973

Hillbald, Thorolf (ed.), *Twilight of the Gods – A Swedish Waffen-SS Volunteer's Experiences with the 11th SS-Panzergrenadier Division 'Nordland', Eastern Front 1944–45*, Helion, 2004

Jones, Michael, *Leningrad: State of Siege*, John Murray, 2008

Jurado, Carlos Caballero, *Resistance Warfare 1940–45, Osprey Men-at-Arms series, 1985*

Klapdor, Ewald, *Viking Panzers: The German 5th SS Tank Regiment in the East in World War II*, Stackpole, 2011

Krabbe, Oluf von, *Danske soldaten i kamp pa Ostfronten 1941–1945 (Danish soldiers in battle on the Eastern Front 1941–1945)*, Bogan's Vorlag, 1998

Kurowski, Franz, *Bridgehead Kurland: The Six Epic Battles of Heeresgruppe Kurland, (translated by Fred Steinhardt)*, J. J. Fedorowicz Publishing, 2002

Larsson, Lars T., *Hitler's Swedes – A History of the Swedish Volunteers in the Waffen-SS*, Helion, 2015

Le Tissier, Tony, *With our backs to Berlin – The German Army in Retreat 1945*, Sutton, 2001

Lidegaard, Bo, *Dansk udenrigspolitiks historie. Overleveren – 1914–1945 (A History of Danish Foreign Policy 1914–1945)*, Danmarks Nationalleksikon, 2003

Lindstad, Bjorn, *Den Frivillige – En Frontkjemper Forteller Sin Historie (The Volunteer – a front fighter tells his story)*, Kagge Vorlag, 2010

Littlejohn, David, *The Patriotic Traitors: A History of Collaboration in German-Occupied Europe 1940/1945*, William Heinemann, 1972

Littlejohn, David, *Foreign Legions of the Third Reich Volume 1*, R. James Bender, 1979

McDonough, Frank, *The Gestapo: The Myth and Reality of Hitler's Secret Police*, Coronet, 2015

McKale, Donald M., *The Swastika outside Germany*, Kent State University, 1977

McNab, Chris (ed.), *Hitler's Armies: A History of the German War Machine 1939–45*, Osprey, 2015

McNab, Chris (ed.), *Hitler's Elite: The SS 1939–45*, Osprey, 2013

Merridale, Catherine, *Ivan's War – The Red Army 1939–45*, Faber & Faber, 2005

Michaelis, Rolf, *Panzergrenadier Divisions of the Waffen-SS*, Schiffer, 2010

Michaelis, Rolf, *The 11th SS-Freiwilligen-Panzer-Grenadier-Division 'Nordland'*, Schiffer, 2008

Mitcham Jr, Samuel W., *Hitler's Legions: German Army Order of Battle World War II*, Leo Cooper, 1985

Mitcham Jr, Samuel W., *Hitler's Field Marshals and their Battles*, Guild, 1988

Møller, Magnus J., *I Krig for Danmark (I fought for Denmark)*, Eget Vorlag, 2008

Munk, Jan, *I was a Dutch Volunteer*, self-published, 2008

National Council of the National Front of Democratic Germany Documentation Centre of the State Archives Administration of the German Democratic Republic, *Brown Book: War and Nazi Criminals in West Germany*, Verlag Zeit im Bild, 1965

Overmans, Rüdiger, *Soldaten hinter Stacheldraht*, Deutsche Kriegsgefangene des Zweiten Weltkriege, Ullstein

Parrish, Michael, *The Lesser Terror: Soviet State Security, 1939–1953*, Praeger Press, 1996

Ravn, Ole, *Fører uden folk: Frits Clausen og Danmarks National Socialistiske Arbejder-Parti*, University of Southern Denmark, 2007

Rees, Philip, *Who's Who in the Extreme Right Since 1890: An International Biographical Dictionary*, 1990

Reitlinger, Gerald, *The SS: Alibi of a Nation, 1939–1945*, Heinemann, 1956

Rikmanspoel, Marc J., *Soldiers of the Waffen-SS – Many Nations, One Motto*, J. J. Fedorowicz Publishing, 1999

Rikmanspoel, Marc J., *Sunwheels and Siegrunen – Wiking Nordland, Nederland and the Germanic Waffen-SS volume 1*, Helion, 2015

Rikmanspoel, Marc J., *Waffen-SS Encyclopedia*, Aberjona, 2004
Roberts, Geoffrey, *Stalin's General – The Life of Georgy Zhukov*, Icon, 2012
Roberts, Geoffrey, *Stalin's Wars – From the World War to Cold War 1939–1953*, Yale University Press, 2006
Sydnor, Jr, Charles W., *Soldiers of Destruction: The Death's Head Division, 1933–1945*, Princeton University Press, 1977
Taylor, Brian, *Barbarossa to Berlin Volume Two: The Defeat of Germany, 19 November 1942 to 15 May 1945*, Spellmount, 2004
Tieke, Wilhelm, *The Finnish Volunteer Battalion of the Waffen-SS*, (translated by Klaus Scharley), J. J. Fedorowicz Publishing, 2013
Villani, Gerry, *Voices of the Waffen-SS*, self-published, 2015
Weale, Adrian, *The SS – A New History*, Abacus, 2010
Westberg, Lennart & Gyllenhaal, Lars, *Swedes at War: Willing Warriors of a Neutral Nation, 1914–1945* (translated by Carl Gustav Finstrom) Aberjona, 2004
Williamson, Gordon, *The Blood-Soaked Soil*, Blitz Editions, 1997
Williamson, Gordon, *Loyalty is my Honor*, Brown, 1995
Williamson, Gordon, *The SS: Hitler's Instrument of Terror*, Sidgwick & Jackson, 1994
Willmott, H. P., *The Great Crusade: A New Complete History of the Second World War*, Pimlico, 1992
Winchester, Charles D., *Hitler's War on Russia*, Osprey, 2007

INDEX

Also available from Amberley Publishing

Available from all good bookshops or to order direct
Please call **01453-847-800**
www.amberley-books.com